The United States Coast Guard in World War II

The United States Coast Guard in World War II

A History of Domestic and Overseas Actions

THOMAS P. OSTROM

with a Foreword by John Galluzzo

To Jerry Savage

MMI USN

Regards,
Thomas P. Ostrom

McFarland & Company, Inc., Publishers
Jefferson, North Carolina, and London

All photographs are courtesy of the United States Coast Guard (USCG) and the United States Coast Guard Historian's Office (USCGHO); maps created by Nicholas Edward King, cartography student, University of Wisconsin–Eau Claire.

LIBRARY OF CONGRESS CATALOGUING-IN-PUBLICATION DATA

Ostrom, Thomas P.
 The United States Coast Guard in World War II : a history of domestic and overseas actions / Thomas P. Ostrom ; with a foreword by John Galluzzo.
  p. cm.
 Includes bibliographical references and index.

 ISBN 978-0-7864-4256-0
 softcover : 50# alkaline paper ∞

 1. United States. Coast Guard. 2. World War, 1939–1945—Naval operations, American. 3. United States. Coast Guard—History—World War, 1939–1945. I. Title.
 D773.O88 2009
 940.54'5973—dc22   2009014100

British Library cataloguing data are available

On the cover: the 327-foot USCGC *Duane* (WPG-33) on convoy escort patrol in heavy North Atlantic seas

Manufactured in the United States of America

McFarland & Company, Inc., Publishers
 Box 611, Jefferson, North Carolina 28640
  www.mcfarlandpub.com

To the men and women of the multi-mission U.S. Coast Guard, who have bravely served the nation in peace and war, at home and overseas since 1790, forging and enriching the service motto, "Semper Paratus" (Always Ready).

Contents

Documents

Acknowledgments

The motivation for writing *The United States Coast Guard in World War II* evolved from the respect and admiration I acquired during and since my service in the U.S. Coast Guard Reserve (1961–1969).

The expertise, articles, documents, and photographs provided by U.S. Coast Guard historian Dr. Robert Browning and assistant historians Scott T. Price, Christopher Havern, and Richard T. Boonisar at Coast Guard Head-quarters, Washington, D.C., were extensive and invaluable, as were the suggestions of Dr. William H. Thiesen, Atlantic Area Coast Guard historian, Dr. David Rosen, Pacific Area Coast Guard historian, and the Coast Guard Museum Northwest in Seattle, Washington.

I am indebted to Elderberry Press editor David St. John for his expertise in the publication of my first two books, *The USCG, 1790 to the Present* and *The USCG on the Great Lakes*.

Steve Plunkett and his parents, Roger and Elizabeth Plunkett, proprietors of the Extraordinary Bookseller in Rochester, Minnesota, secured essential sources for my research. University of Wisconsin-Superior staff members Al Miller, a maritime author, and the Maritime Collection archivist, Laura Jacobs, provided guidance and sources for my research on Great Lakes Coast Guard missions and the shipbuilding industry in the Lake Superior port cities of Duluth and Superior.

The Foundation for Coast Guard History, former FCGH executive director Capt. Fred Herzberg (USCG, Ret.), and the present executive director, Capt. Robert L. Desh (USCG, Ret.), provided encouragement and sources. Capt. Desh advised me "to keep writing about Coast Guard history."

John J. Galluzzo, a prolific author and editor of Coast Guard books and articles and editor at the United States Life-Saving Service Heritage Association (USLSSHA), provided me with sources and writing opportunities and wrote the scholarly foreword to this book.

Naval historian and author Richard P. Klobuchar inspired me with his friendship, humor, writing skills, and books and lectures on Pearl Harbor and the U.S. Navy. Klobuchar's magnificent book *The USS Ward* (McFarland, 2006) includes valuable information about Coast Guard operations at Pearl Harbor before, during and after the 7 December 1941 Japanese attack.

Mary Kreigh, an expert on the USS *Utah* as well as a writer, coordinator of naval history conferences, and graphic artist, assisted me with the initial planning and organization of maps for this book. My deepest appreciation and gratitude are extended to Dr. Brady Foust, chairman of the University of Wisconsin-Eau Claire Geography Department, and his talented cartography student, Nicholas Edward King. Mr. King's exemplary maps are a significant contribution to the historical geography of World War II military missions.

Tom Hosier and Tom Brinkman, codirectors of the Scott Hosier World War II Round Table in Rochester, Minnesota, offered me a 2005 speaking invitation that stimulated this writing project. The popular forum allows veterans to share and preserve their stories of service and sacrifice.

I have been inspired by Major James H. Eddy (USMC, Ret.) and his son, Chief Petty Officer Christopher J. Eddy (USCG, Ret.). Dr. James Eddy, a retired Winona State University political science professor, expressed his pride in CPO Eddy, and respect for the Coast Guard and its historic missions. Dr. Eddy encouraged my research with this written assertion: "A book about the United States Coast Guard in World War II is needed. The USCG is truly the silent service in terms of its wartime role in World War II, and subsequent national defense missions. Full speed ahead."

Colonel Walter T. Halloran (United States Army, Ret.) is a distinguished World War II combat photographer who emerged from a landing craft at Normandy just ahead of a squad of U.S. Army combat engineers. Col. Halloran acquainted me with the missions of combat photographers and landing craft crews, whose ranks included Navy and Coast Guard personnel.

Captain Ralph W. Niesz (USCG, Ret.) offered positive comments about my first book, *The USCG, 1790 to the Present*. The decorated Vietnam combat veteran encouraged me to keep writing about Coast Guard history.

Lt. Roy Watson (USNR) shared stories of his World War II naval service on the USS *Makassar Strait* (CVE-91) in the Pacific. Lt. Watson's regard for the USCG motivated him to present me with a magnificent model and photograph of a Coast Guard cutter. Roy's wife, Beverly, and her friend Shirley Nygren shared their professional experiences as wartime administrative assistants in the Washington, D.C., offices of the U.S. Navy and U.S. Coast Guard respectively.

Cmdr. Marc Carpenter (USNR), a bomber patrol pilot in the South Pacific, helped me understand the surveillance, search and rescue, and combat missions carried out by U.S. Navy and Coast Guard aviators in the formidable amphibious PBY floatplanes.

SN2 Seymour Wittek exemplifies the significance of the World War II Coast Guard Port Security mission. Wittek and his courageous colleagues extinguished an ammunition ship fire which, had the ship exploded, could have detonated adjacent fuel and ammunition depots and tankers and caused thousands of civilian casualties in the New York and New Jersey harbor and port region. In a November 2008 telephone conversation, Wittek, an energetic octogenarian, updated me on his belated Veterans Day Coast Guard award ceremony, an event heralded in the *New York Times* and attended by the USCG vice commandant.

BMC Christopher Browning, author of *Coast Guard* magazine articles, encouraged my continued writing and honored me with the coveted Chief's Mess coin from the USCGC *Dauntless*.

The time, energy, travel, and resources needed to complete this book would have been impossible without the patience and support of my accomplished wife, Mary Lamal Ostrom.

Foreword
by John Galluzzo

It is easy to look at World War II and place the Marines at Iwo Jima, the Navy at Midway, and the Army on the battlefields of France. But what of the United States Coast Guard? The public knowledge about the Coast Guard at war is generally vague, even though the Coast Guard and its predecessor agencies have been involved in every American war since 1798. Since that time, the U.S. Coast Guard has been mandated by Congress to fall under the command of the U.S. Navy in time of declared war.

In World War II, the Coast Guard cutter *Taney* responded to the surprise attack upon Pearl Harbor on 7 December 1941. The USCGC *Taney* is now a floating museum on the Baltimore waterfront. The Service was protecting merchant ships from German U-boat "Wolf Packs" crossing the North Atlantic before that fateful Pearl Harbor day. Typical of the Service's history, the Coast Guard assumed many roles in the 1940s. Already charged with search and rescue, marine inspections, antismuggling activities, ice patrols, aids to navigation, weather patrols, and more, the maritime Service expanded its port security mission, performed antisubmarine patrols in the air and at sea, experimented with military helicopters in lifesaving missions, and was an essential element of America's amphibious warfare machine.

Early in the conflict, America's top military officials realized that many Atlantic and Mediterranean beachheads and the innumerable Japanese-held islands of the South Pacific had to be assaulted by massive troop strength carried to shore in small boats. Air and naval bombardment could soften an entrenched enemy, but not wipe him out. The U.S. Navy had never focused its training efforts on small boats and landing craft. The Coast Guard and its predecessor, the U.S. Life-Saving Service, had been handling small boats in varied surf conditions since the middle of the nineteenth century. Their coxswains were ideally suited for taking the helm of the thousands of LCVPs (Landing Craft, Vehicle, Personnel)) which rolled out of the Higgins Industries boatyard in New Orleans. The Coast Guard's only Medal of Honor recipient, Signalman First Class Douglas Albert Munro, died at the helm of a Higgins boat while leading the evacuation of U.S. Marines from Guadalcanal on 27 September 1942.

1

The Coast Guard's World War II contributions ranged from air, land, and sea from Pearl Harbor to V-J Day. The missions stretched from the Aleutians to the South Pacific, from the West Coast, across the Great Lakes, to the East Coast, and across the Atlantic from Greenland to the beaches of Normandy, into the heart of the Mediterranean Sea.

In his typical, thorough fashion, Tom Ostrom has laid out the story of the Coast Guard in World War II. Tom is a "no-stones-left-unturned" researcher, well capable of capturing the depth, width, and breadth of the maritime Service's tale in the most significant conflict of the twentieth century. Once you have finished reading this book, you will be thoroughly educated about the history of one of the most fascinating chapters in the maritime history of the United States.

John Galluzzo is the editor of *Wreck and Rescue Journal,* the executive director of the U.S. Life-Saving Service Heritage Association, and author and contributor to numerous books and articles on maritime and U.S. Coast Guard history.

Preface

The United States Coast Guard, contrary to the image suggested by its name, has performed its war and peacetime missions not only on inland and coastal waters but also on the high seas since its founding as the U.S. Revenue Cutter Service in 1790.

Under the administration of President George Washington and the first Treasury secretary, Alexander Hamilton, the USRCS enforced import duty laws, surveyed coastal and inland waterways, and saved lives and property at sea.

The USRCS partnered with the USN in the Undeclared Naval War with France, the War of 1812 against Britain, in the interdiction of pirate ships and slave traders, and in the Seminole Wars, Mexican War, Civil War, and the Spanish American War. During World War I the U.S. Revenue Cutter Service merged with the U.S. Life-Saving Service to form the U.S. Coast Guard in 1915. The U.S. Coast Guard and the U.S. Navy have joined forces in national defense missions from World War I to the present.

Since the American purchase of Alaska in 1867, the Coast Guard has assumed law enforcement, maritime safety, search and rescue, and national security responsibilities in Alaskan, Bering Sea, and Arctic waters. The cutters and crews of the USRCS and USCG gained reputations as ice sailors with expertise in icebreaking, oceanography, maritime weather station patrols, and the tracking of icebergs by ship and aircraft. This multi-mission experience would serve America well in World War II.

The Coast Guard's early experience in seaplane and maritime reconnaissance patrols was skillfully applied in World War II when President Roosevelt assigned the Sea Service to strategic and dangerous convoy escort, antisubmarine, and Greenland Ice Patrol duties.

During World War I the USCG had conducted convoy and antisubmarine patrols from the Atlantic coast to the European continent and suffered ship and crew casualties in the process. In World War II, the Coast Guard expanded upon that experience and carried out convoy escort, search and rescue, and antisubmarine patrols while manning Coast Guard, Army, and Navy ships. Coast Guard crews ran troop, cargo and tanker transports, and the combat destroyers and landing craft vessels that supported military operations around the globe.

3

A wide range of historical literature covers specific, specialized Coast Guard missions and theaters of operation in World War II. The best general treatment of the war is the 1957 publication *The Coast Guard in World War II*, by Malcolm T. Willoughby, which was reprinted in 1989. Robert Erwin Johnson's Coast Guard history, *Guardians of the Sea* (1985), covers World War II in chapters 12–15. This book, *The United States Coast Guard in World War II* is a modest attempt to supplement and update those magnificent histories with a broad narrative synthesis of World War II. This history is written at a time when the population of World War II military veterans is rapidly diminishing, and it represents a modest attempt to chronicle the achievements of the maritime veterans who served America and the world at home and overseas.

Members of the U.S. Coast Guard and their colleagues in the other military services carried out their missions on land and sea and in the air—in the Atlantic, Gulf of Mexico and the Caribbean; from Greenland to Normandy to the Mediterranean Sea; and in the Pacific from Pearl Harbor to Australia, the Aleutians, the Philippines, and countless other islands.

The geostrategic, tactical, and logistical challenges were enormous. This book attempts to chronicle that inspirational story of courage, sacrifice, and success, and the tremendous cost of that effort.

Introduction

The United States Coast Guard traces its origins to the U.S. Revenue Cutter Service (initially referred to as the Revenue Marine) established under the Treasury Department in 1790. The USRCS merged with the U.S. Life-Saving Service to form the U.S. Coast Guard in 1915.

Throughout its history, the USCG has been assigned maritime safety, law enforcement, lifesaving, environmental protection, contraband interdiction, and national defense responsibilities. The Coast Guard has partnered with the U.S. Navy in national defense missions at home and overseas in peace and war throughout its history and to the present.

In World War I, the Coast Guard used its land, sea and air platforms to continue its peacetime duties and to protect Allied troop and supply convoys from torpedo and deck gun attacks by German submarines (U-boats). The danger of convoy escort duty was illustrated on 26 September 1918 when the U.S. Coast Guard cutter *Tampa* was torpedoed by a U-boat in the English Channel with the loss of more than 100 Coast Guard officers and enlisted men. That maritime combat experience prepared the Coast Guard to serve jointly with the other U.S. Armed Forces, and contribute to victory in World War II. *The United States Coast Guard in World War II* chronicles that costly and complex mission.

World War II quickly came to American shores. Coast Guard Captains of the Port (COTPs) supervised port security, marine safety, explosives loading, Coast Guard Beach Patrols, and the positioning of antisubmarine nets at strategic harbor entrances. Great Lakes ports, economic infrastructure, cargo vessels, and the strategic Sault Ste. Marie Locks were conduits for the shipment of strategic mineral resources, food, and manufactured goods essential to the war effort at home and overseas.

On the foggy night of 13 June 1942, Coast Guard Seaman John C. Cullen was on Beach Patrol along the sandy shores of Long Island (New York). SN Cullen confronted four German saboteurs just put ashore from a German submarine. Cullen pretended to cooperate with the German agents and hurriedly returned to his Coast Guard station. Coast Guard officials contacted the Federal Bureau of Investigation. Within days the Long Island saboteurs and four other German agents reported by Florida fishermen were apprehended.

World War II naval casualties were high. In just one U-boat attack on 13 June 1943 the Great Lakes icebreaker USCGC *Escanaba* (WPG-77) was sunk in the frigid and rolling seas of the North Atlantic with the loss of 101 Coastguardsmen and only two survivors. The CGC *Alexander Hamilton* (WPG-34), sunk by a U-boat off Iceland on 29 January 1942, was the first U.S. Navy vessel lost in action after Pearl Harbor. The 165-foot CGC *Icarus* (WPC-110) out of Staten Island (New York) sank *U-352* in the Eastern Sea Frontier of the Atlantic on 9 May 1942 and rescued the surviving German, seamen, who became prisoners of war.

Coast Guard–manned vessels served in all of the maritime combat theaters. The first Coast Guard combat casualties of the war occurred when the attack transport USS *Leonard Wood* (APA-12) was attacked by Japanese aircraft at the Asian port of Singapore on 8 December 1941. Between 1941 and 1945 the *Leonard Wood* carried U.S. Army and Marine Corps troops into combat zones in the Mediterranean (North Africa and Southern Europe), and to the Pacific islands of Kwajalein, Eniwetok, Saipan, and Leyte in the Philippines.

The USCGC *Taney* (WHEC-37) shot at Japanese aircraft during the Pearl Harbor attack on 7 December 1941. The *Taney* later patrolled the Atlantic and Pacific, was decommissioned in 1986, and home-ported as a maritime museum vessel in Baltimore (Maryland). The USCGC *Ingham* (WPG/WAGC-35) sank German submarine *U-626* in the North Atlantic and served as a U.S. Navy flagship in the Philippine landings. At the end of its sailing career, the CGC *Ingham* was decommissioned and home-ported as a museum ship in Charleston Harbor (South Carolina).

The USCGC *Duane* (WPG-33) assisted the USCGC *Spencer* (WPG/WAGC-36) in the sinking of *U-175* on 17 April 1943. The *Spencer* escorted convoys in the Caribbean and Mediterranean, and served as a Navy flagship in the Philippine landings in 1945. The 327-foot USCGC *Campbell* (WPG/WAGC-32) rammed and sank *U-606* in the Atlantic in February 1943.

Numerous other cutters, rescue boats, and Coast Guard–manned Army and Navy transports, combat ships, and landing craft participated in the Normandy invasion of 1944, and shot down ("splashed") Japanese suicide (*kamikaze*) aircraft in the Pacific. Coast Guard search and rescue (SAR) and aids to navigation (ATN) teams performed maritime safety missions during the war, including explosives loading, port security and fire fighting, and rescued downed aviators and sailors on land and sea in often extreme geographic environments.

Then there are the stories of the excitement and danger the cutter crews and aviators endured dodging icebergs and breaking up ice floes on the Greenland Patrol. Coast Guard, Navy and Army personnel suffered injuries and fatalities on land and in cyclonic storms and winds, and on icy and heavy seas in waves that exceeded 10 to 20 feet or more in height.

Coast Guardsmen rescued civilian and military personnel in polar seas and off the glacial ice cap. Cutters, weighed down by ice that could and did capsize ships, rolled in high seas searching for the lethal U-boats. Coast Guard personnel captured German vessels and enemy personnel at isolated bases and weather stations. The exploits of "ice captains" like Capt. Charles W. Thomas, commander of the 216-foot USCGC *Northland* (WPG-49), and the tactical leadership of Commander Edward "Iceberg" Smith (USCG) determined the success of the Greenland Patrol.

Coast Guard personnel mingled with American ground troops on faraway shores as beach masters, cargo handlers, and combat photographers. After World Wars I and II, congressional budget hawks and appreciative U.S. Navy officers and administrators considered placing the Coast Guard permanently under Defense Department and Navy control. The distinguished wartime Coast Guard commandants, Captain Ellsworth P. Bertholf (World War I) and Admiral Russell R. Waesche (World War II), utilized their significant leadership skills to prevent the well-intentioned postwar assimilation schemes.

The contributions to the war effort by civilian industrial leaders and workers, and the brave sailors and Navy gunners of the U.S. Merchant Marine, are noted. But the primary emphasis of this book is on the men and women of the Coast Guard in World War II. The spotlight is placed on members of the Coast Guard and their colleagues in the other U.S. Armed Forces who served at home and in the Aleutians, Atlantic, Gulf of Mexico, Caribbean, Pacific, and Mediterranean. These active duty Coast Guard officers, enlisted personnel, reservists, Auxiliary, and civilian employees added to the legacy of the Service, and its motto, "Semper Paratus" (Always Ready).

1

Prelude to Pearl Harbor

The significant role the United States Coast Guard played at home and overseas may surprise observers whose perceptions of that naval service might be circumscribed by the word "Coast."

A brief history of the service puts its missions into perspective. In 1789 the U.S. Lighthouse Service was established under the Treasury Department. In 1790 Congress created the U.S. Revenue Marine and authorized the construction of ten sailing vessels ("cutters") to enforce tariff laws. Treasury Secretary Alexander Hamilton organized and administered the Revenue Marine and established its training and missions.

The Revenue Marine, later known as the U.S. Revenue Cutter Service, was the first federal navy. The Continental Congress had established a Navy that fought gallantly in the Revolutionary War, but was subsequently disbanded. In 1794 the United States Congress authorized the U.S. Navy and launched its fledgling fleet in 1797.

From 1799 to 1800, the Revenue Marine and the Navy waged war against France in the "Quasi" Undeclared Naval War. After the war, the Revenue Cutter Service returned to domestic law enforcement, coastal security, and lifesaving missions. In 1812 the Revenue Marine and the Navy battled the British navy. In the 19th century the Revenue Cutter Service saw action in the Seminole Indian wars, subdued pirates, and supported the Navy in the Mexican War, Civil War, and Spanish American War.

In 1915 the U.S. Life-Saving Service, which had been directed by Sumner Kimball since 1871, and the USRCS merged to form the U.S. Coast Guard (USCG). During World War I the Coast Guard served national defense by inspecting vessels, administering port security, conducting antisubmarine warfare (ASW) patrols, and guarding merchant ship convoys across the Atlantic to supply our European Allies, primarily Britain and France, in the war against the Central Powers (Germany and the Ottoman (Turkish) and Austro-Hungarian Empires).

Between and after those wars, the USRCS/USCG participated in the evolving peacetime missions of lifesaving and search and rescue (SAR), aids to navigation (ATN), maritime law enforcement, ship inspection, scientific and oceanographic expeditions, monitoring iceberg locations as part of the International Ice Patrol, weather station duty, icebreaking to maintain navigation lanes, drug and immigration interdiction, and environmental protection.

The maritime domain of the Coast Guard included U.S. coastal regions, inland waterways, Alaska, Hawaii, and the international high seas. The Coast Guard joined with the Navy at home and overseas in combat and SAR missions in World Wars I and II, Korea, Vietnam, the Persian Gulf wars of the 20th and 21st centuries and the war on terror at home and abroad.

In 1939 the U.S. Lighthouse Service merged with the USCG. In 1940 the Coast Guard was preparing for what became World War II. After the Japanese attack on the U.S. Naval Base at Pearl Harbor on 7 December 1941, the Coast Guard, Navy, Marines, and Army confronted the Axis Powers of Germany, Japan, and Italy.[1]

The apex of the Coast Guard command structure is the Coast Guard commandant. Captain-Commandant Ellsworth Bertholf was the commander of the Revenue Cutter Service when the USLSS and the USRCS merged into the U.S. Coast Guard in 1915. Capt. Bertholf achieved fame as a young lieutenant in the Arctic Overland Expedition of 1898 and as a Revenue Service cutter commander in the Alaska-Bering Sea region. Commandant Bertholf led the Coast Guard through World War I. He consistently and successfully persuaded Congress to keep the USRCS/USCG in the Treasury Department rather than permanently assign the service to the U.S. Navy.[2]

Coast Guard commandant Russell R. Waesche led the Coast Guard through World War II. Appointed in 1936, Admiral Waesche is the Coast Guard's longest serving commandant.[3] Adm. Waesche's exemplary wartime leadership enhanced the Coast Guard's reputation as a military combat service, and the admiral himself earned the respect and appreciation of his U.S. Navy, Army, and Marine Corps colleagues.

An essential element of wartime logistics and security at home and abroad is the management and control of ports and harbors. The Coast Guard has played a significant historic and contemporary role in port security and national defense. The USCG has monitored port security through its Captains of the Port. COTPs coordinate operations with local, state, and federal law enforcement, civilian commercial and harbor authorities, and the U.S. Armed Forces. COTP authorities have facilitated national defense activities and maintained safe commercial and military maritime supply lines from World War I to the present.

The Coast Guard utilized World War I experiences to carry out World War II port security, convoy, search and rescue, national defense and combat responsibilities. During the Prohibition era (1920–1933) the Coast Guard–manned patrol boats and Navy destroyers to carry out its law enforcement m ission. That experience facilitated joint U.S. Coast Guard and U.S. Navy combined crew and vessel operations in World War II.[4] The war clouds of World War II (1939–1945) were visible in prewar European border quarrels, military alliances, nationalist passions, and prewar Axis aggression in Europe, Africa, and Asia. The League of Nations seemed powerless to act.

The embers of the Great War (World War I) continued to smolder under the blanket of the flawed Treaty of Versailles, the United States hosted international disarmament conferences in the 1920s to no avail. Great Britain and France declared war on Germany after Nazi dictator Adolf Hitler invaded Poland. President Franklin D. Roosevelt (FDR) and the U.S. Congress officially followed a policy of neutrality; but FDR aided the Allies with supply convoys, U.S. Atlantic naval patrols, and the controversial but generous Lend-Lease policy (1941) with Britain. FDR maintained regular communications with British prime minister Winston Churchill and met with him secretly off the Canadian coast of Newfoundland (August 1941) where they crafted international objectives and war policy.

Congress voted to strengthen U.S. military forces with appropriations and the drafting (conscription) of civilians for military service through the Selective Service and Training Act of 1940. Roosevelt claimed his policies were intended as a deterrent to Axis aggression and were necessary for military preparedness in his role as commander-in-chief of the Armed Forces.

Nonetheless, Germany perceived U.S. actions as decidedly non-neutral and initiated submarine warfare activity against U.S. vessels. Japan reacted after FDR cut off the flow of iron ore and petroleum to that insular nation. Japan's subsequent sneak attack upon Pearl Harbor occurred because Japanese war planners saw the U.S. as the only military power capable of thwarting Nippon's Asian-Pacific imperial expansion in quest of territory and resources. Japanese military and political leaders hoped that after Pearl Harbor a chastened United States would negotiate for peace and allow Japan to keep some of her Asian empire.[5]

An interesting prewar episode involved the Coast Guard in the flight and disappearance of famous aviator Amelia Earhart in 1937. Relations with Japan were so contentious that some observers speculated the Japanese military shot down and captured Earhart and navigator Fred Noonan because they may have flown over a secret Pacific base. Evidence has not confirmed the conspiracy theory. The U.S. Coast Guard Cutter *Itasca* was in the vicinity of Earhart's Howland Island destination to provide a radio beacon on the scheduled flight path. Radio transmission failures from the aircraft and navigation errors and fuel problems may have contributed to the disappearance. The U.S. Navy aircraft carrier *Lexington* joined the CGC *Itasca* in the unsuccessful search for survivors.[6]

Tensions between the United States and Japan would lead to the Japanese attack on the U.S. Naval Base at Pearl Harbor, after which the United States entered the war against Japan and Germany. During the period of prewar American neutrality, U.S. naval forces were involved in naval hostilities in an incident with Japan in China and between the United Kingdom and Germany.

German submarines fired at American naval vessels as U.S. ships began to escort supply convoys to Britain and track and report the location of German U-boats in the North Atlantic.

On 4 September 1941 two torpedoes were fired from a German submarine at the U.S. Navy destroyer *Greer*. President Roosevelt then issued his "shoot on sight" orders against German U-boats that entered American defense perimeters. On 17 October the U.S. Navy destroyer *Kearney* attacked a German submarine that retaliated. The USS *Kearney* was severely damaged and suffered the loss of eleven sailors in the German torpedo attack.[7] The crew from the USCGC *Eastwind* captured a German trawler crew in the North Atlantic and German military personnel on the Danish island of Greenland.[8]

Coast Guard cutters found themselves in the middle of the famed North Atlantic battle between the British and German navies. The 240-foot USCGC *Modoc*, launched in 1922, was within six miles of the German battleship *Bismarck* in the North Atlantic between 24 and 27 May 1941. The crew of the *Modoc* saw the British naval attack on the gigantic 800-foot German battleship *Bismarck*. Armed with two five-inch and two three-inch guns and a crew complement of 140, the 15-knot *Modoc*, almost targeted in the battle, was no match for the German leviathan.[9]

The 216-foot USCGC *Northland*, launched in 1927, a cruising gunboat designed for Arctic missions, was armed with two 3-inch guns, had a crew complement of 105, and was in the *Bismarck* area of operations from 20 to 23 May 1941.[10]

The *Bismarck* was armed with 20 guns, 8 torpedo tubes and a complement of more than 2,000 crew members, and had a flank speed of 30 knots. The *Bismarck* was sunk on 27 May 1941 after several days of tracking and battle by British torpedo planes, which took off from two British aircraft carrier decks, and British battleship action.[11]

The British warship HMS *Prince of Wales* was damaged in the battle with the *Bismarck*, and the battle cruiser HMS *Hood* was sunk by the German battleship, which in turn was severely damaged by HMS *King George V* and HMS *Rodney*.[12]

On 12 December 1937 Japanese aircraft bombed and sank the USS *Panay* while the U.S. Navy gunboat lay at anchor on the Yangtze River in China, with a casualty toll of two American sailors killed and 30 wounded.[13] Prewar military action against the United States by the Tokyo-Berlin Axis intensified animosities that led the United States into World War II. The crowning catalyst was the attack by the Japanese Navy at Pearl Harbor.

2

The Day of Infamy: Pearl Harbor

President Franklin D. Roosevelt supported, and Congress imposed, an economic embargo upon Japan that was intended to deter further Japanese military expansion in the insular regions of the Eastern Pacific Ocean and continental East Asia. Japanese militarists and Emperor Hirohito believed these imperial acquisitions were necessary to balance the power and threat of American and European colonization in the region and acquire the land and resources needed to support Nippon's expanding population. Ironically, America's refusal to sell iron ore and petroleum to Japan not only failed to deter that nation's expansion, but the U.S. policy also seemed to support the rationalizations of most of Japan's political and military leaders.

In early December 1941, while two earnest Japanese diplomats were in Washington, D.C., preparing to discuss the diplomatic conflicts with Cordell Hull, FDR's secretary of state, a formidable Japanese Strike Force (JSF) was sailing undetected toward the U.S. military and naval base at Pearl Harbor, Hawaii.[1] American military and civilian officials expected a Japanese attack somewhere in Southeast Asia, perhaps in the Dutch East Indies (today's Indonesia), in British or French possessions, or perhaps the U.S. colony of the Philippines. Pearl Harbor was not a suspected target because of the perceived logistical and tactical challenges involved in traversing such a vast maritime expanse. Nonetheless, U.S. cryptographic experts had successfully decoded Japanese electronic transmissions and were properly suspicious of Japanese intentions.[2]

When the Japanese Strike Force bombed Pearl Harbor on 7 December 1941, President Roosevelt declared it "a day that would live in Infamy."[3] Washington had not advised the Pearl Harbor military commanders that an attack was imminent, but Adm. Husband E. Kimmel (USN) and Lt. Gen. Walter C. Short (USA) had been given a "war warning." Following the attack, Kimmel and Short were relieved of their commands.[4]

By 1941 American cryptographers could intercept and translate the Japanese code called PURPLE, which circumstance served as a strategic advantage prior to Pearl Harbor and throughout the Pacific war. The U.S. military and civilian policy planners also had the technological benefit of RADAR, detected

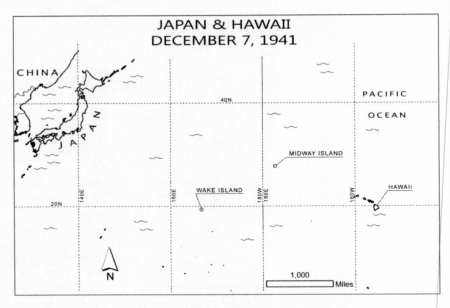

JAPAN & HAWAII
DECEMBER 7, 1941

which tracks air and sea craft at considerable distances. Radar screens in fact had illustrated the images of the approaching Japanese naval strike one hour to the north of the Hawaiian island of Oahu. Communications failures prevented that information from being utilized in a timely fashion.[5]

American cryptologists called the project to intercept and decode Japanese code MAGIC. The talented civilian and military code breakers included U.S. Navy officers Laurence F. Stafford and Robert J. Rochefort and Major William Friedman (U.S. Army) and his wife, Elizabeth.[6] Major Friedman had previously assisted the Coast Guard in the Prohibition era (1920–1933) with the development of radio codes to conceal USCG law enforcement patrol locations from the ears of radio equipped rumrunners and their armada of contraband-carrying water craft.[7]

The Office of Naval Intelligence provided strategic and national security information to the federal government and the other military services prior to Pearl Harbor and throughout World War II. The staff of Adm. Chester W. Nimitz (USN), commander of the U.S. Pacific Fleet, expanded to nearly 2,000 personnel in the Joint Intelligence Command Pacific Ocean Area (JICPOA). JICPOA comprised U.S. Army, Navy, Marine and Coast Guard personnel,[8] and included Cmdr. Edwin Thomas Layton (USN), the Pacific Fleet intelligence officer,[9] and the legendary Lt. Joseph Rochefort (USN), who had worked with Lt. Laurence Stafford (USN) in cryptographic research at the Office of Naval Communication (ONC) in Washington, D.C.[10] Coast Guard intelligence operatives assisted military at Pearl Harbor and in the Pacific and Atlantic theaters of operation.

The Coast Guard also contributed personnel to the Office of Strategic Services (OSS), the predecessor of the Central Intelligence Agency. The OSS protected national security by conducting espionage missions, and it utilized Coast Guard signals and information intercepts. Coast Guard Regulars and the civilian Coast Guard Auxiliary were used in Port Security operations. Well-trained Coast Guard personnel contributed signaling, intelligence, swimming, boat handling, and diving skills to OSS operations.

Of the 56 USCG members who worked for the OSS, Lt. John Babb (USNR), chief of the OSS Maritime Unit in the Asian area of operations, said, "They were engaged in the infiltration of agents and working their way into enemy lines through mangrove swamps under enemy outposts" and evading enemy patrols.[11] Several OSS operatives in Operational Swimmer Group 2 (OSG 2) were Coastguardsmen. Lt. John P. Booth (USCGR), the OSG 2 field commanding officer in Burma, earned the Bronze Star. OSG 2 "frogmen" were the predecessors of the U.S. Navy SEALS.[12]

Diplomatic tensions during the year prior to the Pearl Harbor attack and concern about potential espionage by Japanese aliens and even Japanese citizens of the United States led to Coast Guard patrols being assigned to keep fishing boats from operating in the strategic waters off Diamond Head Cape on southeast Oahu island near Honolulu.[13] The stunning attack by the Japanese Imperial Navy upon Pearl Harbor was intended to prevent the U.S. fleet from interfering with Japan's East Asian conquests, and to force the United States into a negotiated diplomatic settlement and acceptance of the status quo. The attack had the opposite effect. It united America and led to the eventual U.S. and Allied defeat of Japan.[14]

The U.S. Navy, Marine, Army, and Coast Guard installations in Hawaii included ten battleships; three aircraft carriers carrying 250 aircraft; 500 land-based aircraft; dozens of warships, submarines, support ships, cutters and boats; and two infantry divisions. The military infrastructure included maintenance facilities, warehouses, and fuel depots that the Japanese Strike Force (JSF) failed to completely destroy.[15] The JSF struck from a point 250 miles north of Hawaii. The enemy aircraft arrived in Pearl Harbor at 7:55 Sunday morning. The first wave of JSF combat planes was composed of more than 140 torpedo planes and dive-bombers and 42 fighter escorts.

U.S. Fleet antiaircraft guns and several military aircraft swiftly struck back at the invaders; but within the first hour of the attack, eight battleships and ten warships of other classifications were sunk or damaged. Two hundred American aircraft were destroyed, most while sitting on airstrips. Two thousand three hundred and eighty-eight military and civilian personnel were killed and 1,178 were wounded. Three aircraft carriers were out to sea and survived to fight future battles. JSF losses were minimal and included nine midget submarines and their crews, 55 aviators, and 29 warplanes.[16]

U.S. naval patrol vessels made suspicious contacts with unauthorized ves-

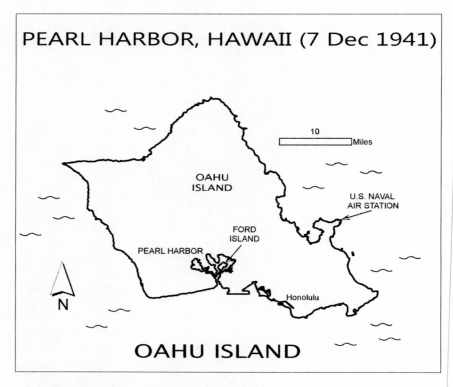

PEARL HARBOR, HAWAII (7 Dec 1941)

OAHU ISLAND

sels in the Pearl Harbor area prior to the JSF attack. The USS *Ward*, under the command of Lt. William W. Outerbridge (USN), was on patrol off the harbor entrance and picked up sonar evidence of a possible enemy submarine at 0703. The *Ward*, crewed by U.S. Navy reservists from Minnesota, depth-charged the intruder. Outerbridge submitted radio information about the incident and requested that a U.S. Coast Guard cutter be sent to escort a suspicious sampan boat out of the unauthorized area of the harbor. The cutter escorted the sampan to shore and impounded the vessel. Lt. Outerbridge's radio message about the submarine incident got no immediate response.[17] Before the Pearl Harbor attack, an Imperial Japanese Navy (IJN) submarine, identified by one source as HA-19, was sighted by harbor tug *YT-153* and the USCGC *Tiger* (WPC-152) and narrowly escaped a ramming attempt.[18]

Coast Guard activities before, during, and after 7 December were varied and extensive. In April 1942 a new naval base was being built adjacent to the U.S. Marine Corps (USMC) base at Ewa on Oahu. The Barbers Point Naval Air Station accommodated several military units, including a U.S. Coast Guard Station.[19]

Among the Coast Guard personnel who joined his U.S. Armed Forces colleagues in responding to 7 December was Lt. Frank Erickson (USCG). Erickson had been assigned to the U.S. Navy since August 1941 when the Coast Guard was shifted from the Treasury Department to the Navy Department in the Hawaiian area of operations. The USCG was fully incorporated into the U.S. Navy in all operations areas on 1 November 1941. Prior to August 1941, Lt. Erickson was an aviator assigned to the USCGC *Taney* (W-37). After that date, he was a naval station duty officer at the aircraft control tower. From the control tower Erickson observed the JSF attacks, vessel destruction, brave American responses, casualties, and the flaming harbor waters into which sailors, airmen, and marines leaped and from which survivors tried to swim to shore on Ford Island.

An enthusiastic student of the new and innovative helicopter aircraft, Lt. Erickson foresaw the search and rescue (SAR) mission possibilities of the rotor-winged craft. In the bloodshed and chaos of Pearl Harbor, he could only imagine the lives that could have been saved with helicopters. A future legendary helicopter pilot, Lt. Erickson devoted the rest of his career to making the Sikorsky helicopter a tactical and SAR reality in the Coast Guard and other Armed Forces. In that mission, Erickson had the help and support of other intrepid Coast Guard, Navy, Marine and Army aviators but had to battle cynics, critics, and obstructionists along the way.

For the next ten days following 7 December, Lt. Erickson flew naval patrols in search of any remnants of the Japanese fleet that some analysts believed would return for another air attack and even a ground invasion. Erickson and his airborne colleagues flew Grumman J2F and Sikorsky JRS seaplanes (flying boats) initially armed only with shotguns and rifles. The more lethal machine guns would be added to the floatplanes and amphibious aircraft at a later date.[20]

Radioman First Class (RM1/c) George C. Larsen (USCG) enlisted in the Coast Guard on 29 October 1939 at the Customs House in San Francisco, California, had basic training at Port Townsend, Washington in the Pacific Northwest, and was assigned to Government (now Coast Guard) Island in Alameda, California. Between 1939 and 1941 Petty Officer (PO) Larsen served on the decommissioned Coast Guard icebreaker *Northland*, the 165-foot CGC *Ariadne* (WPC-101), on patrol off the California coast, the CGC *Taney* (WPG-37/WAGC-37) at Oahu, Hawaii, and the 185-foot buoy tender *Kukui* (WAGL-225). As Seaman First Class (SN 1/c), Larsen maintained range and tower lights and then learned to monitor classified radio communications at Diamond Head Lighthouse on Oahu Island. Because of international diplomatic tension between the United States and Japan in November 1941, Coast Guard personnel were armed with .45 pistols while on duty.

On 7 December 1941, at 7:55 A.M., the "Day of Infamy" in President Roosevelt's words, PO Larsen witnessed the Japanese attack on Pearl Harbor from his shore post and was informed that the U.S. Navy destroyer USS *Ward* (DD-139) had depth charged and shot at a Japanese submarine near the entry channel to Pearl Harbor. While on radio watch, PO Larsen received a distress call from a sinking fishing boat that had been attacked by a U.S. Army airplane. In anticipation of a Japanese land invasion, Larsen was ordered to conduct an armed beach patrol on the 7th and 8th of December. While on patrol, PO Larsen watched as nervous Army machine gunners shot down three low flying U.S. Navy aircraft.

On 8 December Radioman (RM) Larsen was temporarily assigned to the CGC *Kukui* (WAGL-225) on a mission to extinguish automatic tower and lighthouse lights in its area of responsibility (AOR). The *Kukui* sailed close to shore to avoid a reported Imperial Japanese Navy submarine (I-boat), picked up a squad of USA troops, and then embarked to an island where a Japanese aviator had reportedly crashed. The Army squad and four armed Coastguardsmen went ashore and discovered that the Japanese pilot had been subdued and killed by a 6-foot 6-inch Hawaiian male who had been shot three times by the invader. The CGC *Kukui* transported the courageous islander to Port Allen for hospitalization and recovery.

The *Kukui* crew then extinguished the aids to navigation lights in the Kauai Island area and then returned to mark shipping hazards in the devastated Pearl Harbor area. Upon completion of that mission the *Kukui* docked at Pier Four in Honolulu Harbor, adjacent to the submarine-chasing USCGC *Tiger* (WSC-152). Larsen requested and was granted a transfer to the CGC *Tiger*. Soon after reporting for duty, the commanding officer of the *Tiger* assigned the young radioman to his station with a promotion. RM2 George C. Larsen proudly assumed his new billet and prepared for action in the Pacific theater of naval operations.[21]

Many outer island residents and fishermen who had been at sea in the days before 7 December 1941 were unaware of the attack on Pearl Harbor and the subsequent radio broadcast blackout. Therefore fishermen in boats and sampans suffered surprise and casualties when Japanese and American combat aircraft attacked them. Newspapers warned that watercraft approaching the Hawaiian Islands would be targeted. The Japanese alien cohort of fishermen was considered by many observers to be spies for Imperial Japan.

Coast Guard boats and cutters approached suspicious vessels, gave fishing crews flags to display, escorted fishing boats to shore and some crews to internment. Abandoned sampans were allowed to drift away. At least six fishermen were killed during post–December 7 panics. Wounded boaters were given medical aid and hospitalization, and some became prisoners of war (POWs).[22]

Observation posts were quickly established throughout the Islands and staffed by male and female civilian volunteers and members of the Armed Forces. Reports about suspicious activities and air- and watercraft movements were provided to police and military officials. By 1942 lookout towers were built or utilized at strategically located Coast Guard lighthouses. Trained civilian Coast Guard Auxiliary members participated in lookout duties and conducted surveillance patrols at sea to release Coast Guard regulars for other national defense operations.[23]

With the cooperation of the U.S. Army, Navy, and Marines, the Coast Guard assumed the responsibility of waterfront port security, firefighting, and the supervision of loading dangerous military cargoes and continued its regular search and rescue and aids to navigation duties. Coast Guard members built, modified, and crewed fireboats and land-based firefighting vehicles and equipment. The Coast Guard Captain of the Port (COTP) at Pearl Harbor administered a force of about 600 military personnel.[24]

On 23 November 1942 Congress authorized the establishment of the Coast Guard Women's Reserve. Captain Dorothy Stratton transferred from the U.S. Navy to train and lead the unit. Capt. Stratton called the women Coast Guard members "SPARS," from the USCG motto, "Semper Paratus" (Always Ready). Twelve thousand women served in officer and enlisted ranks in a variety of administrative and technical support roles during World War II. SPARS in Hawaii and throughout the United States played an essential role in carrying out Coast Guard missions that released male members of the service for other military duties at home and overseas.[25]

The SPARS joined their female counterparts in the U.S. Navy's Women Accepted for Volunteer Emergency Service (WAVES), Marines (Marine Corps Women's Reserve), Army Air Force (Women's Air Service Pilots, or WASPS), and Women's Army Corps (WACS) in the war effort and paved the way for women to serve with honor and courage in all of the branches of the Armed Forces in the postwar years. But by the end of 1945 most of the women who had served in the U.S. military in Hawaii had been released from duty and returned to civilian life.[26]

In her magnificent book on women in the Armed Forces in World War II, Sally Van Wagenen Keil reported that by 1945 the totals of women in the respective services were WACs: 150,000, WAVES: 100,000, Women Marines: 23,000, and SPARS: 13,000. However, Van Wagenen Keil's reference to SPARS as members of the "Women's Coast Guard auxiliary" is misleading.[27] The SPARS were members of the Women's Reserve of the Coast Guard, not members of the civilian Coast Guard Auxiliary. Their ranks included 955 officers. Civilian employees, like SPARS, did do Coast Guard clerical work.

Enlisted SPARS had access to 43 ratings ranging from yeoman to boatswain's mate. SPARS ran LORAN (Long Range Navigation) units that involved familiarity with highly classified navigation systems. By 1944 SPARS were serving outside the contiguous boundaries of the United States in Alaska and in Hawaii, where more than 200 women served.[28] U.S. Navy units in Hawaii were stationed at the Hilo Naval Air Station, at Upolu Point, where the Coast Guard ran two LORAN stations, and Port Allen on Kauai. Coast Guard Headquarters was located at the U.S. Customs House at the port of Hilo on the "Big Island" of Hawaii.[29]

Richard P. Klobuchar is the author of two exemplary World War II naval histories. Klobuchar's first book covers the attack upon Pearl Harbor. The second book considers the history of the USS *Ward* (DD-139), crewed by Minnesota U.S Navy reservists, which sank a Japanese I-boat one hour before the Pearl Harbor attack. Klobuchar considered the role the Coast Guard played at Pearl Harbor before, during, and after the Japanese attack. Cutters were assigned to ocean patrol, port security, search and rescue, and aids to navigation duties before 7 December 1941. During the attack, the Coast Guard responded with gunfire, protected and escorted private watercraft, fishing boats, and tourist ships out of restricted Harbor areas, and impounded vessels.

Commander John Wooley (USN) headed the Inshore Patrol Command, which included four Navy destroyers, four USN minesweepers, and three Coast Guard cutters: USS *Taney* (WPG-37), USS *Tiger* (WPG-152), and USS *Reliance* (WPG-150). The cutters were tasked with patrolling shoreline areas to prevent espionage and the transfer and landing of illegal contraband and people. In 1941 the Navy temporarily absorbed the Coast Guard in preparation for what looked liked the coming of war. Coast Guard cutters were assigned submarine tracking duties in the Atlantic, Pacific and Gulf. To carry out these duties, cutters were gradually equipped with the newest classified sonar and depth charge technology to supplement the traditional deck guns and small arms component already on Coast Guard vessels.

The USCGC *Taney* was a destroyer-size 327-foot cutter with a 41-foot beam and 2,216-ton displacement. *Taney* armament included small arms and six 3-inch and six 5-inch guns. The smaller 125-foot cutters *Reliance* and *Tiger* were each equipped with small arms and a 3-inch deck gun.[30] The CGC *Taney* performed distinguished combat service at Pearl Harbor and throughout the Pacific. At Pearl Harbor the cutter crew drove away several Japanese aircraft and depth charged an enemy submarine.[31]

During the Battle of Okinawa (1945) in the Pacific, the *Taney* shot down five enemy aircraft. Later, in the Korean War (1950–1953), the *Taney* would provide weather and communications support to United Nations forces while on ocean station duty in the Pacific. In the Vietnam War (1969) the *Taney* patrolled the Vietnamese coast, monitoring Viet Cong and North Vietnamese Army (NVA) activities, and assisted U.S. and GSV (Government of South Vietnam) military and naval forces with transportation and combat support missions.[32]

Stationed in Hawaii on 7 December 1941 with the 327-foot CGC *Taney* (WPG-37) were the 190-foot buoy tender *Kukui*, the two 125-foot patrol craft, *Tiger* and *Reliance*, which because of their lengths were called the "Buck and a Quarter Class" cutters, two 78-foot patrol cutters, and several craft too small (less than 65 feet) to be called "cutters."

The *Taney*, under Cmdr. G.B. Gelly (USCG), was a Treasury Class cutter

Top: USCGC *Taney* (WPG-37). The Taney fought off Japanese combat aircraft at Pearl harbor on 7 December 1941. The 327-foot "Secretary Class" cutter operated as an escort vessel in the Mediterranean and as a command ship and combat information center in the Pacific. *Bottom:* USCGC *Tiger* (WSC-152). While patrolling by the Pearl Harbor entrance before the Japanese attack on 7 December 1941, the 125-foot Submarine Chaser *Tiger* picked up a sonar contact. During the attack, enemy aircraft fired upon the *Tiger*.

(named after secretaries of the U.S. Treasury) commissioned in 1937. The ship's armament included two 5"/51-caliber guns, several .50-caliber machine guns, and four 3"/50-caliber weapons. Home-ported at pier six in Honolulu, the *Taney* was six miles from the main U.S. Navy anchorage when the Japanese attack occurred. Without orders to steam out from the pier, the crew went to general quarters at first sight of the enemy aircraft and commenced firing as the second wave of Japanese planes passed overhead.

The *Kukui* was unarmed and remained moored during the attack. The CGC *Tiger* (WSC-152), under the command of Chief Warrant Officer (CWO) William J. Mazzoni (USCG), carried two depth charge racks, several machine guns, and one 3"/23-caliber gun. Commissioned in 1927 as a Prohibition enforcement patrol craft, the *Tiger* had been designed to intercept rumrunners in small boats that received contraband from larger vessels anchored outside the sovereign boundaries of American waters.[33]

While on patrol at 6:45 A.M. on 7 December, the CGC *Tiger* received a U.S. Navy message that reported the sinking of a Japanese submarine by the Navy destroyer USS *Ward*. In proximity to Barber's Point Lighthouse one half-hour later, the *Tiger* made sonar contact with a probable submarine, lost contact, and continued on patrol. At 8:00 A.M. the *Tiger* was fired upon by an unknown source, resumed her assigned station outside of Honolulu Harbor, observed the continuing Japanese air attack, and received undamaging "friendly fire" from nervous shoreside U.S. Army units that evening.

Other Pearl Harbor area cutters on patrol were the 78-foot cutters *CG-400* and *CG-403*; the 60-foot *CG-27*; *CG-4818*; and *CG-517*, a small buoy boat. Boatswain Mate First Class Boyd C. Maddox was in charge of the 78-foot *CG-8* (83360) that was armed with one machine gun. BM1 Maddox and a crew of six sailed out in the midst of the attack and dodged bombs and strafing attacks by Japanese warplanes. *CG-8* prevented civilian small boats from moving until Naval Intelligence personnel checked out the owners. *CG-8* (Ensign Richard S. Peer) then assisted in extinguishing and blacking out navigational aids as guards took positions at waterfront stations.

The buoy tender USCGC *Walnut* (WAGL-252) came under enemy shell fire 1,000 miles northwest of Hawaii when Japanese destroyers attacked Midway Island. The unarmed tender escaped unscathed and returned to Hawaii to receive depth charges and guns and carry out wartime aids to navigation missions.

Keeper John L. Sweeney (USCG) stood watch at Barbers Point Light Station, where he observed the Pearl Harbor attack and chronicled the action in an official report.[34]

The CGC *Taney* served gallantly throughout World War II in the Atlantic and Pacific in convoy and combat duty. The wartime commanders of the *Taney* were Cmdr. Eugene A. Coffin, Cmdr. George B. Gelly, Cmdr. Louis B. Olson, Capt. Henry C. Perkins, Cmdr. Henry J. Wuensch, Cmdr. George D.

Synon, and Cmdr. Carl G. Bowman. The *Taney* sailed on to serve in the Pacific Okinawa campaign in 1945 where her gun crews made hits on Japanese bombers, downed four suicide planes, and assisted in several kills and splash-downs.[35]

3

U.S. Coast
Guard Organization

During World War II, the United States Coast Guard was temporarily transferred from the Treasury Department to the War Department and placed under U.S. Navy jurisdiction. Between 1940 and 1945 the number of Coast Guard personnel increased from 13,756 to 171,192. The officer ranks increased from 1,351 to 12,683. Enlisted personnel increased from 12,261 to 158,290. The U.S. Coast Guard Academy cadet population grew from 144 to 219.

At its maximum 1945 numbers, the Coast Guard crews manned 802 ocean-going cutters (boats and ships ranging from 65 feet to over 300 feet in length), 351 Navy vessels, and 288 U.S. Army watercraft. As of 30 June 1945, the Coast Guard manned 1,677 vessels, including 600 cutters, and smaller craft assigned to port security and escort missions.

Wartime Coast Guard duties included national defense and port security missions at major ports and harbors under the jurisdiction of Captains of the Port at home and overseas. COTP and Coast Guard missions included the regulation of merchant shipping; guarding harbor infrastructure from espionage, sabotage, and fires; supervision of explosives loading on and off of civilian and military ships; and manning landing craft, troop transports, and supply ships.

The Coast Guard supported domestic Navy defense operations using foot, mounted, and canine beach patrols. Lookout stations were manned, and Coastguardsmen personnel joined Navy personnel at shore stations and on sea and air patrols under the operational jurisdiction of U.S. Navy Sea Frontier Commanders.

During the war, Coast Guard aviation tripled in size as its aviators performed traditional search and rescue missions, convoy protection, surveillance, antisubmarine warfare (ASW), aerial mapping, iceberg monitoring, and Great Lakes icebreaking missions to aid the wartime shipping of strategic cargo. In 1945 the USCG operated nine Coast Guard air stations on the Great Lakes and ocean coasts, with 165 aircraft. Coast Guard aviators responded to 5,357 medical emergencies and saved more than 780 lives in SAR missions.[1]

Coast Guard Reserve female personnel in World War II were called SPARS, a term constructed from the Coast Guard motto, "Semper Paratus"

(Always Ready). Captain Dorothy Stratton directed the Women's Coast Guard Reserve from 1942 to 1946. The former college professor and dean transferred from the U.S. Navy to lead the SPARS, which reached a wartime maximum of 1,000 officers and 10,000 enlisted personnel. SPARS performed administrative, recruiting, and hospital duties in Alaska, Hawaii, and throughout the continental United States. The SPARS were demobilized in 1946, but women were welcomed into Coast Guard Reserve and Regular units and the U.S. Coast Guard Academy in later decades.[2]

The Coast Guard Reserve in World War II totaled over 50,000 volunteer members. The Department of Commerce transferred the Bureau of Marine Inspection and Navigation to the USCG in 1942, adding to the defense and maritime safety missions the service performed in World War II and in the postwar period.

Twenty-eight Coast Guard cutters and boats and Navy vessels manned by Coast Guard personnel were sunk during the war. Wartime Coast Guard death tolls reached 1,030, including 572 killed in action (KIA). Coast Guard crew members on Coast Guard and Navy vessels participated in the sinking of 11 enemy submarines and the rescue of 4,000 people from sunken or damaged vessels at sea. A USCG aviator sunk a twelfth submarine.

Interesting missions, people and historical firsts occurred in the Coast Guard during World War II. Lieutenant Commander Edward H. "Iceberg" Smith commanded the Greenland Patrol that included several tugs, small boats and cutters. The cutter *Northland* captured a radio equipped German naval vessel in Greenland waters in September 1941 before the United States entered World War II. In June 1944 the first helicopter landing on the deck of a naval vessel occurred on the USCGC *Cobb*. In 1944 the cutter *Sea Cloud* led the way with its racially integrated United States navy crew.[3]

During the war the United States enlisted 11,260,000 soldiers, 4,183,466 sailors, 669,000 Marines, and 241,093 Coast Guard members. Civilian patriots built 296,000 aircraft, 102,000 tanks, and more than 88,000 landing craft, boats and ships.

The Coast Guard Reserve Act of 1939 was intended to train civilians to assist the Coast Guard in monitoring watercraft activities and pleasure boat and marine safety in classrooms, to perform free boat equipment and safety inspections, and to relieve active duty Coast Guard personnel to make them available for military duties at home and overseas. In 1941 Congress restructured the Reserve. The civilian component was renamed the Coast Guard Auxiliary and the Coast Guard Reserve was mandated to provide a pool of trained military personnel similar in function to the U.S. Army, Navy and Marine reserves. Reservists were assigned when and where needed, could be called up for full-time active duty, and were paid while on duty. Temporary Reservists (TRs) were unpaid volunteers who served for a limited time close to home.

Congress created the Women's Reserve of the Coast Guard (SPARS) in

U.S. Coast Guard civilian Auxiliary patrol and search and rescue vessels out of the port of Savannah, Georgia.

1942 and modeled it after the newly created U.S. Navy Women's Reserve (WAVES) and the Women Marines. SPARS performed their duties at Coast Guard Headquarters in Washington, D.C., and throughout the nation in ranks and rates ranging from yeoman to boatswain to chief petty officer and warrant and commissioned officers.

In 1944 the Coast Guard lifted the ban on stationing women outside the continental United States. After the war, women served in regular and reserve Coast Guard units. In the 1970s women were accepted in all branches of the U.S. Armed Forces and at the respective service academies. The Coast Guard Reserve and Coast Guard Auxiliary acquired permanent status after World War II.

Active duty Regular Coast Guard personnel were aided in World War II, and have been ever since, by the exemplary contributions of dedicated and well trained Reserve, Auxiliary, and civilian personnel who became part of what came to be called Team Coast Guard.

To meet wartime ship safety and construction needs, the Coast Guard recruited U.S. Merchant Marine officers and placed Temporary and Reserve Coast Guard personnel in Marine Inspection Offices within the Bureau of Marine Inspection and Navigation (BMIN). Marine Inspection Office responsibilities included regular inspection of merchant vessels to insure compliance with federal regulations, proper operation and maintenance of loading, fire safety and lifesaving equipment, the training and legality of crew members, inspection of mariner casualties and discipline problems, and the issuance and credibility of licenses and certificates.

Coast Guard personnel investigated ships' logs and manifests. Violations subjected merchant marine officers, crews, and ship owners to Coast Guard hearings, fines, and license and certificate suspension or revocation. The Bureau of Merchant Marine Inspection (BMMI) monitored maritime safety and security. BMMI specialists made essential contributions to maritime safety in peace and war, and continue to do so today.[4] The well-trained personnel in the civilian U.S. Merchant Marine provided a corps of disciplined seafarers that the naval services welcomed into their ranks as officers and enlisted personnel and as inspectors in the Bureau of Merchant Marine Inspection.

The U.S. War Shipping Administration took over merchant marine shipping in 1942. The federal government supervised 131 ship operators, oversaw the maritime unions, and trained the merchant seamen who served on the Victory and Liberty ships in various wartime tasks and responsibilities. The U.S. Navy and Coast Guard communicated and cooperated with the U.S. Merchant Marine academies to facilitate their respective and reciprocal operations and interests.

The commercial merchant vessels suffered sinking and high casualties from 1941 to 1943 from the torpedoes and deck guns of Axis (German and Japanese) submarines. The Merchant Marine carried supplies and troops into combat theaters in the Atlantic Ocean and across to Normandy, the Pacific Ocean, the Mediterranean (Southern Europe and North Africa), along the Atlantic shores of the United States, and the Gulf of Mexico. These maritime regions were rich hunting grounds for enemy vessels. The stormy and freezing waters of the North Atlantic and the shipping lanes to northern Russia were dangerous enough without the menace of German U-boats. Out of the two hundred and fifty thousand brave seamen who served in the World War II Merchant Marine, 5,368 mariners lost their lives to Axis naval and air attacks.[5]

Liberty Ships were merchant cargo vessels that were mass-produced by the nation's shipyards and the U.S. Maritime Commission to meet wartime needs. Simple and uniform construction techniques and reciprocating turbine, diesel and electric engines and motors were built to allow such rapid construction that the U-boats could not sink them fast enough to severely restrict wartime supply flows to U.S. allies and combat theaters. The ships carried tanks, trucks, aircraft, military supplies and food, and liquid fuel.

The Maritime Commission built 5,777 cargo vessels between 1939 and 1945, most of which were Liberty ships. The U.S. Navy used some of the ships, but civilian shipping companies operated most of them.[6] Mass-produced Victory Ships succeeded the Liberty Ships. Victory ships were designed by the Maritime Commission to operate at higher rates of speed and for postwar commercial use. The engines were more powerful and the Navy used some of these ships as APA attack transports that could carry an infantry regiment and serve as regimental headquarters.[7]

Frederic C. Lane and several contributors chronicled an extensive history of the building of the Victory and Liberty ships and the Coast Guard and Navy ships, boats and other craft which helped win World War II. The history of the prewar and wartime shipbuilding under the U.S. Maritime Commission included the story of the dedicated and skillful civilian men and women who built the ships, the support of military and other government agencies and the U.S. Maritime Academy.

The shipbuilding companies, which were located along the coasts and on the Great Lakes, cooperated with the Coast Guard and the Bureau of Marine Inspection and Navigation. The Maritime Commission accepted American Bureau of Shipping Standards for engines, shafting, and structure and Coast Guard standards for firefighting equipment, lifeboats, and all procedures, recommendations, and regulations involving communications and safety at sea.

The expertise and efficiency of cooperating corporate and government entities is illustrated by a board inquiry into the design, construction and welding of the ships. Board members included the secretary of war, the secretary of the Navy, several Navy admirals, and Admiral R.R. Waesche, the wartime commandant of the United States Coast Guard.[8]

During World War II, U.S. Navy and Coast Guard gun crews were placed onboard civilian merchant ships to provide some measure of self-defense. The well-trained crews used machine guns and 3" to 5" naval deck guns. The Naval Armed Guard saved many ships and crews, and some Naval Armed Guards went down with their ships and were casualties of war.[9]

4

Port Security, Navigation, and Aviation

The World War II national defense missions of the U.S. Coast Guard included port and harbor security, beach patrols, and operations on land, sea, and in the air. The USCG also performed some of these missions overseas as the war progressed, The Coast Guard began to carry out its wartime missions soon after the commencement of World War II (1939–1945), even though the United States did not enter the war until 1941.

Coast Guard Captains of the Port coordinated their responsibilities with local, state and federal law enforcement and other public safety agencies, civilian commercial and port authorities, and the other Armed Forces. As a result of several domestic and foreign ship disasters and explosions in North American waters, and concern about World War I era espionage and sabotage, the federal government designated USCG officers as Captains of the Port. In 1916 COTP offices were set up in Philadelphia, New York City, Norfolk, Virginia, and on the Great Lakes. Subsequently, COTP offices were established at other major U.S. ports.

The USCG had previously acquired port security authority in the River and Harbor Act of 1915, and then expanded authority by the Espionage Act of 1917. COTP authority included safety, espionage and sabotage surveillance, and the supervision of explosives loading on and off ships in U.S. harbors.

The first and largest COTP office in World War I was established in the port of New York City under the command of Captain Godfrey L. Cardin (USCG). Capt. Cardin supervised 1,400 employees and nine in the U.S. Army Corps of Engineers and Coast Guard ships and boats. On Capt. Cardin's watch the port of New York suffered no disasters despite servicing 1,000 ships and loading 300 million tons of explosives.[1]

To enforce prewar U.S. neutrality, the Coast Guard sealed the radios of foreign ships in American ports to prevent the broadcast of intelligence information overseas. The USCG did shipboard weapons checks. In 1940 the Dangerous Cargo Act expanded COTP authority in hazardous cargo loading. Harbor and shipboard fire prevention was also assigned to the COTPs, which necessitated the acquisition and building of fire boats manned by Reserve and

Temporary Coast Guard personnel who also guarded onshore waterfront infrastructure in designated security zones and ship gangways and inspected railroad cars.

Coast Guard boat, jeep, canine and mounted patrols supplemented port security operations in harbor areas and on coastal beaches. Civilian ship and merchant personnel inspectors came into the Coast Guard with the 1942 merger of the Bureau of Marine Inspection and Navigation. BMIN personnel had the opportunity to accept Coast Guard officer commissions.

The ten-thousand member Coast Guard Women's Reserve (SPARS) contributed personnel to port security duties. More than 170,000 Coast Guard personnel served in port security in World War II.[2]

Commander Quentin R. Walsh (USCG) assumed COTP functions at the French port of Cherbourg in 1944. Cmdr. Walsh earned the Navy Cross for subduing elements of German military control at the port after conducting a joint Navy–Coast Guard reconnaissance mission that opened Cherbourg for Allied supplies.[3]

Captain Miles Imlay (USCG), a combat veteran of the Sicily and Salerno invasions in Italy, commanded a Coast Guard landing craft flotilla in the Normandy invasion of 1944. Capt. Imlay also directed beachhead traffic and performed port director duties in the Normandy (D-Day) Omaha Beach area.[4]

Captains of the Port were designated for 29 strategic U.S. ports. Several COTP offices were established on the Great Lakes. The Inland Sea ports included Sault Ste. Marie, Detroit and Marquette, Michigan; Cleveland, Ohio, the headquarters of the Ninth (Great Lakes) Coast Guard District; Chicago, Illinois; Oswego and Buffalo, New York; and the Twin Ports of Duluth, Minnesota, and Superior, Wisconsin, at the western terminus of Lake Superior.

The cargoes transported on lake freighters illustrate the strategic significance of Great Lakes shipping. The merchant vessels transported manufactured goods, agricultural products (grain, corn), and natural resources (lumber, coal, iron ore). These cargoes had to pass through the Sault Ste. Marie Locks, which made port security concerns paramount. The several boat and shipbuilding yards are added to the economic infrastructure, and the significance of wartime port security and ship inspections on the Great Lakes is apparent. Coast Guard Temporary and Reserve members and civilian Auxiliary personnel provided invaluable mission support to Regular Coast Guard personnel.

In addition to the building and maintenance of freighters, the Great Lakes shipyards constructed military vessels, including 180-foot Coast Guard buoy tenders and icebreakers which carried out commercial, law enforcement, port security, search and rescue, and national defense missions in the United States and in the Atlantic and Pacific campaigns.[5] In cooperation with the U.S. Navy, Army, Marines, local law enforcement and the Federal Bureau of Investigation (FBI), the Coast Guard administered Beach Patrols and sentries on the Great Lakes, Atlantic, Gulf, and Pacific coasts.

The U.S. Coast Guard acquired beach patrol experience from its predecessor agencies, the U.S. Life-Saving Service and the U.S. Lighthouse Service. The USCG absorbed the USLSS and USLHS in 1915 and 1939, respectively.

The wisdom of establishing the Beach Patrol with Coast Guard personnel on foot patrol and using canines, horses, jeeps, and small boats, was affirmed in June 1942. While on foot patrol, Seaman Second Class John C. Cullen approached four suspicious German-speaking persons on a foggy Long Island, New York, shore. The suspects first threatened and then bribed Cullen with money. SN2 Cullen calmly withdrew and returned to the Coast Guard station. FBI agents were contacted and subsequently apprehended the Nazi saboteurs, who had been put ashore from a submarine. The enemy agents were tried and imprisoned. Petty Officer Cullen was awarded the Legion of Merit for his actions.[6] Other instances of enemy espionage and sabotage agents coming ashore occurred along the Atlantic coast. As in the Cullen incident, incriminating supplies and equipment were discovered. Trials, imprisonment and executions resulted.

The Beach Patrols were initially and primarily under the command of the regional Coast Guard Captain of the Port. The patrols were later integrated into Naval Coastal and Sea Frontiers and attached to U.S. Navy and Army Defense commands.[7]

Beach Patrol personnel usually traveled in pairs armed with pistols, rifles, flares, radio receivers-transmitters, and compasses. Temporary Reserves (TRs) often carried out patrols that allowed Reserve and Regular Coast Guard personnel to be assigned to other active duty missions, including combat. Fifteen percent of the TRs in the Lake Michigan region served in lifeboat stations and on beach patrols. Beach Patrol units reported suspicious objects, found booby traps, and reported ships in distress, including torpedoed vessels. Beach Patrol teams rescued injured and endangered victims on and off shore, and radioed rescue boats and float planes to come to the aid of downed or drowning military aircrews, sailors and civilians.[8]

Beach Patrols enhanced port security and communicated with COTPs and ACOTPs (Assistant COTPS). Captains of the Port enforced anchorage and shipping regulations and tracked the positions and movements of aircraft and foreign and domestic vessels. The COTPs forwarded tracking information to interested sources, including the White House, U.S. Customs, FBI, Immigration and Naturalization, and the Navy and Army. They worked closely with local fire departments, law enforcement agencies, shipping companies, and private security agencies that cooperated with the Coast Guard to check the identities of merchant seafarers and longshoremen, prevent and fight shore and ship fires, defend against espionage and sabotage, guard ships and boats in the harbor, and provide security for shore infrastructure like piers, warehouses, and fuel facilities.[9]

Coast Guard personnel throughout the United States earned medals and commendations from military and civilian agencies for numerous acts of courage in responding to fires and explosions, and for lifesaving in storms and floods and other hazardous situations.[10]

The Great Lakes (Inland Seas) were not free from national security threats. In 1942 a highway bridge inspector in Toledo, Ohio, discovered material evidence of Nazi agent activities that was passed on to Coast Guard headquarters and the FBI. The Sturgeon Bay, Wisconsin, COTP reported the sabotage of shipyard firefighting equipment.

Guards were placed on Great Lakes and Mississippi River merchant and military vessels. The Coast Guard furnished pilots for ships traversing strategic interior and coastal waterways. Fire and safety incidents and port security operations were extensive in the strategic harbors and commercial and military infrastructures in Seattle, Washington, Honolulu and Pearl Harbor, and the numerous but smaller ports on Alaskan navigable waters.[11]

SN2 John Cullen (USCG) on Beach Patrol confronted six German saboteurs landed from *U-202* on a foggy Long Island, New York, beach in 1942. The Nazi agents were apprehended and convicted.

The port security responsibilities of the Coast Guard in the World War II era were overwhelming. Coast Guard personnel took preventive and reactive measures to keep domestic waterways, ports and harbors safe. The Coast Guard protected America by adhering to the USCG motto: "Semper Paratus" (Always Ready).

An added Coast Guard responsibility and contribution in the war era was the development and maintenance of a reliable all-weather communication and direction finding system to aid ship and aircraft navigation. The Coast Guard already had the domestic responsibility of maintaining such aids to navigation as buoys, lighthouses, and other kinds of light stations, lightships, channel markers, and radio communications. World War II military operations in a variety of global theatres of operation necessitated the establishment of an accurate navigational and direction finding system on land and sea and in the air.

In 1940 the British developed radar to track incoming German bombers. In 1941 civilian scientists from the Massachusetts Institute of Technology (MIT) and American Telephone and Telegraph (AT&T) learned about a British radio navigation system designed to guide bombers to targets on the European continent.

Admiral Russell R. Waesche, the Coast Guard Commandant, assigned Lt. Cmdr. Lawrence M. Harding, an expert on radio aids to navigation, to cooperate with federal agencies, and, later, the Canadian and British governments and their respective military services, the Royal Canadian Navy, the Royal British Navy, U.S. Navy and Coast Guard. Cmdr. Harding was charged with the development of an accurate triangulation method for precisely determining ship and aircraft location.[12] He named the electronic system LORAN. The system supplemented the navigation and radio communication systems of civilian and military sea and aircraft.

The LORAN system was installed on the oceangoing medium and high endurance cutters assigned to search and rescue and weather station (Ocean Station) patrols in the Atlantic and Pacific oceans. Ocean Station cutters radioed weather and iceberg reports, collected oceanographic data, and performed SAR or directed other sea and aircraft to ships, boats, and aircraft in distress.[13] The pulse-transmitting Loran navigation aid exceeded the radar range by 50 to 100 miles. To experiment with the system, civilian scientists used two inactive Coast Guard lifeboat stations in Delaware (Fenwick Island) and New York (Montauk, Long Island).

After the 7 December 1941 Pearl Harbor attack, Rear Adm. Julius A. Furer, the U.S. Navy Research and Development Coordinator, expressed interest in LORAN. U.S. Navy officials requested the assistance of the Coast Guard. Newly promoted Captain Lawrence Harding coordinated his research and activities with the U.S. Navy, U.S. Army, MIT, and the Royal Canadian Navy. The RCN provided an experimental site in Nova Scotia.

In 1943 the British Admiralty and the Royal Navy became involved in the project. LORAN stations were constructed in the United Kingdom, Canada, Iceland, Danish Greenland, the Alaskan Aleutian Islands, and Asian and Pacific locations as Allied Forces pushed into Japanese held islands.[14] The building projects posed daunting logistical challenges in a variety of often extreme topographic, climatic, and meteorological conditions. Military and civilian engineers and building personnel performed heroic and often dangerous duty in the successful completion of their missions.

Coast Guard personnel have served civilian and military communication and safety needs from LORAN stations around the world from World War II to the present. The duty stations have ranged from pleasant to extreme in lonely, dangerous and vulnerable posts in the World War II Pacific, Korea, and in territory close to enemy troops in Vietnam.[15]

World War II historian and author Bill D. Ross paid a 1980s visit to the historic Iwo Jima battlefield, where U.S. Marines and a Navy corpsman had raised the American flag on Mt. Suribachi. Ross described the contemporary Coast Guard contingent and Loran Station: "Twenty-seven United States Coast

Guardsmen operated a LORAN navigational aids and weather station for civilian and military aircraft" in "a dismal, lonely, and uncomfortable outpost" on
a one year tour of duty. "A Coast Guard C-130 Hercules transport makes a
weekly roundtrip flight from the U.S. Navy Base at Yakota, Japan," carrying
supplies and mail "and an occasional visitor" to the "single-story cinder block
barracks and operational buildings of the LORAN station."[16]

Active Coast Guard aviation began during World War I when the service
acquired a flying lifeboat and began air SAR and reconnaissance. Coast Guard
connections to aviation initially occurred in 1903 when members of the Kill
Devil Life-Saving Station assisted the Wright Brothers in securing their gliders and aircraft in heavy winds, A Kill Devil Station surfman photographed the
famous first flight at Kitty Hawk, North Carolina, in 1903.[17] Lt. Cmdr. Tom
Beard (USCG, Ret.), an aviator, author, and historian, wrote: "From this beginning through the following century, the fledgling service expanded the use of
seaplanes, developed the naval helicopter, and eventually saw its aviators in
space."[18]

Commander Elmer Stone (USCG) was the pilot of the U.S. Navy NC-4
seaplane that flew the first transatlantic flight in 1919. Cmdr. Stone earned the
Navy Cross for the achievement and led the way in the use of flying boats for
reconnaissance and SAR.[19]

Coast Guard aviators joined their World War II Navy and Army colleagues
flying the versatile PBY Catalina.[20] PBY1 was put into service in 1936. The
wingtip floats could be retracted in flight. Two 1,200 horsepower engines provided a speed of 175 miles per hour and a range of 2,350 miles. With a 104-
foot wing span; gross weight of 18 tons; .50- and .30-caliber machine guns
mounted in the nose, ventral hatch, and glass side blisters aft the wings; and
four thousand pound bomb load, the PBY was functional—and ominous.[21]

A generation before World War II, the crew of the USCGC *Onondaga*
experimented with launching and retrieving seaplanes and developed boat/air-
plane coordination tactics. A contentious rivalry developed between Coast
Guard supporters of seaplanes and proponents of the new helicopters that
eventually replaced the seaplanes. Lt. Frank Erickson (USCG) saw the potential for the use of rotor aircraft in 1940 when helicopter inventor Dr. Igor Sikorsky flew his experimental aircraft. Lt. (later Commander) Erickson, a seaplane
pilot off the CGC *Taney* at the Pearl Harbor Navy Base, worked with Dr. Sikorsky to develop the helicopter for Coast Guard missions.

Captain William J. Kossler (USCG), chief of aircraft engineering at Coast
Guard Headquarters in Washington, D.C., echoed Cmdr. Erickson's helicopter vision. As early as 1941, Capt. Kossler had envisioned helicopter use in SAR,
environmental, and antisubmarine warfare missions, and promoted the util-
ity of the aircraft for Navy and Coast Guard missions.

Commander Erickson's crews at Coast Guard Air Station (CGAS) Brooklyn, New York, successfully replaced helicopter wheels with skids, an innova-

tion that served the Coast Guard well in a variety of geographical environments.

The Coast Guard initially trained U.S. Navy helicopter pilots, but later it established helicopter-training classes and welcomed USCG aviation students. By 1944 the naval services were training qualified enlisted personnel and officers as helicopter pilots.[22]

Although eventually replaced by helicopters, during World War II fixed wing aircraft dominated the aviation units of the Coast Guard, Navy, Marines and Army. Antisubmarine warfare required armed floatplanes. The Coast Guard developed a .50-caliber gun for seaplane installation at CGAS Brooklyn. The PH-3 seaplane was a popular Coast Guard flying boat. The PH-3 resembled the PBY, but featured a hull that replicated lifesaving surfboats, unlike the PBY floats suspended from the wings.

During the period of U-boat activity off the Atlantic coast of the United States, seaplanes located more than one thousand torpedoed ship survivors for boat rescues and made water landings to rescue 100 other victims. On occasion, when sea and wind conditions prohibited seaplane takeoffs, floatplanes had to taxi significant distances to reach shore.[23]

The first Coast Guard Air Station was established in 1925 at Cloucester, Massachusetts, from which a radio equipped seaplane-tracked rumrunners during Prohibition. By the end of 1926 the Coast Guard had acquired five additional aircraft. By 1942 the Coast Guard expanded to 27 pilots and 45 aircraft at nine USCG air stations located along the Atlantic, Gulf, and Pacific coasts.[24]

Between 1939 and 1940 the Coast Guard was assigned primary responsibility for the Coast Neutrality Patrol. After the United States entered World War II on 8 December 1941, Navy and Coast Guard aviation significantly increased to cover ASW, SAR, and convoy escort duty.[25]

In the World War II era Coast Guard aircraft included twin engine amphibian planes, which by definition landed on land or water; the PH2 flying boat; the single engine SOC-4 reconnaissance plane; the J4F and JRF Grumman amphibians; the Navy VOS scout plane; and Catalina PBYs, which dropped emergency equipment at sea to mariners in distress. The equipment included markers, transmitters, and life rafts. Aircraft included helicopters, fixed-wing propeller planes and lighter-than-air blimps. At the height of the German U-boat menace off the Atlantic coast of the United States between 1941 and 1943, USCG planes delivered 61 bombing attacks on enemy submarines.[26]

Coast Guard seaplanes and crews performed extraordinary SAR missions. Coast Guard Air Station Elizabeth City, North Carolina, aviators Lt. Richard J. Burke and Lt. R. W. Blouin rescued seven German sailors after a U.S. Army plane sunk their U-boat. Lt. J.N. Schrader, on patrol out of Coast Guard Air Station Miami, Florida, landed at sea to rescue several survivors of a tanker badly damaged in a torpedo attack. Lt. Schrader did not get airborne until other rescue planes came on scene in the shark invested waters.[27]

USCG Amphibious PBY Flying Boat Patrol Bomber. The Coast Guard PBY missions included cargo and passenger transportation, search and rescue, reconnaissance, and antisubmarine patrol.

Besides rescuing civilian mariners and aviators at sea, USCG pilots alone and in joint operations with the other Armed Forces, attacked enemy submarines and went to the aid of downed U.S. National Guard, Army, Navy, and Marine Corps personnel. In a few instances, USCG helicopters performed humanitarian and military missions.[28]

Lt. Cmdr. Tom Beard (USCG, Ret.) chronicled the history of a courageous Coast Guard aviator who gave his life after successful rescues of Armed Forces personnel in treacherous Arctic Greenland. Lt. John H. Pritchard (USCG) was a pilot on the Grumman J2F amphibian plane. Lt. Pritchard was stationed on the CGC *Northland*. The J2F was lowered by crane from the cutter to the sea. On the return flight the aircraft would be lifted from the sea onto the deck of the ship.

In November 1942 Lt. Pritchard landed in the icy Arctic waters adjacent to the Greenland ice cap, found the downed Canadian aircrew, led them to the J2F, and flew them to the warmth and safety of the *Northland*. Five days later, facing the threat of Greenland's fog, winds, ice, rain, and snowstorms, Pritchard volunteered to return to the ice cap, land with the wheels retracted, and rescue the crew of a downed U.S. Army Air Corps B-17 bomber. After bringing three of the crewmen back to the CGC *Northland*, Lt. Pritchard ignored a snowstorm and flew back for the remaining airman. On the return flight Lt. Pritchard, his radioman, Benjamin A. Bottoms, and the Army airman crashed. Pritchard and Bottoms posthumously received the Distinguished Flying Cross.[29]

In April 1941, by agreement with Denmark, the United States assumed the defense of Greenland. Commander Edward H. Smith (USCG) was given

Grumman J2-F Seaplane. The armed bi-wing floatplane performed reconnaissance, search and rescue, and depth charge missions. Coast Guard cutters *Northland* and *North Star* carried the seaplanes on the Greenland Patrol.

command of the defense operation. Cmdr. Smith reported directly to the U.S. Navy Commander of the Atlantic Fleet. The mission assumed greater significance after the United States entered World War II.

Patrol Squadron Six (VP-6 CG) was established by the USN in 1943 at Argentia, Newfoundland, Canada, The squadron was based at Narsarssuak, Greenland, under the command of Cmdr. Donald B. MacDiarmid (USCG), an experienced seaplane pilot. The extreme weather conditions challenged the 30 Coast Guard officers and 145 enlisted personnel responsible for the ten PBY-5A Catalina patrol planes. The PBYs were equipped with machine guns and bombs. By the end of the war the USCG had acquired 114 PBYs.

The PBY carried a crew of 9 for its multimission tasks of SAR, ASW, convoy air support, iceberg tracking, delivering mail and supplies to regional military bases, LORAN station support, and surveillance in U-boat infested waters. The Coast Guard area of operations included two PBYs and crews at Reykjavik, Iceland, mission support over eastern Canada, and coordination with the British Royal Air Force Coastal Command. The U.S. Coast Guard rescued downed American, British and Canadian aircrews.

Greenland (1800 miles in length and 800 miles wide) is mostly ice cap. Coast Guard aircraft radioed cutters at sea to rescue mariners and ships in distress in often heavy seas, strong winds, bitter cold, ice fields, blizzards, and fog.[30]

5

Coast Guard Crews and Navy Ships

The historical chronology section of this book provides a concise summation of Coast Guard ships and craft and combat and rescue missions in World War I and World War II. More detailed descriptions of Coast Guard crews on cutters and Navy and Army vessels are chronicled in this chapter and throughout the book.

To meet wartime combat and cargo requirements, thousands of new boats and ships had to be built at American shipyards. The growing number of Navy, Coast Guard and Army troop, transport, combat and cargo vessels required expanded military recruitment and training. Coast Guard regular and reserve volunteers and conscripted personnel helped fill the gap. Regular, Reserve, Temporary Reserve, Women's Reserve (SPARS), and civilian Auxiliary and civil service personnel cooperated on the home front and allowed more regular and reserve personnel to transfer to oceangoing vessels in combat zones off the American shores and in the Atlantic, Mediterranean, and Pacific.

During World War II, Coast Guard crews manned hundreds of cutters and 351 Navy and 288 Army vessels. Coast Guard crews manned troop transports, fuel tankers, cargo ships, and combat vessels. The Coast Guard ran landing ship tanks (LSTs), patrol frigates and vessels (PF and YP), destroyer escorts (DE), transports (AP), gasoline tankers (AOG), cargo ships (AK), large landing craft infantry ships (LCI-L), auxiliary transports (APA), gunboats and corvettes (PG), submarine chasers (SC, PC, and WPC), auxiliary attack cargo ships (AKA), coastal yachts (PYC), launches and ferryboats (YFB), ambulance boats (YHB), motor torpedo boat tenders (AGP), and a variety of unclassified and miscellaneous vessels. Army vessels manned by the USCG included freight and supply ships and boats (FS and F), large tugboats (LT), tankers (TY), and repair ships (AMRS).

Coast Guard–manned vessels designated for combat included patrol and destroyer escorts, troop and vehicle transports, amphibious landing vessels, convoy escorts, weather observation ships, and supply vessels. Most of the USCG-manned vessels were armed. Oceangoing cutters and destroyer escorts carried deck guns and depth charge devices for antisubmarine warfare. Landing craft carried machine guns and rockets.

Coast Guard cutters by definition were from 65 feet in length to over 300 feet. Small to large transport vessels ranged from 500 to more than 600 feet in length and could carry up to 5,000 troops and several hundred CG officers and men. The larger vessels displaced from 12,000 to 18,000 gross tons, had beam widths of 70 to 75 feet, and average speeds of 17–20 knots. The troop transports carried American and Allied soldiers.[1]

Coast Guard–manned attack transport ships were equipped with smaller amphibious landing craft. Soldiers, sailors and Marines loaded with supplies and combat gear descended treacherous rope ladders from the sides of the ships into the rolling and pitching landing craft that took them to hostile enemy shores. Attack transports and landing craft operated off and onto the islands and shores of North Africa, Italy, France, the Alaskan Aleutians, the Philippine archipelago, and numerous other Japanese held Pacific islands. Coast Guard–operated gasoline and oil tankers fueled Navy and Army vessels inside and outside the combat theaters. The attack vessels and smaller craft destroyed enemy aircraft and submarines and rescued downed and drowning Allied and enemy military personnel.

LSTs were 328-foot, twin-screwed diesel powered boats with 50-foot beams and a seagoing draft of eight feet at the bow and fourteen feet aft. LSTs needed to be seaworthy and with a shallow enough draft to land in shoal water for beach landings. Water-filled ballast tanks provided stability at sea. Emptied ballast tanks allowed shallow-water maneuvering and landing. Landing Ship Tanks (LSTs) unloaded heavy equipment and vehicles (trucks, tanks, jeeps) and combat troops. Landing craft designed to carry tanks were called LCTs (Landing Craft, Tank).[2]

Designated hull numbers identified LSTs. *LST-327*, commanded by Lieutenant A. Volton, and later Lt. L. Wedemeyer, sailed from New York in April 1943. It participated in the Italian campaigns at Sicily and Salerno, and then the Anzio invasion of January 1944. In May *LST-327* loaded troops and vehicles in Britain for the June Normandy invasion. After unloading on the beaches of Normandy, *LST-327* returned to the United Kingdom with 76 German prisoners of war, and then returned to France with more combat personnel and equipment.[3]

U.S. Coast Guard cutters served as AGCs (Amphibious Force Flagships) in World War II. The USCGC *Ingham* (WPG-WHEC-35) served as the flagship for Rear Adm. Arthur D. Struble (USN) during the amphibious assault on the Japanese-held Philippine Islands in 1944. After the war, the AGC cutters were again designated WHEC (high endurance) cutters.[4]

The 327-foot *Ingham* was built at the Philadelphia [Pennsylvania] Navy Yard in 1935 and launched in 1936. It was transferred to U.S. Navy duty in July 1941 and assigned to North Atlantic escort duty in 1942–43. On 15 December 1942 the *Ingham* sank German submarine *U-626*.[5]

The 327-foot CGC *Ingham* (WPG-35) sank *U-626* in the Atlantic on 17 December 1942, rescued survivors of sunken ships, escorted Mediterranean convoys, and served as a combat vessel, flagship, and communications center in the Pacific.

Navy patrol craft (PCs) were not as large, well armed or fast as battleships and destroyers, but national security needs necessitated the building and use of these smaller Coast Guard and Navy vessels. The PCs served as convoy escorts, submarine hunters, and search and rescue vessels; they also led landing craft to invasion beaches. PCs sank U-boats and shot down enemy aircraft. Fifty thousand sailors, mostly reservists without seafaring experience, contributed courageously to the war effort and suffered significant casualties.[6]

The U-boat menace off the Atlantic coast commenced in 1942. U-boats caused carnage from the sinking of hundreds of cargo ships and tankers and associated crew casualties. The U-boat "Wolf Packs" operated off the U.S. Atlantic and Gulf coasts to disrupt the supply lines to Britain.

The Atlantic Coast region was called the Eastern Sea Frontier (ESF). The ESF commander, Rear Admiral Adolphus Andrews (USN), had to rely on a limited number of Coast Guard cutters, Navy destroyers, and Army Air Corps, Navy and Coast Guard aircraft to cope with the U-boat onslaught. The Navy even used lighter than air blimps.

Private yachts and fishing boats were gradually armed by the Navy with depth charges, machine guns, and sound (sonar) gear. Patriotic yacht owners, many with Reserve officer commissions, manned their vulnerable vessels far out to sea in often stormy waters at significant cost and risk. The fledgling crews stood by to report submarine activity and initiate rescue missions.

Some of the patrol craft had the Coast Guard ("CG") letters and numbers stenciled on the hull. U.S. Navy and Coast Guard PCs were identified by numbers, but not ship names, which some observers believe diminished the pride of the dedicated mariners.

By the end of 1943 the Atlantic sea patrols, land and carrier-based air reconnaissance (including Navy and Coast Guard floatplanes), improved radar, and better defensive tactics saved hundreds of merchant ships and mariners. The missions identified, damaged, sunk, and forced more U-boats out of action, and influenced the German Admiralty to change tactics and theaters of operation.[7]

PCs were generally 450-ton, 173-foot vessels with twin screws and a flank speed of 21 knots. High seas caused PCs to dramatically pitch and roll (60 degrees and more) and subjected crews to rough, dangerous, and injurious rides. Sixteen shipyards located on the Atlantic, Gulf and Pacific coasts, and the Great Lakes built most of the PCs. The highly skilled employees at the DeFoe Shipbuilding Company in Bay City, Michigan and the Commercial Iron Works in Portland, Oregon represented the shipbuilding industry at its best.[8]

PCs were crewed by well trained U.S. Navy and Coast Guard officers and enlisted men and conducted joint patrols with cutters. *PC-793* and the USCGC *Cyane* used sonar and depth charges while on ASW patrol outside Adak Harbor in the Aleutian Islands in 1945. Debris floating to the surface indicated a successful attack but unproven kill upon a Japanese submarine (I-boat).[9]

The 165-foot CGC *Cyane* (WPC-105) was launched at the Lake Union Dry Dock in Seattle, Washington in 1934, assigned to the Northwestern Sea Frontier, and stationed at Ketchikan, Alaska.[10] In May and June 1942, the *Cyane*, under the command of Lt. Cmdr. Leslie B. Tollaksen, was part of the U.S. Navy fleet tasked with thwarting two Japanese naval task forces sailing toward the Aleutians.[11]

The weather challenge faced by PCs is illustrated by the 9 October 1945 typhoon disaster that struck U.S. Navy and Coast Guard vessels stationed at Okinawa. Two hundred naval vessels were damaged or destroyed and more than 100 sailors drowned. Typhoon Louise struck as the Coast Guard–manned *PC-590* dropped anchor in Buckner Bay, Okinawa, after a mail run between Formosa and Okinawa. Gale force winds of 100 knots and 30-foot waves broke the anchor chain and forced the cutter onto the reefs. Ships and small craft adrift steered to avoid collisions. Crews tried to pull sailors from the water as they floated past the helpless vessels; they also worked to secure depth charges on foundering craft. The Coast Guard crewmembers were eventually rescued from *PC-590* and plucked out of the sea by the courageous crew of the *Mona Island* (ARG-91).[12]

The 83-foot wooden hull patrol boat was the SAR and ASW watercraft used off the American Atlantic coast, and in the amphibious assaults in Europe and Asia. *CG-83306* was one of the 230 boats built for the Coast Guard during World War II. The 83-footers were long enough to be called cutters, carried a 12-man crew, were gasoline or diesel powered, and were armed with a "depth charge" weapon called a "Y" gun. Cramped sleeping quarters and galleys and bridges characterized the vessels and high seas guaranteed what some sailors called "roller coaster rides."[13]

On 2 January 1944 *CG-83306* was on night patrol outside of the submarine nets of New York Harbor. Heavy winds, sleet and snow challenged the crew as they continued their patrol in the vicinity of the anchored U.S. Navy destroyer USS *Turner* (DD-648). At approximately 6:15 A.M. on 3 January a tremendous explosion ripped through the USS *Turner*, followed by three more explosions and then the capsizing of the destroyer at 7:50 AM, which activated depth charges set for 30 feet, causing another horrendous explosion. The cause of the explosions was never satisfactorily determined, but reported sonar "pings" suggested a U-boat might have been in the area.

CG-83306 was the first rescue vessel on scene. Several Coast Guard vessels later converged on the site and assisted the rescue mission. *CG-83306* commander Lt. (jg) John C. Dean placed his vessel against the burning destroyer. Lt. Dean's courageous crew rescued 55 badly burned Navy survivors from the ocean and the burning destroyer. *CG-83306* then sliced its way through the cold and snowy waters to the Sandy Hook, New Jersey, Coast Guard Base. Waiting ambulances took the wounded and traumatized sailors to Ft. Hancock Army Hospital.

The rescue mission made Coast Guard aviation history when Lt. Cmdr. F.A. Erickson flew two cases of blood plasma through the snowstorm in a USCG Sikorsky HNS-1 helicopter to the hospital to save the lives of several of the severely injured *Turner* crew, of whom 154 survived and 138 died.[14] Members of the crew of *CG-83306* received letters of commendation from the U.S. Coast Guard signed by Rear Adm. Stanley V. Parker, Third Naval District, which stated, "Your courageous conduct ... was in keeping with the highest traditions of the Naval Service."[15]

The Coast Guard ran 18 Navy auxiliary gasoline oil tankers (AOGs). Coast Guard AOG crews received training at the Navy Submarine Chaser Training Center in Miami, Florida and Coast Guard Yard in Curtis Bay, Maryland. The AOGs fueled U.S. Navy vessels in combat zones. The USS *Calamus*, commanded by Lt. William Hord (USCG), shot down a Japanese aircraft in the invasion of Okinawa. The USS *Sheepscot* under the command of Lt. George A. Wagner (USCGR) grounded and capsized off of Iwo Jima in the 6 June 1945 hurricane.[16]

Specially trained USCG crews manned U.S. Navy attack cargo auxiliary vessels (AKAs) that carried landing craft personnel. Among the AKAs was the USS *Theenim* (Capt. Gordon A. Littlefield, USCG). During the Okinawa invasion, the *Theenim* fired at Japanese aircraft and claimed a hit ("splash") on a suicide plane on the evening of 15 April 1945.[17]

The 459-foot USS *Theenim* (AKA-63) was launched and commissioned in 1944. It carried a 5-inch stern gun, four 40mm twin mounts, and eighteen

20mm antiaircraft guns. The AKA was 63 feet wide and had a 10-foot draft unloaded and more than 25 feet fully loaded. *AKA-63* and her sister ships had a flank speed of 16-knots; a 400-man crew, 100 of whom were assigned to the 24 landing craft onboard; and berthing for 56 soldiers or Marines.[18]

The *Theenim* participated in a successful diversionary attack on a portion of the island of Okinawa, drawing Japanese troops away from the main landing force. The enormity of the logistical and tactical challenges of the Pacific island invasions is illustrated by the components of the U.S. naval armada against Okinawa: 1,457 ships, including more than 400 transports, 50 submarines, 18 battleships, dozens of cruisers, and 150 destroyers (DDs) and destroyer escorts (DEs). The U.S. Army Air Force (USAAF) contributed 300 B-29 bombers to the initial softening up phase of the attack.[19]

AKA-63 manned its guns 24 hours per day for 16 days and survived attacks by kamikaze suicide planes, suicide boats, one-man submarines, and suicide swimmers.[20] Before retiring from the battle zone, the *Theenim* received credit for shooting down two Japanese fighter planes, one of which passed within 30 feet of the bridge, and an enemy bomber. On the way to Guam, *AKA-63* captured two appreciative Japanese prisoners from a dugout canoe and brought them to intelligence officers.[21]

The Coast Guard utilized several kinds of watercraft and crews to complete the prewar and wartime missions assigned to the service. It acquired private pleasure craft to patrol harbor areas. Coast Guard reservists ran hundreds of these craft, with "CGR" and a designated number stenciled on the bow. The CGR numbers, unlike CG boat numbers, did not indicate the length of the boat. The Coast Guard usually designated a name on craft more than 100 feet in length and put a number on the hull of craft less than 100 feet. Most of the watercraft were returned to the owners after the war.[22]

The World War II era civilian Coast Guard Auxiliary consisted of more than 11,000 members and 10,000 boats. The Coast Guard acquired many of these boats, and their owners and crewmembers often joined the Temporary U.S. Coast Guard Reserve (USCGR-T). Coast Guard Auxiliary craft were identified with the letters "CGA" and a hull number.[23] During the war, Coast Guard crews manned 351 U.S. Navy craft. By mid–August 1945 more than 45,000 enlisted Coast Guard personnel and 3,350 officers crewed Navy ships.[24] The Navy ships were identified as USS vessels. Individual ships were classified by function (AGP, AK, LST, AOG, DD, DE, etc.) and assigned a hull number.

In March 1944 the Coast Guard began to man U.S. Army Transportation Corps ships. By the end of World War II the USCG crewed 288 United States Army boats and ships, mostly in the South Pacific. The letters F and FS and a hull number usually identified USA freight and supply ships.[25]

Coast Guard–manned vessels engaged in combat rescue operations. On 20 April 1944 the USS *Menges* (DE-320) and USS *Newell* (DE-322) rescued 230 U.S. Navy crewmembers when the USS *Lansdale* was sunk by a German air-

The Coast Guard–manned destroyer USS Menges (DE-320).

craft attack in the Mediterranean. The *Menges* shot down one German plane. Among those rescued was Lt. Robert M. Morgenthau (USNR), the son of President Roosevelt's Treasury secretary.[26]

On 3 May 1944 destroyer escort *Menges* was struck by a torpedo off the North African nation of Algeria with the loss of two officers, 29 enlisted men, and one-third of her hull. The *Menges* was towed to port. After the ship was repaired, it joined three other destroyer escorts and was given shared credit in the sinking of *U-866* on 18 March 1945.[27] Lt. Cmdr. F.M. McCabe (USCG) commanded the USS *Menges* in the successful U-boat hunt and acquired German documents from the surface debris.[28]

Edgar M. Nash, a Hawaiian resident, enlisted in the Coast Guard on 27 November 1941. On 7 December Nash observed the attack on Pearl Harbor, after which he was transferred from sentry duty at 14th Coast Guard District Headquarters to the USCGC *Taney* and Pacific patrol duty. Exemplary test scores got Petty Officer Third Class (PO3) Nash transferred to the U.S. Coast Guard Academy at New London, Connecticut. Nash earned a USCGR officer commission and admission to the U.S. Navy SCTC (Sub-Chaser Training Center) school in Miami, Florida. Lieutenant (jg) Nash was assigned Gunnery Officer on the 306-foot USS *Menges* (DE-320) that had a crew complement of 186 and a flank speed of 21 knots.

The *Menges* was launched and commissioned in 1943 by Consolidated Steel Corporation in Orange, Texas. The destroyer escort featured considerable combat armament: 15 guns (3"/50, 40mm, and 20mm); three torpedo tubes; two depth charge tracks; one hedgehog; and eight depth charge projectors. The USS *Menges* earned two battle stars for its combat achievements in World War II.[29]

As gunnery officer in a ship complement of 15 officers and 200 enlisted personnel, Lt. (jg) Nash was responsible for crew weapons instruction and the maintenance of small caliber weapons, three 3-inch guns, three .40 mm anti-aircraft guns, and depth charge technology and operations. Destroyer escort duty on the *Menges* required the protection of merchant convoys, regular battle station duty, ASW patrols, and vigilance against German Air Force (Luftwaffe) attacks. On the evening of 30 March 1944, Lt. Nash experienced a convoy attack by thirty German torpedo bombers using illumination flares. The *Menges* gunners shot down one bomber, damaged another, and the crew rescued 107 Navy sailors from a torpedoed vessel, and two downed German aviators.

On the evening of 3 May 1944 a U-boat sent an acoustic torpedo into the *Menges*, blowing off the stern of the ship, killing 31 crew members and wounding twenty-five. A French tugboat towed the *Menges* to the port of Oran, Algeria for repairs.

Coast Guard escort ships USS *Pride* (DE-323) and USS *Mosley* (DE-321) and two other DEs tracked the enemy submarine (*U-271*), depth charged the U-boat to the surface, and captured the enemy commander and several crewmembers. Lt. (jg) Nash was later assigned to an 83-foot Coast Guard cutter in the 1944 D-Day invasion of Normandy.[30]

The USCGC *Eastwind* (WAG-279) was constructed by Western Pipe and Steel Company in Los Angeles, California, in 1942, launched in 1943, and commissioned in 1944. The 269-foot "Wind" Class icebreaker had a 63-foot beam, 25-foot draft, three propellers (twin aft, one forward), and a complement of 295 enlisted personnel and 21 officers. The *Eastwind* carried one J2F floatplane, radar and sonar, 7 guns and small arms, and depth charges. The heavy icebreaker and other "Wind" Class cutters were assigned to provide military access to Arctic bases, especially on Greenland.[31]

On 4 October 1944 crewmembers from CGC *Eastwind* captured a German weather station in Greenland and took 12 enemy prisoners. On 15 October 1944 the *Eastwind* captured the German trawler *Externsteine* and took 17 prisoners.[32] The new icebreaker *Eastwind*, under the command of Captain Charles W. Thomas (USCG), was on the Greenland Patrol searching for Nazi radio and weather stations, which transmitted helpful information to the German military and more particularly the U-boat fleet.

Captain Thomas received word of the presence of the German trawler from the cutter's reconnaissance floatplane. Thomas sailed his cutter 100 miles through thick pack ice to intercept the German crew, equipment, and documents. Subsequently the trawler and its crew and equipment were captured by a landing party under the command of Lt. (jg) Alden Lewis on North Little Koldewey Island. The German prisoners from the captures were placed on the *Eastwind* and eventually transferred to Navy intelligence operatives. The *Externstein* was taken over under the command of Lt. Curtis Howard (USCG), sailed to Iceland and turned over to the U.S. Navy.[33]

Warren D. Bonner, Motor Machinist Mate 3rd Class (USCG), was a crewman on the CGC *Eastwind* between 1944 and 1946. Bonner dedicated his compilation of the cutter's history, *The Mighty "E": A Ship and Her Crew*, to the men who performed "their daily duties under freezing, rigorous, and dangerous conditions in the polar seas" in the Greenland Patrol of the North Atlantic Campaign.[34] MM3 Bonner's manuscript included Coast Guard and crew photographs, documents, letters, and autobiographies. One source Bonner used was *Ice is Where You Find It* (1951), by former *Eastwind* commander Captain Charles W. Thomas (USCG).[35] Capt. Thomas dedicated his book to "three outstanding Ice Admirals: Richard E. Byrd, Rear Adm., USN (Ret.), Edward H. Smith, Rear Admiral, USCG (Ret.), and Richard H. Cruzen, Rear Admiral, USN." In the foreword to *Ice*, famed polar explorer Adm. Richard Byrd (USN) credited Capt. Thomas with courage and leadership in the profession of "ice navigation."[36]

MM3 Bonner served under Capt. Thomas and he revealed that President Franklin Roosevelt and First Lady Eleanor Roosevelt corresponded with Capt. Thomas and the *Eastwind* crew and expressed appreciation for their significant strategic North Atlantic service in World War Two.[37]

MM3 Bonner described attacks on the CGC *Eastwind* by a "wolf-pack of U-boats" between Newfoundland, Canada and Narsarssuak, Greenland in which torpedoes missed the cutter by from five feet to 50 yards. Skilled *Eastwind* maneuvers "confused the U-Boat commanders."[38] The *Eastwind* floatplane was a Grumman J2F-5 biplane used to search for enemy submarines, outposts, and ships. The seaplanes of the icebreaking cutters performed reconnaissance missions to find cracks in the ice fields through which the cutters could more easily navigate. While those missions were carried out in Arctic temperatures, *Eastwind* engine room crews operated in 120 degree Fahrenheit temperatures, while on deck readings dipped to minus 60 degrees.[39]

The North Atlantic was still a hotbed of U-boat attacks on convoys in 1943. While the CGC *Eastwind* was cutting through 7-foot ice fields at 17 knots[40] with its six diesel engines under full power,[41] further west the USCG cutters *Bibb*, *Campbell*, and *Spencer* were on convoy duty dodging enemy torpedoes and depth charging U-boats. USCGC *Spencer* dodged torpedoes from *U-600* and *U-628*, and the CGC *Campbell* had to be taken in tow by two naval ships after being heavily damaged in its ramming attack on a surfaced U-boat. The B-17 and other aircraft flew ASW and SAR patrols from coastal Canada and the United States.[42]

Amphibious Landing Ship Tanks (LSTs) were constructed to discharge cargo directly onto shore and then back off for the return to sea and other ports. Cargoes included equipment, supplies, and military vehicles (tanks, amtracks, trucks, and jeeps). LSTs ranged from 200 to 300 feet or more in length. Smaller vessels were simply called LCs (Landing Craft). Specific hull numbers identified both vessel types. LSTs were built at river shipyards on the Great Lakes and along the Ohio River at such yards as Ambridge, Pennsylvania, and Evansville, Indiana. Launched sideways into the Ohio River, the vessels were then sailed down the Ohio and Mississippi rivers to the Gulf of Mexico and then overseas.[43]

LST crew complements generally consisted of 8 to 10 officers and 100 to 120 enlisted personnel. Most were U.S. Navy and Coast Guard reservists. Of the 933 LSTs manned by the USN and USCG, 39 were destroyed by enemy activity, grounding, storms (typhoons) and heavy seas, fire, and cargo explosions. Enemy activity included mines, torpedoes, bombing, artillery, and kamikaze suicide plane attacks.

LSTs operated in European and Pacific waters carrying supplies to shore, wounded military personnel back to hospital ships and shore stations, and enemy prisoners of war to Allied ports for interrogation and internment. Their shallow draft, flat bottoms, and high vertical hulls made LSTs relatively unseaworthy and rough to ride on the high seas.[44] LSTs and LCVPs (Landing Craft, Vehicles and Personnel) were armed with antiaircraft (AA) mounts and water-cooled machine guns.[45] Some LSTs were equipped as hospital ships and staffed with Army and Navy nurses, medics, corpsmen, and medical and dental officers. Other LSTs served as ammunition ships for naval cruisers and battleships.[46]

Lieutenant (jg) George Alton (USCGR) was the watch officer and executive officer (XO) on the 177-foot U.S. Army freight supply ship *FS-268* in the Pacific in World War II. Lt. Alton chronicled the Pacific ports of call from Australia and New Guinea to the Philippines, stormy seas, combat areas, navigational challenges, and the leadership strengths and shortcomings of officers and enlisted personnel he met along the way. His massive manuscript contains photographs, maps, letters, the autobiographies of surviving crew members, newspaper articles, and official Coast Guard documents.

Lt. Alton described supply and logistical challenges in the far reaches of the Pacific, military strategies and tactics, and battle action between Japanese and American naval and military forces. Ultimate dissatisfaction with the leadership style and personality of the *FS-268* commander and a desire to be on a combat vessel motivated Lt. Alton to transfer to the combat patrol craft *PC(C)-469* in the Pacific Seventh Fleet. On that patrol craft Alton experienced kamikaze attacks, antisubmarine warfare missions, defensive activity against Japanese torpedo boats, and a horrific typhoon in the Philippines that caused the sinking of U.S. naval vessels and the drowning of crew members and other military personnel.

The sturdy shallow draft freight ships, which ranged from 99 to 180 feet in length, had to navigate treacherous Pacific inlets and coral reefs and were crammed with equipment, supplies, powerful engines, machine guns and anti-aircraft deck weapons. Lt. Alton credited the leadership and seamanship skills of Captain John Bender (USCG) on *PC(C)-469* with his survival in Pacific storms and combat.[47]

Lt. Alton researched the construction history of the World War II FS ships built between 1943 and 1945. The FS shipyards in the United States were located along the Great Lakes, and on the Atlantic and Gulf coasts and on inland rivers. The builders included Higgins Industries in New Orleans, Louisiana, and ship-yards in the states of New Jersey, Washington, California, Georgia, Maine, New York, Illinois, and Wisconsin (at Kewaunee and Sturgeon Bay).[48]

Coast Guard port and harbor security on the domestic front during the war was critical to homeland security. Wartime reporter and British Broad-casting Company correspondent Alistair Cooke noted the Coast Guard role in his cross-country travels in 1941 and 1942.

Cooke noticed a Coast Guard patrol plane off the coast of Maine and out of the morning mist heard "the drone of a Coast Guard patrol boat."[49] Cooke reported that Coast Guard port security and national defense policies required fishermen, farmers with guns, and local boats to carry special Coast Guard licenses. Boats had to be in port by nightfall. The USCG supervised shipyards and explosives loading. Island dwellers were identified and licensed. Foreign vessels obtained permission for military clearance and port entry. Lighthouses had been under USCG jurisdiction since the U.S. Lighthouse Service merged with the Coast Guard in 1939.

Alistair Cooke reported that fishermen were recruited by the Coast Guard into the enlisted ranks, and yachtsmen were offered officer commissions because of their knowledge of local waters, inlets and rivers and their abilities to place mines, submarine nets, and underwater obstructions in strategic loca-tions.[50] The harbor of Portland, Maine, Cooke explained, "was the end of the safe continent, the beginning of the Atlantic and the real war."[51]

Harvard historian and World War II U.S. naval officer Samuel Eliot Mori-son chronicled the history of the U.S. Navy and Coast Guard in World War II in his magnificent five-volume work and follow-up one volume synthesis. Admiral Morison sailed on Navy and Coast Guard vessels in the Atlantic and Pacific theaters and dedicated the massive one-volume "short history" to his "wartime shipmates" on seven U.S. Navy vessels and the "USCGC *Campbell*."[52]

Morison wrote that the CGC *Campbell* was such an effective destroyer-escort that "most of her sister ships of the Treasury class were devoted to this duty." The danger the naval escorts faced was described concisely by Adm. Morison: "USCGC *Hamilton* was torpedoed and sunk ten miles off Iceland 29 January 1942 while towing a disabled store (supply) ship."[53]

Professor Morison contended Cmdr. P.R. Heineman of the USCGC

Campbell was an exemplary escort commander who, in June 1941, protected Convoy ONS-102, a 63-ship convoy with three cutters, five Canadian warships, and the USS *Leary* (USN) on a voyage from Londonderry, United Kingdom to Halifax, Nova Scotia, Canada.[54]

In 1943 westbound transatlantic Convoy ON-166, with more than 60 ships, was escorted by now Capt. P.R. Heineman (USCG). ON-166 included five British and Canadian warships and the Polish destroyer *Burza*. On that mission two U-boats were sunk. "One," Morison wrote, "by USCGC *Spencer* with depth charges, one by USCGC *Campbell* with gunfire and ramming after *Burza* had depth charged it."[55] Professor Morison wrote that other Coast Guard cutter commanders "rank high among our anti-submarine *fighters*," including another *Campbell* skipper, Cmdr. Jesse Sowell, and Capt. H.S. Berdine (USCG) on the USS *Decatur*.[56]

The noted naval historian commended the regular and reserve Coast Guard personnel who operated small craft on the oceans and were "forced to perform functions and make long voyages for which they were not designed."[57] Admiral Morison did not neglect the U.S. Merchant Marine. The civilian maritime service, he noted, "deserves high praise for its world wide operations which were indispensable to the Navy, Army, and our Allies." The merchant sailors and U.S. Navy Armed Guards on the merchant vessels, Professor Morison concluded, "showed exemplary courage in convoy duty" in the Atlantic and Pacific combat theaters.[58]

By mid–1943, U.S. naval warships had sunk 11 German submarines, six by USCG oceangoing cutters. A Coast Guard patrol seaplane sank one of the 24 U-boats sunk by U.S. Navy aircraft. Ensign Henry C. White, flying a Grumman J4F, sank *U-166* with a depth charge in the Gulf of Mexico on 1 August 1942.[59]

Clay Blair's two-volume history of submarine warfare surveyed Navy, Coast Guard and U-boat action in the Atlantic. Of the many USCG cutters that contributed to the war effort, Blair credited the CG cutter *Thetis* under the command of Lt. (jg) Nelson C. McCormick with the sinking of *U-157* off Key West, Florida, in June 1942.[60]

In his official reports combined in the federal publication *U.S. Navy at War: 1941-1945*, Admiral Ernest J. King (USN) chronicled the contributions of the USCG in the Atlantic, Mediterranean, and Pacific combat theatres. Adm. King, U.S. fleet commander and Chief of Naval Operations, wrote: "During the period of this report, the Navy, the fleet and shore establishments, the Marine Corps, the Coast Guard, the WAVES, the Seabees, have all nobly done their parts ... but hereafter all are included in the term, 'The Navy.'"[61]

Admiral Chester W. Nimitz succeeded Adm. King as the postwar Fleet Admiral and Chief of Naval Operations. Admiral Nimitz paid tribute to the thousands of Regular, Reserve, Auxiliary and civilian Coast Guard personnel who served during World War II.

Admiral Nimitz held wartime USCG Commandant Admiral Russell R. Waesche "in the highest esteem." He wrote, "It was my privilege to have many of his combatant units under my command during the War." The Coast Guard performed its domestic and overseas duties, Nimitz concluded, with "dependability" and served "in the highest traditions of their Service to prove themselves worthy of their Service motto, Semper Paratus ... Always Ready."[62]

6

Defense from the Great Lakes to the Oceans

The Coast Guard's wartime responsibilities and missions had antecedents from the days of the U.S. Revenue Cutter Service and since 1915. The Coast Guard had experience throughout its history in national defense in peace and war, at home and abroad, in partnership with the U.S. Navy, Marines, Army, and with local, state and federal public safety and law enforcement agencies.

The national defense responsibilities of the Coast Guard have been incrementally expanded. In the World War II era the areas of geostrategic responsibility would extend from the Great Lakes and other U.S. inland waterways to the Gulf of Mexico, Caribbean Sea, Alaska and the Bering Sea, Atlantic and Pacific oceans, and the Mediterranean Sea.

To prepare its personnel for the extended missions and dangers, the United States Navy prepared a manual titled *Survival on Land and Sea*. The plethora of professionals who prepared the 187-page pocket sized wartime edition included staff members from the Smithsonian Institution and Navy experts from the Bureaus of Aeronautics, Medicine and Surgery, and the Office of Naval Intelligence.

Maps, illustrations, diagrams and charts guided the reader and potential survivors in response to potential wartime accidents, disasters, and circumstances. Major topics included navigation without instruments; tips on fishing with improvised bait and tackle; water and food sources on land and sea; vegetation types; protection from the sun, insects and dangerous critters; and a survey of geographic regions, climates, challenges, and survival techniques. Traveling, clothing, and signaling techniques were included.[i]

Creative, controversial and sometimes dubious counsel was included in the narrative. Examples include: "Sea snakes do not attack swimmers but are poisonous, and should be left alone. Their flesh is edible, but you might be bitten trying to land one…. Turtles are good to eat and their blood is suitable for drinking…. Sharks sometimes rub against lifeboats or rafts to scratch off sea lice rather than as an attempt to overturn the boat. The nose is their most sensitive spot and a blow here may drive them away. Kicking, slapping the water, and shouting may also have the same effect."

During World War I, President Woodrow Wilson signed the Espionage Act of 1917 into a law that shifted port security responsibilities from the U.S. Army Corps of Engineers to the Treasury Department and U.S. Coast Guard. The newly created Captain of the Port (COTP) position was initially assigned to USCG officers at the strategic ports of Norfolk, Virginia, Philadelphia, Pennsylvania, New York City, and the Great Lakes port of Sault Ste. Marie, Michigan, where the "Soo" Locks were located.

The Soo Locks connected the Great Lakes commercial waterways from the Twin Ports (Duluth, Minnesota, and Superior, Wisconsin) at the western terminus of Lake Superior, to the St. Lawrence River between Canada and the United States, and then to the Atlantic Ocean. The Great Lakes–St. Lawrence Seaway accommodated large freshwater and saltwater cargo ships from the United States and nations throughout the world.

The lake carriers and saltwater vessels carried agricultural crops, manufactured goods, coal, iron ore, steel, and other goods and supplies to American and foreign ports. The goods and supplies were essential to national economies and the war effort and gave the Great Lakes Seaway ports and the Soo Locks an economic and strategic significance which required the attention and cooperation of local, state, federal, and private public safety and security agencies.

During World War II, President Roosevelt expanded the mission of COTPs to 29 strategic U.S. ports. With that expansion the Great Lakes ports administered by Coast Guard COTPs came to include the previously mentioned Sault Ste. Marie, Michigan, and the additional ports of Duluth-Superior, Detroit and Marquette, Michigan, Cleveland, Ohio, Oswego and Buffalo, New York, and Chicago, Illinois.

COTPs tracked and inspected foreign merchant vessels in U.S. ports in search of enemy espionage, sabotage, and contraband. Axis Power vessels were impounded. Anchorage regulations were enforced. Dangerous cargo loading on commercial and military vessels was closely supervised. Public safety considerations (maritime rules, law enforcement, firefighting, and preventative and preemptive regulations) were responded to, expanded, and enforced.

The Coast Guard conducted fire inspections and assumed firefighting responsibilities onshore, in harbor areas where critical infrastructure was present, and at sea. Coast Guard patrol boats were equipped with firefighting equipment. USCG crews responded to ship, boat, and port fires throughout the war, and saved port facilities, vessels and other property, and, most important, human lives. With its inspection and civilian and military crew-training operations, the Coast Guard probably prevented many more potentially serious disasters from occurring, and confined the repercussions of the incidents that did happen.

To prepare the Coast Guard for its expanded wartime duties at home and overseas, President Roosevelt sighed executive orders that authorized the USCG to carry out COTP functions, recruit more personnel, and upgrade vessels, aircraft, shorestations, weapons, and vehicles.

The significance of the wartime duties of Coast Guard units and Captains of the Port along the Atlantic coast in the World War II era is illustrated by the outline of assets and missions in a 240-page file from the offices of the COTP and commander of the Marine Safety Office in Charleston, South Carolina. Volumes one and two of the *History of the U.S. Coast Guard in the Sixth Naval District during World War II* chronicled USCG activities in the ports and offshore areas of South Carolina in World War I, Prohibition, and World War II.

Charleston area Coast Guard cutters included the *Modoc, Yamacraw, Tallapoosa, Agassiz, Palmetto, Mangrove,* and *Cyprus.* The records included descriptions of coastal geography, major seaports, shipping, shore establishments, industrial plants and infrastructure, patrol operations, and the assets and activities at U.S. Coast Guard Air Base Charleston.

Aids to navigation, blackouts, anti-sabotage operations, firefighting, explosives loading, cutter patrols, and merchant ship control were described, as were administrative structures and operations between the Coast Guard and Navy in the Coast Guard Sixth and Navy Seventh Districts. Assistant COTPs administered the regional ports of Beaufort and Georgetown, South Carolina and Brunswick, Georgia.

The contributions of the civilian Coast Guard Auxiliary, coastal picket boat patrols, Temporary Reserves, Coast Guard Police, Beach Patrols, and civilian personnel were chronicled. Communications systems, legal administration, Coast Guard Intelligence, marine and civil engineering, merchant marine inspections, public relations, the Coast Guard Women's Reserve (SPARS), health services, civil aviation, defensive mines, blimp patrols, equipment status, training, and submarine patrols were described and assessed. Seventeen pages of the history file were devoted to the 9 May 1942 sinking of the German submarine *U-352* by the USCGC *Icarus* in the western Atlantic, and the follow-up Sixth Naval District Intelligence Report. Coast Guard photographs were included in the World War II file. A gracious letter of introduction from the Charleston COTP explained the circumstances of the historical documents from the Coast Guard to the South Carolina Historical Society.

Motor Machinist Mate First Class (MMM1) Richard L. Cariens responded to an explosion on U.S. Army Boat 234 in Charleston Harbor on 21 September 1943. Coast Guard Fireboat CG-30041-F rescued a civilian in the water and MMM1 Cariens boarded the burning vessel and repaired the leaking gas line. Coastguard personnel removed explosives that had been secured to the deck and retrieved classified documents. Cariens was awarded the Navy and Marine Corps medal.

On 6 October 1944 a railroad pier in the port of Charleston caught fire. Coast Guard fireboats and firefighting teams aided the Charleston Fire Department in containing the blaze. The CFD Chief credited the USCG with saving adjoining port infrastructure. Further north, up the North Carolina coast, on 15 March 1942 an oil tanker was torpedoed by a U-boat off the port of Southport. The COTP at Wilmington ordered several Coast Guard and Coast Guard Auxiliary boats to the scene where USCG crews spent several hours in the burning waters and on the flaming ship rescuing wounded merchant sailors. Coast Guard Temporary Reservists in picket boats out of Charleston Harbor boarded merchant ships for inspections in all kinds of weather 24-hours a day. Ports around the nation were challenged daily during World War II because of greatly increased shipping tonnage, and the necessity of enhanced port security measures for national defense.

A U.S. Navy landing craft ship tank (LST) was navigating downstream on the Mississippi River near New Orleans on 20 October 1944. Nine oil barge cargo containers pushed by a tugboat collided with the LST. Two barges and the LST ignited. One hundred thousand gallons of burning crude oil spilled into the Mississippi River. Four Coast Guard vessels (a cutter, picket boat, and 2 fireboats) arrived on the scene from New Orleans and extinguished the fires, dispersed the flaming waters, blocked the intake pipes to the New Orleans water purification plant, and tied up the runaway barges. The LST fire was put out by Navy firefighters.

The strategic Gulf of Mexico region, the Central Plains and the Upper Midwest posed national security scrutiny because of their essential wartime industrial, mineral, and agricultural production, and the strategic maritime transportation highways such as the Missouri, Ohio, and Mississippi rivers, major connecting tributaries and channels, and the Great Lakes.

In April 1944 the USCG COTP of the Port of Galveston, Texas responded to a fierce rain and wind storm that capsized several watercraft near a transportation causeway. Several boaters drowned. Coast Guard personnel from the Galveston Life Boat Station rescued 41 people and accounted for the missing persons in a one-week mission. Five watercraft were eventually recovered.

In the region of the Great Lakes, port security alerts, maritime accidents, and the potential of espionage against ships and the transportation and industrial infrastructure were a continuing threat. In July 1942 a bridge guard found evidence of sabotage equipment on a Toledo, Ohio, bridge. The evidence was given to Coast Guard officials and the Federal Bureau of Investigation. In August 1944 the Sturgeon Bay, Wisconsin, COTP received a reliable report of damaged firefighting equipment near the shipyards.

The Chicago waterfront contained refineries, steel mills and other industrial plants, railroad properties, and shipyards. The Chicago area Coast Guard COTP increased boat patrols in the region and enhanced firefighting prevention and response capacities. Guards were placed on U.S. Navy vessels for the voyages from the Great Lakes and river tributaries to the Gulf and Atlantic coasts. Numerous incidents were prevented or successfully responded to.

On 20 October 1944 Coast Guard Temporary Reservists responded to liquid gas tank explosions and fires at the East Ohio Gas Company in Cleveland, Ohio. Hundreds of homes were incinerated. More than 100 people died. Area Coast Guard and Navy personnel responded at great personal risk to fight the fires, save lives, carry out law enforcement functions in coordination with local public safety agencies, protect waterfront industrial infrastructure, prevent additional explosions and fires and the spread of lethal fumes from other petrochemical and flammable sites. The mission was successful after three days of hard and dangerous work. Temporary Reservists and Auxiliary conducted inspections, patrolled harbor waters and waterfronts, guarded docks, vessels, and bridges, manned lookout posts, and saved lives on land and sea. Those activities released thousands of Coast Guard Regulars and active-duty Reserves for duty on the high seas off America's coasts and overseas.

In World War Two the Ninth Coast Guard District included St. Louis, Missouri. Today the Ninth District encompasses the Great Lakes region, and St. Louis is in the Eighth Coast Guard District. The wartime Ninth District then included the Midwest (North Central Plains) inland navigable waters region south to Memphis, Tennessee, and north and east to Minneapolis, Minnesota, and Pittsburgh, Pennsylvania. Rural and metropolitan areas and thousands of miles of river shoreline need security patrols and protection. About 2,500 Temporary Reservists with military credentials, ranks and rates, were transferred from the civilian Coast Guard Auxiliary to serve under 20 Coast Guard COTPs. The TRs conducted boat and jeep patrols, sentry, vessel boarding and inspection duties, manned fireboats, stood telephone and radio watches, and piloted surveillance aircraft.

President Franklin D. Roosevelt directed the Coast Guard to expand its icebreaking operations to the Inland Seas (Great Lakes) to keep the shipping season open longer in the winter months. Shipyards scattered throughout the Great Lakes region constructed several new Coast Guard icebreakers and buoy tenders for that purpose. Among them were the rugged 180-foot buoy tenders, several of which were built at Duluth-Superior (Twin Ports) shipyards, and the gigantic 290-foot icebreaker USCGC *Mackinaw* that was launched in 1944 and home-ported in Cheboygan, Michigan.

For greater administrative efficiency, FDR merged the U.S. Lighthouse Service into the U.S. Coast Guard in 1939. That merger expanded the aids to navigation responsibilities of the Coast Guard, required U.S. lighthouse keepers and assistants to become members of the U.S. Armed Forces, and added 10 lighthouse tender boats (now cutters), 51 radio beacons and weather broadcast stations, 58 small boat stations, and 78 weather bureau observation stations to the Great Lakes Coast Guard equipment and personnel component.

In 1941 President Roosevelt signed into law the establishment of the Coast Guard Women's Reserve under the command of Lt. Cmdr. (later Capt.) Dorothy Stratton (USN, USCG). In 1944 the Ninth (Great Lakes) Naval District headquarters in Cleveland, Ohio listed nearly 400 SPARS. By 1945 more than 600 SPARS were serving Ninth District Coast Guard units in office support and management positions, hospitals, and communications stations.

The USCGC *Escanaba* (WPG-77) illustrates the contribution of Great Lakes Coast Guard personnel to World War II. Built at Defoe Works in Bay City, Michigan, launched in 1932, and home-ported at Grand Haven, Michigan, the 165-foot icebreaker/gunboat was transferred to the Atlantic Sea Frontier for SAR and convoy duty. On 13 June 1943, while escorting a U.S. Army supply ship through icebergs and fog between the North Atlantic island of Greenland and New Foundland, Canada, the *Escanaba* was torpedoed and sunk by a U-boat.

Lt. Cmdr. Carl Petersen and 100 other officers and enlisted personnel were lost. Two survivors, Seaman First Class (SN1) Raymond O'Malley and Boatswain Mate Second Class (BM2) Melvin Baldwin, were rescued by passing convoy ships. Four months prior to its sinking, the *Escanaba* rescued 133 survivors from a torpedoed transport ship.

During the war years of 1941–1945 the shipyards in the Twin Ports of Duluth, Minnesota, and Superior, Wisconsin, at the southwestern terminus of Lake Superior built several 180-foot Coast Guard icebreaker/buoy tenders. The "180s" served the Great Lakes for several decades. The Marine Iron and Shipbuilding Corporation and the Zenith Dredge Company laid the keels of 20 Coast Guard cutters, one of which served in the Pacific.

After the war, in January 1946, the USCG was transferred back from U.S. Navy and War Department jurisdiction to the Treasury Department. From 1946 to 1950 Commodore James A. Hirshfield (USCG) commanded the Ninth (Great Lakes) Coast Guard District. During the war, on 23 February 1943, as commanding officer of the USCGC *Campbell*, Cmdr. Hirshfield rammed and sank *U-606* in the Atlantic and received the Navy Cross for his action.

In May 1944 Yeoman First Class (YN1) Ray Thomas (USCG) was stationed in Duluth after South Pacific combat duty. The Traverse City, Michigan, native had joined the Coast Guard in 1940 at the age of eighteen. In 1942 YN Thomas served on ships carrying Army and Marine Corps personnel overseas and supplies from New Zealand to various South Pacific ports and islands. From the deck of a troop transport, Petty Officer Thomas witnessed the sinking of four U.S. Navy cruisers by Japanese warships. Thomas participated in the recovery of wounded and dead American sailors and Japanese military personnel. Japanese survivors were transferred to prisoner of war camps.

Lake Superior Journal maritime writer James R. Marshall chronicled the missions of a World War II buoy tender that was constructed in a Twin Ports (Duluth-Superior) shipyard. Marshall described Chief Boatswain Mate (BMC) Vermont Johnson's wartime experiences in the Pacific on the USCGC *Balsam* (WLB-62). The *Balsam* sank a Japanese submarine (I-boat) with rockets and depth charges and then stood by to ram the I-boat if necessary with the *Bal-*

sam's reinforced Great Lakes icebreaker bow. A Bayfield, Wisconsin, native, BMC Johnson recalled how Lt. Cmdr. L.P. Toolin depth charged the I-boat while escorting a U.S. Navy fuel and ammunition tanker. The CGC *Balsam* was credited with the submarine kill and subsequently placed a symbol of the Japanese flag and its telltale "Rising Sun" image on the starboard bridge of the cutter. In 1985 Johnson wrote a letter to the Zenith Dredge Company of Duluth describing his service aboard the buoy tender "built in 1942 by your company."

From 1942 to 1945 the CGC *Balsam* was assigned to ATN duties in the South Pacific. The *Balsam* crew assisted in the construction and maintenance of LORAN stations. In June and July of 1945 the *Balsam* performed general duty in the Okinawa Island area and fought fires on the USS *Rawlins* after the Navy warship had been struck by Japanese suicide aircraft.

The CGC *Balsam* participated in a joint naval mission and the successful rescue of 12 U.S., Navy aviators whose plane went down off Howland Island (the landing site missing civilian aviator Amelia Earhart failed to reach in her 1937 transoceanic flight). The *Balsam* then returned to Baker Island 31 miles to the south to land LORAN station materials during a two week period of gale force winds, tropical rain, and dangerous surf. The *Balsam* transported military landing parties to isolated Pacific island LORAN sites where dogs, sentries, machine guns, grenades and small arms were the arsenals with which Coast Guard and other military crews might have to defend themselves against Japanese forces interested in acquiring LORAN equipment.[1]

Boatswain Mate Chief (BMC) Manny Greenwald enlisted in the Coast Guard in 1942 and subsequently served on active and reserve port security duty in Philadelphia, Pennsylvania. After leaving the USCGR, Greenwald joined the civilian Coast Guard Auxiliary and continued his service in the Marine Safety Office (MSO), Philadelphia. In 2003, when Greenwald was 92, President George W. Bush honored him after Vice Adm. James Hull (USCG), the Ninth Coast Guard District commander, informed Bush about Greenwald's long and dedicated service.[2]

Great Lakes shipyards and the highly skilled and motivated men and women who worked in them built the vessels that sustained the war effort and made victory possible. The Globe Shipbuilding Company of Superior, Wisconsin, built commercial cargo vessels and U.S. Navy and Coast Guard boats, ships and cutters. McDougal Duluth Company launched cutters as early as 1941. Marine Iron and Shipbuilding Corporation launched five Coast Guard cutters in 1942 and 1943.[3]

The strategic and logistical significance of the Duluth-Superior shipyards in World War II was indicated by the consistent presence of federal law enforcement officials (Treasury, FBI, and Coast Guard) to monitor port security, deter sabotage and espionage, and investigate allegations of security threats.[4]

Twin Ports shipyards hired more than 14,000 workers to build 200 ships in seven yards. These shipyards were Zenith, Dredge, Marine Iron and Ship-

The USCGC *Balsam* (WAGL-62) was built by the Zenith Dredger Company of Duluth, Minnesota, in 1941. The 180-foot buoy tender's crews served on SAR. Aids to Navigation, LORAN station supply, salvage, firefighter, and combat missions in the South Pacific.

building, Globe Shipbuilding, Lake Superior Shipbuilding, Barnes Duluth Shipbuilding, and Walter Butler Shipbuilders. The shipbuilding tradition in the Twin Ports dated back to the 1870s. The Zenith Dredge and Marine Iron companies built 38 buoy tenders and other Coast Guard cutters between 1942 and 1944. Globe Shipbuilding launched 27 cargo vessels, tugboats, and U.S. Navy frigates in the same time period.

Twin Ports area civilians also contributed to the war effort by their service in the U.S. Merchant Marine fleet that plied the dangerous waters of the world combat zones to bring essential supplies to the Allies in their battle against the Rome-Berlin-Tokyo Axis.[5] Hundreds of merchant mariners suffered injuries in the stormy waters of the global combat zones. Hundreds of maritime seamen were killed in enemy air and sea attacks against their vessels.

The shipbuilding companies hired buses to pick up their skilled employees, bring them to the Twin Ports yards, and return them to their Duluth-Superior homes and hotel rooms, the outlying towns of Philips and Ashland, Wisconsin, and the Iron Range mining region of northern Minnesota. The Northern Pacific Railroad transported the hundreds of men and women shipyard and railroad workers who made critical contributions to the national defense and economy.[6]

Among the many industrial managers and entrepreneurs who contributed their knowledge, skills, and patriotism to victory was Clarence Skamser. In his capacity as president of Globe Shipbuilding Company, Skamser, a former chamber of commerce director, traveled to Washington, D.C., to negotiate for federal construction contracts. By the end of 1942 Mr. Skamser had acquired contracts for the building of eight U.S. Navy frigates and ten tugboats.[7]

With the termination of World War II, however, the loss of U.S. Navy and Coast Guard ship- and boatbuilding contracts dried up the dry docks. The American Shipbuilding Company in Superior was sold to Knutson Brothers Construction. Twin Ports natives Robert Fraser and Byron Nelson then purchased the Knutson shipyard and formed Fraser-Nelson Shipbuilding and Dry Dock Company. The Fraser-Nelson Company transitioned into the peacetime economy and built technologically advanced lake freighters.[8]

Throughout World War II the Duluth "Black Hull Fleet" of 180-foot buoy tenders served as icebreakers, maintained aids to navigation, and performed SAR and law enforcement duties on the Great Lakes, and served with distinction in traditional and combat missions in the Atlantic and Pacific.[9]

National security concerns overseas and on the home front focused the attention of civilian and military officials. The vulnerability and significance of wartime shipping and the strategic infrastructure of the Twin Ports of Duluth-Superior led a Coast Guard official to assure public safety agencies that a minimum of five armed patrol boats would provide security to the Twin Ports 24 hours a day, seven days a week.[10] Civilian yachtsmen contributed their skills as members of the Coast Guard Auxiliary to patrolling and monitoring Great Lakes port security. A Port Security Unit (PSU) was established in Duluth during the war that included a personnel complement of 15 members.[11]

Great Lakes Coast Guard cutters left their mark in World War II maritime combat zones with significant contributions and costs. The U-boat torpedo attack on the USCGC *Escanaba* (WPG-77) on 12 June 1943 caused the loss of 101 crewmembers with only two survivors. Grand Haven, Michigan was the homeport of the *Escanaba*. Grand Haven residents held annual tributes to the courageous cutter crew and raised the money to construct a new cutter of the same name. Grand Haven's support of the Coast Guard resulted in the U.S. Coast Guard officially designating the community "Coast Guard City USA."[12]

The new 270-foot medium endurance oceangoing cutter *Escanaba* (WMEC-907) was launched in 1985. The deepwater WMEC-907 was the third Coast Guard vessel to be named *Escanaba*, the Native American term for "flat rock." WMEC-907 was built by R.E. Derecktor Shipyard in Middleton, Rhode Island and appropriately commissioned at Grand Haven in 1987. Although stationed in Boston, Massachusetts, the CGC *Escanaba* (WMEC-907) has served as the flagship for the annual Grand Haven tribute to the World War II era 165-foot USCGC *Escanaba* (WPG-77). The World War II *Escanaba* was built by Defoe Boat and Motor Works in Bay City, Michigan, in 1932.[13]

The 165-foot USCGC *Escanaba* (WPG-77) stationed at Grand Haven, Michigan, in 1935. The Great Lakes icebreaker served on convoy and SAR duty in the North Atlantic. On 13 June 1943 the *Escanaba* was sunk by a German submarine with the loss of 101 men. Other naval vessels rescued two *Escanaba* Coastguardsmen.

The Great Lakes served as a training area for naval crews and vessels. The lakes were a U-boat free region on which to train Navy personnel on gunboats and ships modified as aircraft carriers. Navy aviators, other officers, enlisted personnel, and Reservists received essential training before being sent to combat zones. World War II historian Richard P. Klobuchar chronicled the training of U.S. Navy Reservists on the Great Lakes out of the ports of Chicago, Illinois, Detroit, Michigan, and Duluth, Minnesota, and the interaction between Navy and U.S. Coast Guard units.[14]

After World War II, as Coast Guard members remained on overseas active duty awaiting matriculation to civilian life, the U.S. Coast Guard Auxiliary (USCGAUX) continued to serve on the home front. When personnel shortages stimulated federal plans to close selected Great Lakes stations, USCGAUX volunteers stepped forward to perform permissible Coast Guard duties until active duty personnel could return to carry out their traditional responsibilities.[15]

7

Admiral Russell R. Waesche: Wartime Commandant

At the direction of Presidents Woodrow Wilson and Franklin D. Roosevelt, the Coast Guard was placed under U.S. Navy jurisdiction in World War One and World War Two. Founded in 1790 as the U.S. Revenue Marine under the direction of Treasury secretary Alexander Hamilton, the Sea Service evolved into the U.S. Revenue Cutter Service (USRCS) and then, in 1915, the U.S. Coast Guard (USCG). The Coast Guard would subsequently be transferred to the Department of Transportation (1967) and the Department of Homeland Security (2003), maintaining liaison connections to the War Department (World Wars I and II) and then the Defense Department since 1947.

A captain-commandant headquartered in Washington, D.C., headed the Coast Guard during World War I. The Coast Guard commandant has held admiral rank since World War II.[1] Commodore Ellsworth P. Bertholf was appointed captain-commandant of the USRCS in 1911 and the USCG from 1915 to 1919. Captain Bertholf led the Sea Service through World War I, and then through the postwar transition to expanded peacetime missions. Admiral Russell R. Waesche served as the Coast Guard commandant from 1936 to 1945, through the World War II era. Adm. Waesche prepared the Coast Guard for war at home and overseas.[2]

In 1942 Waesche was promoted from vice admiral to rear admiral and then full admiral in 1945. Adm. Waesche's successors have generally had four-star admiral rank.[3]

Waesche's early career opportunities prepared him to lead the Coast Guard during World War II and then protect the service's postwar autonomy when congressional budget cutters advocated the permanent transfer of the USCG into the U.S. Navy. Waesche began his naval career in 1904 as a cadet at the USRCS School of Instruction. He graduated from the School of Instruction as a commissioned officer in 1906. Ensign Waesche then served in the Pacific Northwest and the North Atlantic, and on the Great Lakes. In 1911 he commanded the U.S. Revenue Cutter *Arcata*, served on the RC *Pamlico* in 1912, and was assigned to USCG Headquarters in Washington, D.C., from 1915 to 1918 throughout World War I.

After World War I, Waesche commanded Coast Guard patrol boats and cutters and had shore postings at the Philadelphia Navy Yard and the War Plans Division. In the latter assignment he developed fortuitous plans for the integration of the Coast Guard and Navy in time of war. In June 1936, Cmdr. Waesche was promoted to rear admiral and appointed commandant of the Coast Guard, serving as commandant throughout World War II.[4] Commander Waesche had been nominated for that leadership post by President Roosevelt's Treasury secretary, Henry Morganthau, and promoted over 4 commanders and 20 captains.[5]

In 1936, three years before World War II began in Europe and five years before the attack on Pearl Harbor brought the U.S. into the war, Commandant Waesche accepted seven new 327-foot oceangoing cutters. Named after Treasury Department secretaries, the sleek, new "Treasury Class" cutters were the *Campbell, Ingham, Duane, Spencer, Taney, Bibb*, and *Hamilton*. Each of these vessels and their crews would go on to perform valiantly in World War II maritime combat zones. Cutters equipped with cranes for lifting flying-boat floatplanes on and off the decks were designated as "Seaplane Tenders." Each of these 327-foot cutters initially carried two 5-inch .50 caliber deck guns and assorted small arms; they would receive armament upgrades during the war years.

Rear Adm. Waesche administered the 1939 merger of the U.S. Lighthouse Service (USLHS) and its personnel and tenders (now classified as cutters) into the Coast Guard. The USLHS guided military and merchant ships through dangerous coastal and shoal waters with intensely illuminated lighthouse lights. USLHS personnel and equipment enhanced the Coast Guard Aids to Navigation (ATN) mission. Adm. Waesche administered the logistics of war preparation with skill and creativity. In addition, the commandant was assigned the controversial task of transferring ten cutters to British control as required by presidential order and the Lend-Lease Act of 1941.

Coast Guard cutters had to be scheduled for shipyard construction to accommodate increased armament needs that gradually included larger deck guns, explosive depth charges for use against enemy submarines, sound-detecting sonar equipment, advanced radio communications, and image transmitting radar screens for the detection of air and seacraft. Adm. Waesche and his headquarters staff also planned for the coming North Atlantic and Greenland convoy and antisubmarine warfare patrols.[6]

President Roosevelt directed the transfer of two civilian agencies to the Coast Guard in February 1942 by Executive Order Number 9083: The U.S. Maritime Service (USMS), a merchant marine reserve, and the Bureau of Marine Inspection and Navigation. BMIN dealt with safety at sea issues. Its personnel inspected, certified and licensed merchant marine seamen, officers and pilots. Coast Guard personnel were assigned to merchant vessels to train merchant seafarers and man merchant ships. Adm. Waesche designed training programs for this mission and assigned Coast Guard and civilian instructors and inspectors to the tasks of monitoring crew competence, discipline, and ship safety. Regulations were enforced by fines and license suspensions. Skilled and courageous merchant mariners ran the ships that got supplies to ports around the world and suffered accidents and wartime casualties while carrying out those missions. Merchant ship crews were instrumental in securing victory over the Axis nations.

Shipyards were open throughout the nation for the construction of the gigantic vessels needed for wartime shipping. Coast Guard crews acquired valuable experience manning the largest vessels the Sea Service had sailed prior to World War II. The 7,000-ton maritime commission steamship *American Seaman*, for example, had a complement of 18 officers, 100 enlisted men, and 250 student trainees.[7]

Adm. Russell R. Waesche, the World War II Coast Guard commandant. Adm. Waesche prepared the USCG for the war, led the Service throughout the war, and earned the commendations of U.S. Navy and civilian leaders.

The success of the merchant marine training, inspection, safety and certification program led to the permanent transfer of the Bureau of Navigation and Marine Inspection to the Coast Guard after World War II.[8] Under Commandant Waesche's wartime leadership, the Coast Guard manned 290 U.S. Navy vessels, 255 U.S. Army craft, 750 cutters, more than 3,000 assorted small craft, and a variety of amphibious attack vessels, patrol boats, and landing craft in every theater of war. Coast Guard seamen and aviators carried out ASW, SAR, and convoy escort missions. After the war, Waesche secured congressional support for the return of the USCG from U.S. Navy to Treasury Department control.[9]

The contributions of Adm. Waesche to the Coast Guard and the history of World War II are difficult to overestimate. The commandant contributed to the creation of Coast Guard Reserve and Auxiliary units that would play a significant postwar role, and laid the groundwork for the massive demobilization and rate and rank reductions necessitated by the end of the war. A delicate balance had to be achieved, because Waesche had to reduce the enormous number of wartime personnel, but, conversely, plan for the increased numbers of men and women needed for the anticipated expansion of the USCG in the looming Cold War period. Adm. Wasche's administrative and human relations skills facilitated the transition from his command to his successor, Admiral Joseph F. Farley. Commandant Farley would serve from 1946 to 1949.[10]

The highest-ranking officers of the U.S. Navy appreciated the contributions Adm. Waesche made to naval operations. Admiral Ernest King (USN), commander of the U.S. Fleet, and Chief of Naval Operations, chronicled the contributions of the U.S. Coast Guard in the Atlantic, Mediterranean, and Pacific theaters of operation, and wrote: "The Navy ... Fleet, ... shore establishments ... Marine Corps ... Coast Guard ... Waves [and] Seabees have all nobly done their parts. Each has earned an individual 'Well Done' [and] are hereafter all included in the term, 'the Navy.'"[11]

Admiral Chester W. Nimitz (USN) succeeded Adm. King as the postwar Chief of Naval Operations (CNO) and commended the thousands of Coast Guard personnel who served in World War II. Admiral Nimitz held wartime Coast Guard commandant Russell R. Waesche "in the highest esteem. It was my privilege," Nimitz asserted, "to have many of his combatant units under my command during the war." The Coast Guard performed its duties on the home front and overseas, concluded Adm. Nimitz, "with dependability ... and served in the highest traditions of their Service, [proving] themselves worthy of their Service Motto, Semper Paratus, Always Ready."[12]

Upon the return of the Coast Guard to the Treasury Department, U.S. Navy secretary James V. Forrestal recalled, "During the arduous war years, the Coast Guard has earned the highest respect and deepest appreciation of the Navy and Marine Corps. Its performance of duty has been without exception in keeping with the highest traditions of the Naval Service."[13]

Admiral Ernest J. King (USN), the Chief of Naval Operations in World War II, expressed high regard for the contributions of Coast Guard commandant Admiral Russell R. Waesche and the USCG in World War II. Admiral Richard S. Edwards (USN), King's deputy assistant, expressed similar sentiments in his letter to Adm. Waesche upon the latter's retirement from the Coast Guard: "No one knows better than I do how much the Navy owes the Coast Guard in general, and you in particular, not only for the outstanding achievements in the war, but also for the painstaking preparation in the years leading up to the war.... I salute the lowering of your flag with a heartfelt 'Well Done.'"[14]

After serving the longest assignment as Coast Guard commandant of any Coast Guard leader in the history of the Service, Russell R. Waesche retired in January 1946. Adm. Waesche died in October of 1946, at the age of 59, and was buried at Arlington National Cemetery.[15]

Russell R. Waesche, Jr., graduated from the Coast Guard Academy in New London, Connecticut, in 1936, the same year his father was appointed the Coast Guard commandant. Russell R. Waesche, Jr., served on convoy duty in the

Atlantic and in the Pacific during World War II. After the war, Waesche commanded six different Coast Guard stations throughout the United States. Rear Adm. Russell R. Waesche, Jr., died in June 1998 at the age of 84.

Admiral Owen W. Siler served as the Coast Guard commandant from 1974 to 1978. Adm. Siler graduated with an engineering degree from the U.S. Coast Guard Academy in 1943 after a compressed three-year cadet-training period to meet the increased need for wartime officers. Siler served in World War II under the command of Coast Guard Commandant, Adm. Russell R. Wasche. Admiral Siler served as a young officer on two attack transports: the *Hunter Liggett* (APA-14) during the invasion of the Solomon Islands in the South Pacific,[16] and the *Bayfield* (APA-33),[17] which participated in amphibious operations on D-Day (1944) in France, and in the Pacific landings at Iwo Jima and Okinawa.[18] Admiral Siler earned the Coast Guard Distinguished Service Medal, Legion of Merit, National Defense Service Medal, and other World War II awards.[19]

Admiral Siler was not alone among the valiant Coast Guard personnel who earned citations, commendations, ribbons and medals under the command of Commandant Waesche. Military records list Coastguardsmen as having earned the Medal of Honor (1), Navy Cross (5), Navy Distinguished Service Medal (1), and the Silver Star (58).[20]

In his magnificent and extensive history of the Coast Guard in World War II, Malcolm F. Willoughby devoted 22 pages to the names of Coast Guard personnel who earned a variety of medals and awards in the conflict. Willoughby lists one Medal of Honor (SM1 Douglas A. Munro) and the winners of the Navy Cross (6), Distinguished Service Medal (2), Silver Star Medal (64), Legion of Merit (96), Distinguished Flying Cross (12), Navy and Marine Corps Medal (170), Bronze Star Medal (277), Air Medal (248), Navy Commendation Ribbon (512), Army Commendation Medal (12), Air Force Commendation Medal (1), Coast Guard Commendation Ribbon (94), Gold Life-Saving Medal (11), Silver Life-Saving Medal (51), Commandant's Citation (119), and Commandant's Letter of Commendation (435). Members of the Coast Guard also assisted and supported the military missions and personnel of foreign nations. The Allied Nations of Belgium, Brazil, Canada, China, Denmark, Dominican Republic, France, Great Britain, Haiti, Italy, Poland, and the Union of Soviet Socialist Republics awarded decorations to 123 members of the United States Coast Guard.

Admiral Russell R. Waesche was the recipient of several U.S. Armed Forces and Allied Nations medals and awards for his contributions to the war effort in his capacity as the World War II commandant of the U.S. Coast Guard. Waesche earned the Distinguished Service Medal, Navy Commendation Ribbon, the Order of the British Empire from the United Kingdom, and the Polania Restituta award from Poland.[21]

8

Coast Guard Air
and Sea Warfare

Lt. Cmdr. Tom Beard (USCG, Ret.) has chronicled the history of Coast Guard aviation in articles and books and has traced Coast Guard air and sea missions from the early 20th century to the present. Lt. Cmdr. Beard described the seaplanes and the amphibious (land and sea) floatplanes as the primary Coast Guard aircraft used in World War II at the advent of the fledgling Sikorsky rotor-wing helicopter. The Coast Guard pioneered in the use of the helicopter in World War II. The transition to rotor-wing aircraft stimulated a contentious tactical debate between Coast Guard seaplane and helicopter advocates.

As the Sikorsky helicopter was being developed and tested, Cmdr. Frank Erickson (USCG) informed U.S. Army brigadier general William Donovan, the head of the Office of Strategic Services (OSS), and Gen. Frank Lowe (USA) about the potential of the rotor-wing aircraft for surveillance and search and rescue missions. Gen. Donovan's OSS was the predecessor of the Central Intelligence Agency (CIA). Cmdr. Erickson taught Gen. Lowe helicopter aviation. In 1943 Cmdr. Erickson commanded the first military helicopter school at Coast Guard Air Station (CGAS), Floyd Bennett Field, in New York.

Coast Guard floatplanes conducted convoy escorts, antisubmarine warfare surveillance and attack, and SAR missions. SAR patrols searched for downed aviators and survivors of German submarine (U-boat) torpedo attacks on military and civilian ships. During World War II, Coast Guard aircraft found more than 1,000 victims of torpedo attacks and saved over 100 people, including crewmembers from a U-boat.[1]

The J4F Widgeon amphibious seaplane, capable of landing on sea and land, carried a 325-pound depth charge beneath its monoplane wing. On 1 August 1942, a J4F Widgeon flown by Coast Guard Aviation Machinist Mate Chief Henry C. White and Radioman First Class George H. Boggs sank U-166 in the Gulf of Mexico. That combat action was the only incident of an enemy submarine being sunk by a Coast Guard aircraft in World War II.[2]

Coast Guard aviators flew North Atlantic and Greenland patrols, often in inclement weather over ice-clogged waters. Coast Guard crews ran U.S. Navy

Patrol Squadron (VP) 6. The Coast Guard performed Ice Patrol and SAR missions in large, rugged PBY Catalina seaplanes. Classified electronic navigation and survey missions were flown by Coast Guard aviators to establish bombing routes, direct U.S. Army Air Force bombers to Japanese targets, and assist U.S. Navy ships.[3]

Coast Guard combat aircraft carried aerial gunners behind machine guns fed by belted chains of high caliber ammunition. Coast Guard aviators performed missions in float planes like the propeller driven PBM Mariner. The Mariner achieved rapid ascent using attached jet assisted takeoff (JATO) containers. The JATO flights predated the jet combat aircraft of the 1950s.[4]

By the early 1960s the Coast Guard phased out the use of flying boats because of the hazards of sea landings and takeoffs. The USCG gradually replaced the seaplanes with amphibious helicopters that would achieve a 20-year history. The floating helicopters were replaced by 1990 with the more reliable all-weather, wheeled land-based helicopters equipped with rescue swimmers and rescue baskets.[5] Nevertheless, the USCG learned a great deal from its seaplane aviation history and the heritage begun by the first Coast Guard aviator, Commander Elmer F. Stone. In 1919, Cmdr. Stone piloted U.S. Navy biplane NC-4 in the first transatlantic flight, for which he earned the Navy Cross.

Coast Guard enlisted and reserve personnel flew over and sailed on the Atlantic Ocean. Petty Officer Glendale Uhlich graduated from high school in 1941 and enlisted in the Coast Guard in 1942. After basic training at Sheepshead Bay, New York, Uhlich was assigned to an LST landing craft that later participated in the South Pacific island invasions. PO Uhlich was transferred from the LST before it went to the Pacific; he was assigned to the USS *Ramsden* (DE-382) as a cook in the galley. "The crew ate well," Uhlich insisted. "We served plenty of chicken, roast beef, meat loaf, and stew."

The Ohio-born Uhlich was assigned to a battle station at one of the destroyer escort's 3-inch deck guns. U.S. Navy crewmembers on the *Ramsden* kidded their Coast Guard colleagues about having previously been in "the Hooligan Navy," Uhlich recalled, but "we sure didn't spend a lot of time guarding the American coastline."

The USS *Ramsden* had a complement of 225 enlisted men and 20 officers who executed ASW missions in the Atlantic Ocean and in the Mediterranean Sea from North Africa to Italy. The *Ramsden* was armed with depth charges and torpedoes. PO Uhlich described how small "flattops provided air cover and that was a big part of antisubmarine warfare." The crew dropped depth charges on detected U-boats, fought off enemy air attacks, and shot down a German bomber. After the war, Glendale Uhlich returned to Ohio, worked in industry, and became a plant supervisor.[6]

Coast Guard convoy escorts and antisubmarine warfare patrols in the Atlantic in World War II illustrate the complexity, diversity, and extensive range of Atlantic naval operations. An overview of the Atlantic, Greenland, and Mediterranean patrols will be considered in this chapter. More extensive treatment of those regional patrols and the formidable Normandy (D-Day) operations in France, and the war in the Pacific from the northern Aleutian Islands to the insular South Pacific, will be covered in subsequent chapters.

The 165-foot USCGC *Algonquin* (WPG-75), built by Pusey & Jones Co. in Wilmington, Delaware, in 1933 and launched the following year, was used in icebreaking missions off the coast of Maine before being assigned to the U.S. Navy (1941–1945) for escort duty on the Greenland Patrol. The *Algonquin* rescued 22 survivors from the SS *Svend Foyne* on 21 March 1943 after the merchant vessel struck an iceberg.[7] On 18 April 1945 the cutter attacked a U-boat in the Atlantic.[8]

The USCGC *Bibb* (WPG-31/WAGC-31) was built at the Charleston, South Carolina, Naval Yard in August of 1935 and launched and commissioned in 1937. The 327-foot cutter was built to carry a floatplane aft. Assigned to the U.S. Navy in the North Atlantic, the *Bibb* rescued 301 survivors from merchant vessels in 1942 and 1943, was a convoy escort to the Mediterranean Sea (1943–1944), and operated as a flagship in the Pacific Fleet. In 1944 the *Bibb* carried a 3"/50 gun, a Hedgehog depth charge mounted on the bow, and a lookout position and radar on the mast.[9] From 1942 to 1944 the CGC *Bibb* was credited with seven attacks on Axis submarines and survived an aircraft attack in the Mediterranean Sea off the North African port of Bizerte, Tunisia.[10]

The 327-foot CGC *Campbell* (WPG-32/WAGC-32) was launched at the Philadelphia, Pennsylvania Navy Yard on 3 June 1936. In September 1939 the *Campbell* was assigned to the Grand Banks Patrol in the North Atlantic as part of Destroyer Division 18, and then to U.S. Navy escort duty from 1941 to 1943. On 22 February 1943 the *Campbell* rammed and sank *U-606* at the cost of damage to the bow, engine room flooding, and the loss of power. Shipyard repairs laid up the CGC *Campbell* until 19 May 1943. From 1943 to 1945 the *Campbell* performed convoy escort duty in the Mediterranean and combat support missions in the Pacific.

Typical of the 327-foot "Treasury Class" cutters, the *Campbell* was initially powered by twin 3-bladed propellers, and 2 Westinghouse turbine engines capable of expending 5,000 horsepower in 1935. By 1945 modified engines provided the *Campbell* with more than 6,000 horsepower and a maximum speed of 19.5 knots. In 1941 the oceangoing cutter's armament included two forward 5"/51s, a 3"/50 in front of the bridge, and three 3"/50s aft.[11]

In October 1942 the *Campbell* was escorting a convoy that lost six commercial vessels to U-boat attacks. Between February 1942 and May 1944 the intrepid Coast Guard cutter participated in 7 submarine and U-boat group (Wolf Pack) attacks and survived an air attack.[12]

The CGC *Duane* (WPG-33/WAGC-6) was constructed at the Philadelphia Navy Yard in 1935 and commissioned in 1936. Between 1940 and 1945, the

USCGC *Bibb* (WPG-31) Gun Turret. The 327-foot cutter served in the North Atlantic on weather patrol and convoy escort duty, in the Mediterranean, and as a USN flagship at Okinawa in the Pacific.

Duane operated as a weather station ship in the Atlantic and participated in a survey of coastal Greenland in a search for airfield sites with the innovative use of an onboard floatplane. The CGC *Duane* also carried out North Atlantic escort duty, rescued survivors of vessel sinkings, guarded Mediterranean and Caribbean convoys, and docked at the harbor of Naples, Italy. In August 1944 the *Duane* was the flagship for the Commander of the Eighth Amphibious Force during the invasion of southern France. On 17 April 1943 the USCGC *Duane* and the USCGC *Spencer* sank *U-175* and rescued 22 of the German survivors.[13]

The 269-foot CGC *Eastwind* (WAG-279) was constructed at Western Pipe and Steel Company in Los Angeles, California and launched in February 1943. The *Eastwind* patrolled the waters off Greenland throughout the war. In October 1944 the *Eastwind* crew captured 12 German prisoners at a Nazi weather station in eastern Greenland,[14] and subsequently captured the German trawler *Externsteine* and 17 prisoners.[15]

Coast Guard cutter gunboats (designated WPG) varied in size and suitability for their assigned missions. Two WPGs, the 327-foot *Hamilton* (WPG-34) and the 165-foot Great Lakes icebreaker *Escanaba* (WPG-77), were

The 327-foot USCGC *Duane* (WPG-33) on convoy escort patrol in heavy North Atlantic seas. The combat cutter carried out weather patrol, SAR, and convoy escort duties in the Atlantic, Caribbean and Mediterranean. The *Duane* served as the flagship for the U.S. Navy commander of the Eighth Amphibious Force in the August 1944 invasion of southern France.

torpedoed in the North Atlantic with heavy loss of life after performing heroic rescues of the survivors of torpedoed ships.[16] The CGC *Hamilton* was sunk 17 miles off the coast of Iceland on 29 January 1942 with the loss of 1 officer and 19 enlisted personnel. Six Coast Guard crewmembers later died of burn injuries.[17] The CGC *Escanaba* was torpedoed and sunk on 13 June 1943 in frigid waters at 60 degrees North Latitude, 52 degrees West Longitude with the loss of 101 Coastguardsmen. Only two crewmembers survived, and they were rescued by nearby ships.[18]

The 165-foot submarine chaser *Icarus* (WPC-110) was constructed at the Bath, Maine Iron Works, Inc., in 1931.[19] In its Atlantic operations between May 1942 and September 1943 the crew of the CGC *Icarus* sank *U-352* and took 32 prisoners, sank *U-626*, participated in other U-boats attacks, and rescued surviving crew members from several torpedoed and damaged merchant vessels.[20]

U.S. Coast Guard cutters in World War II, and since, are identified as USCGC or CGC ships. U.S. Navy vessels manned by Coast Guard crewmembers in World War II are identified as USS vessels. Various Atlantic and Mediterranean Coast Guard patrol and escort operations included weather and ice patrols, rescues of downed air crews and mariners in distress, coastal survey missions, attacks on enemy submarines, extinguishing dangerous shipboard fires, and evading and periodically being struck by enemy air and sea attacks.

The USS *Brisk* attacked an enemy submarine on 27 August 1943. In March 1944 the USS *Calcaterra* (DE-390) attacked U-boat pens on the North African coast of Spanish Morocco. From April through July 1942 the CGC *Comanche* surveyed a section of coastal Greenland and established Ice Cap Station at Comanche Bay.

On 11 May 1945 a German submarine *(U-873)* surrendered to the USS *Durant* (DE-389). The USS *Falgout* (DE-324) rescued four German aviators who had been shot down (July 1944). In May 1945 *U-234* surrendered to the USS *Forsyth* (PF-102). In February 1944 the USS *Harveson* (DE-316) forced to the surface a German submarine that was later sunk by British aircraft. In March and April of 1944 the USS *Joyce* (DE-317) rescued 28 seafarers, participated with two other destroyer escorts in the sinking of *U-550*, and took 12 enemy prisoners. On 9 March 1944 the USS *Leopold* (DE-319) was sunk south of Iceland with the loss of 13 officers and 158 out of an enlisted crew of 186.

In a joint operation with three other destroyer escorts, the USS *Lowe* (DE-325) sank *U-866* on 18 March 1945. On 20 April 1944 the USS *Menges* (DE-320) rescued 113 survivors from the USS *Landsdale* (DD-426) after enemy aircraft sank the USN ship. In May 1944 the *Menges* lost its stern to a U-boat torpedo off the Mediterranean coast of Algeria with the loss of two officers and 29 enlisted personnel. After the ship was repaired the USS *Menges* exacted revenge in a joint destroyer operation that sank *U-866* on 18 March 1945.

In March 1944 the USS *Merrill* (DE-392) attacked enemy submarine sanctuaries off the coast of Morocco. In a joint destroyer attack in May 1945 the USS *Moberly* (PF-63) sank *U-853*. In January 1943 the CGC *Modoc* rescued 128 crewmembers from the merchant vessel SS *Svend Foyne*. From August 1942 through October 1943 the CGC *Mohawk* engaged in three enemy submarine attacks, assisted in the refloating of the U.S. Army transport ship USAT *Fairfax*, and rescued 25 merchant mariners.[21] Between 28 March 1944 and 25 May 1945 the *Modoc* initiated 11 U-boat attacks, went on Ice Patrol and Weather Patrol, and rescued 293 persons from the torpedoed USAT *Chatham* in the Belle Isle Strait between Nova Scotia, Canada and Greenland. The *Chatham* sank in 30 minutes.[22]

The deck guns on destroyer-sized Coast Guard and Navy warships were formidable in the hands of well-trained gun crews. In April 1944 the USS *Mosley* (DE-321) shot down a German combat aircraft off the Algerian coast in the Mediterranean. The *Mosley* joined three other destroyer escorts in March of the following year and sank *U-866*. Between February and August 1942 the appropriately named CGC *Nemesis* (WPC-111) initiated five antisubmarine attacks and saved 28 mariners from a Mexican tanker that had been attacked off the Florida Keys. In May 1942 the CGC *Nike* (WPC-112), a submarine chaser assigned to the Eastern Sea Frontier and the American Atlantic Coast, attacked a U-boat on the ocean surface, and rescued nine mariners from a torpedoed tanker.[23]

The 225-foot gunboat *North Star* (WPG) had a complement of 17 officers and 116 men. The CGC *North Star* armament included two 3"750 and six 20mm/80 guns. The cutter was launched in 1932 by the Berg Shipbuilding Co. in Seattle, Washington. The *North Star* had been designated for icebreaking and patrol duties in Alaskan waters, its unique wooden hull designed for flexibility in ice. One 1500 horsepower diesel engine and a single propeller powered the cutter. In 1941 the U.S. Navy assigned the radar-equipped *North Star* to the Northeast Greenland Patrol. On 12 September 1941, before the attack on Pearl Harbor and U.S. entry into World War II, the CGC *North Star* and the 216-foot CGC *Northland* (WPG-49) took the Norwegian trawler *Boskoe* into custody.

The capture of the *Boskoe* constituted the first wartime U.S. Navy capture of a potential enemy ship, because Norway was then under German conquest.[24] After the *North Star* and the *Northland* took the *Boskoe* into "protective custody," *Northland* crewmembers went ashore and captured three German radiomen.[25]

On 23 July 1943 the *North Star* was attacked by a German warplane off Norway's Jan Mayen Island[26] in the Arctic Ocean 300 miles east of Greenland and 360 miles northeast of Iceland.[27] On 31 August 1943 the crew of the CGC *North Star* investigated an abandoned a German camp in East Greenland.[28]

The USS *Pride* (DE-323), with the support of several other naval vessels, sank *U-371* off the coast of Algeria on 4 May 1944 and *U-866* on 18 March 1945. On 1 April 1944 the USS *Ramsden* (DE-382) downed a German bomber in the Mediterranean Sea. The USS *Rhodes* (DE-384) shot down a German plane the same day.[29] The CGC *Southwind* (WAG-280) assisted in the capture of a German trawler off eastern Greenland on 15 October 1944. Between 7 March 1942 and 21 March 1944 the 327-foot CGC *Spencer* (WPG-36/WAGC-36) attacked 12 different U-boats and sank two others: *U-225* and *U-175*.[30] In 1944 the CGC *Spencer* patrolled from the Atlantic to the Mediterranean. In 1945 the *Spencer* served as a U.S. Navy flagship in the Philippine campaign.[31]

On 13 June 1942 the CGC *Thetis* (WPC-115), patrolling the Eastern Sea Frontier out of Key West, Florida, sank *U-157*.[32] On 11 May 1945 *U-873* surrendered to the USS *Vance* (DE-387).[33] The USS *Richey* (DE-385/WDE-485) rescued 32 survivors from two torpedoed tankers on 9 April 1945.[34] As the aforementioned hull designations and numbers indicate, the *Richey* sailed for both the U.S. Navy and the U.S. Coast Guard and hosted Navy and Coast Guard crews. Built by Brown Shipbuilding Corporation in Houston, Texas, in

1943, the *Richey* patrolled the seas in World War II, and was one of the 12 Coast Guard destroyer escorts on Pacific Ocean station duty assigned to protect troops, aviators, and supplies during the Korean War (1950–1953).[35]

Martin L. Jeter enlisted in the Coast Guard in early 1945 at the age of 17 and was sworn in at St. Louis, Missouri. After 12 weeks of Basic Training at Manhattan Beach in Brooklyn, New York, Jeter was sent to engineering schools in New York City and Newport, Rhode Island. Jeter said he was "assigned duty on the Coast Guard cutter *Richey* (DE-385) at Okinawa, Japan as an oil king." Fireman First Class (FN1) Jeter described his sea voyages from Japan "to China and back through the Panama Canal to Green Cove Springs, Florida."

FN1 Jeter recalled sailing the Asian Pacific Rim in typhoons and hurricanes while monitoring the engine room of the USS *Richey*. Jeter owns a collection of photographs and illustrations of Coast Guard cutters and craft and aids to navigation. Engraved in a paving stone at Soldiers Field Veterans Memorial in Rochester, Minnesota, is an inspirational reference to "Martin L. Jeter, Coast Guard, World War II."[36]

Another World War II warship that served both the Navy and Coast Guard was the USS *Biscayne* (APV-11/WAVP-385). The *Biscayne* was constructed at Puget Sound Naval Shipyard in Washington in 1939 and launched in 1941. The USS *Biscayne* served in combat zones in the Atlantic, Mediterranean, and Pacific. After the war, it was transferred by the Navy to the Coast Guard and named the USCGC *Dexter* (WAVP-385/WHEC-385). The CGC *Dexter* was stationed at Alameda, California, on Government Island from 1958 to 1968 to serve as a training ship for members of the U.S. Coast Guard Reserve (USCGR).[37]

The German naval historians Jurgen Rohwer and Gerhard Hummelchen wrote a detailed chronology of Allied and German naval war action in the Gulf of Mexico, Caribbean, Atlantic, Mediterranean, and Pacific theaters. The magnificent two-volume history *Chronik des Seekrieges* (*Chronology of the War at Sea, 1939–1945*) was translated from the German language by Derek Masters and published between 1972 and 1974. Rohwer and Hummelchen utilized extensive German and Allied historical sources, including civilian, government, and military historical accounts and documents.[38] Interesting and exciting scenarios are described throughout the two-volume chronology of *The War at Sea*. Direct quotes from several entries are noted below:

1 June 1941, North Atlantic: The U.S. Coast Guard organizes the South Greenland Patrol.[39] 29 January 1942, North Atlantic: U-132 (Lt. Cmdr. Vogelsang) in an attack on a convoy sinks the U.S. Coast Guard cutter *Alexander Hamilton* off Reykjavik, Iceland.[40] 26 April–23 May 1942, Western Atlantic: Thirteen U-boats arrive on the American East Coast and in Canadian coastal waters ... against the still largely unorganized coastal traffic.... U352 (Lt. Cmdr. Rathke) is lost on 9 May after an unsuccessful attack on the U.S. Coastguard cutter *Icarus* which then counterattacks.[41]

1 June–24 July 1942, Western Atlantic: U-157 is sunk off Cuba on 13 June by the U.S. Coastguard cutter *Thetis*.[42] 11 June–19 July 1942, Western Atlantic: U-584 (Lt.

Cmdr. Deecke) and U-202 (Lt. Cmdr. Linder) disembark agents on the American East Coast and U-202 sinks two ships in a torpedo operation....[43] 11 July–21 September, Western Atlantic: U-166 lays a mine barrage on 25 July off the estuary of the Mississippi River ... in the Gulf of Mexico. U-166 (Lt. Kuhlman) sinks 4 ships.... U-166 is sunk by a U.S. Coast Guard aircraft off the Mississippi estuary on 1 August.[44]

18–21 August 1942, Western Atlantic: off Trinidad (in the Caribbean Sea) U-565 (Lt. Cmdr. Suhren) found Convoy TAW (S) with 15 ships escorted by HMS *Clarkia*, USS *Courage*, submarine chasers (USS) PC-482, PC-492, SC-504, SC-514, and US coastguard cutters *Antietam* and *Marion*. U-564 sinks 2 ships. U-162 (Cmdr. Wattenberg) on 19 August sank 1 ship in the area of Grenada.[45]

6–25 Sept. 1942, North Atlantic: [7 U-boats] having refueled from U-462 (Lt. Vowe) form a new patrol line on 6 Sept. on the western side of the North Atlantic. On 9 Sept. U-755 [Lt. Cmdr. Going] sinks the US weather observation ship *Muskeget*.[46]

The *Muskeget* (WAG-48) was a U.S. Coast Guard weather ship stationed at Boston, Massachusetts. The 250-foot cutter disappeared from its position at Weather Station #2 (at 52 degrees North Latitude and 42 degrees West Longitude) without a trace on 9 September 1942 with the loss of all 121 crewmen. The cause of the disappearance of the CGC *Muskeget* was unknown until after World War II when the log of *U-755* was revealed.[47]

16–29 Oct. 1942, North Atlantic: On 26 Oct. the convoy HX.212 (45 ships) ... US coastguard cutter *Campbell* runs into the patrol line and is reported by U-436 (Lt. Cmdr. Seibicke) which keeps contact until the next day, while several other boats of the group are driven off. In the night 26–27 Oct. U-436 attacks and with five hits sinks one ship and damages two others....[48]

15–21 Dec. 1942, North Atlantic: On 15 Dec. U-626 happens to be overtaken by the escort group of the Iceland section ... and is sunk by the US coastguard cutter *Ingham*.[49]

In their *Chronology of the War at Sea*, J. Rohwer and G. Hummelchen did not neglect the Allied war against Japanese military forces or Coast Guard operations. The Coast Guard manned its own vessels, including patrol boats, cutters, and landing craft, Army transport vessels, and Navy ships. On the U.S. Navy (USS) vessels, Coast Guard crewmembers operated both independently and as part of U.S. Navy crew complements. Selected Coast Guard missions chronicled in *Chronology* are cited and directly quoted in the following incidents:

24–27 Dec. 1943, South West Pacific: The US VII Amphibious Force (TF 76, Rear Adm. Barbey USN) which sets out on 25 Dec. lands on the following day some 13000 troops of the US 1st Marine Div. (Maj. Gen. Rupertus, USMC) at Cape Gloucester. TG 74.2 comprised US ... and Australian ... transports ... cruisers ... and destroyers ... [which were attacked by] ... 60 Japanese aircraft. (USCG craft) LST-66 and LST-202 [were] lightly damaged.

28 Feb. 1945, South West Pacific: US Coastguard cutter *Spencer* lands 8000 men of the reinforced 186th RCT (41st Inf. Div., Brig. Gen. Haney, USA) on Palawan, Philippines.[50] 18–29 Mar. 1945, South West Pacific: US Coastguard cutter *Ingham* lands 14000 men of the 40th Inf. Div. (Maj. Gen. Brush, USA) by 22 Mar. on the south coast of Panay.[51]

26 Mar.–26 Apr. 1945, South West Pacific: ... headquarters ship US Coastguard cutter *Spencer* lands 14000 men of the Americal Div. (Maj. Gen. Arnold, USA) near Cubu, Philippines.[52] 7–20 June 1945, South West Pacific: On 10 June ... US Coastguard cutter *Spencer* lands 29361 men of the Australian 9th Inf. Div. in Brunei Bay, Borneo.[53]

Rohwer and Hummelchen chronicled the sinking of "US weather observation ship *Meskegat*" on 9 September 1942 in the North Atlantic.[54] U.S. Coast Guard crews manned the weather observation cutters in fair and foul weather hundreds of miles out to sea and forwarded important weather information to shore stations and other vessels by radio communications. The duty was significant and often dangerous. USCGC *Meskegat* (WAG-48) disappeared without a trace with the loss of all hands, including Public Health Service physician Dr. Haskell D. Rosenblum.[55] Weather ships were vulnerable to enemy warships, U-boats, and other vessels in collisions on the high seas, especially at night and in inclement weather. The Weather Patrol cutters were "sitting ducks" in patrol missions of one-month duration. The *Muskeget* was lost 450 miles south of Greenland. Rescue vessels and aircraft searched in an area estimated to contain 20-35 enemy submarines to no avail. No survivors were found from the complement of nine officers, 107 enlisted personnel, four civilians, and one U.S. Public Health Service physician.[56]

9

The Greenland Patrol

The U.S. Coast Guard was ordered by the Roosevelt administration to organize and conduct patrol operations in the Greenland area of the North Atlantic Ocean even before the United States entered World War II. President Franklin Roosevelt concluded that the Danish-owned island was of strategic significance because of its geographic location, a strategic mineral (cryolite) contained on the island, and the necessity of preventing the occupation and control of the island by the German military after the Nazi conquest of Denmark.

Aspects and incidents of the U.S. Coast Guard's Greenland Patrol that applied to pertinent topics are described in other chapters of this book. One of the best and most extensive accounts of the challenges, hardships, and successes of the USCG Greenland Patrol was written in a secret diary kept by Seaman First Class Thaddeus D. Novak on the CGC/USS *Nanok* (WYP-169), a 120-foot wooden ex-fishing trawler out of Boston, Massachusetts. The diary that chronicled Novak's military autobiography was published more than 60 years after the war in *Life and Death on the Greenland Patrol, 1942.* The book contains maps, photographs, professional and personal descriptions and observations of cutter activities and personnel, and information from the files of the U.S. Coast Guard Historian's Office. *Life and Death on the Greenland Patrol* is edited and supplemented with commentary and background information by author and college lecturer P.J. Capelotti, a former USCGR petty officer.[1]

Greenland, the largest island in the world, has a north-south length of 1650 miles and an east-west width of 800 miles and lies mostly within the Arctic Circle. Its Ice Cap interior has a thickness of 11,000 feet. Numerous islands dot a coastline indented with inland sea fjords. Rugged mountainous and glacial topography makes transportation difficult. The highest mountain peak is 12,139 feet. Danish and Inuit population cohorts live in small villages. Human activities and economic resources include fishing, hunting, cryolite, coal, lead, and zinc.[2]

Greenland is located between Canada and Iceland in the North Atlantic Ocean. The geographic sites and ports and U.S. Army, Navy, and Coast Guard bases emphasized in Coastguardsman Novak's 1942 diary and featured on the Greenland maps include Julianahab/Bluie West One (W-1), Godthob, Ivigtuf, Cape Farewell, Comanche Bay, and Angmagssalik.

GREENLAND, WORLD WAR II
(1941 - 1944)

ARCTIC OCEAN

SVALBARD
(NORWAY)

80N

GREENLAND

BAFFIN
BAY

GREENLAND
SEA

BAFFIN
ISLAND
(CANADA)

70N

DAVIS STRAIT

DENMARK STRAIT

ICELAND

Arctic Circle

ANGMAGSSALIK

GODTHAB

COMANCHE BAY

IVIGTUT

ATLANTIC

60N

OCEAN

JULIANEHAB
BLUIE WEST ONE

CAPE FAREWELL

800   Miles

N

Novak wrote vivid descriptions of the Polar and Arctic threats to U.S. Army aircraft, vehicles, and personnel, and U.S. Navy and Coast Guard ships, cutters, officers and enlisted personnel. The challenges included the threat of German U-boats, gale force winds up to 100 miles per hour, mountainous seas of 20 feet or more, fog, drizzle, shifting icebergs, pitch black nights, flying ice blocks that knocked depth charges off the deck, thickening ice which had to be chipped and hammered away from vessel superstructures to prevent capsizing, seasickness, injuries, and the risks to deck crews loading and offloading equipment and supplies at sea and along icy shorelines.

The Coast Guard cutters *Nanok* and the 216-foot CGC/USS *Northland* (WPG-49) assisted in the rescues of downed U.S. and Canadian aircrews. Coast Guard aviator Lt. John H. Pritchard, Jr. (USCG) and Radioman Benjamin A. Bottoms (USCG) landed a floatplane on the ice cap in a successful rescue, but on a return flight crashed and died in fog and a blinding snow squall.[3]

Lt. Magnus G. Magnusson, the *Nanok* commanding officer, joined the Coast Guard while serving as the Danish counsel in Boston. Lt. Magnusson, with thirty years of seafaring experience, joined the USCG in 1940 when Nazi Germany invaded Denmark.[4] Allegedly lax about Coast Guard regulations, ranks, and rates, the maritime experience and skills of Lt. Magnusson in Arctic and North Atlantic waters allowed the *Nanok* and its crew, after several close calls, to successfully complete its mission and return safely to the United States.

The chief of Coast Guard operations in the Greenland Patrol in World War II was Commander Edward H. "Iceberg" Smith. Ensign Smith graduated from the U.S. Revenue Cutter Service School of Instruction in 1913 and continued his career when the USRCS evolved into the Coast Guard in 1915. Smith's assignments on cutters on the International Ice Patrol increased his knowledge of North Atlantic waters and icebergs and navigation. Cmdr. Smith went on to earn a Ph.D. in geology and oceanography at Harvard University. His successful command of the Greenland Ice Patrol during World War II earned Cmdr. Smith the Distinguished Service Medal and advancement in rank. U.S. Navy Secretary James Forrestal commended Adm. Edward Smith, who "under extremely difficult conditions ... successfully operated patrols and escorts, maintained a system of weather stations, and provided full logistic and tactical support" for the U.S. Armed Forces. In 1950, Adm. Smith retired from the USCG to direct the 20-year old Woods Hole Oceanographic Institution on Cape Cod in Massachusetts.[5]

The CGC *Nanok* returned to the United States in time for Christmas 1942. The crew of the 116-foot CGC/USS *Natsek* (WYP-170), a converted wooden fishing trawler, was not so fortunate. In heavy seas and a blinding snowstorm on December 17, 1942, the *Natsek* sank with all hands in the Belle Isle Strait off Newfoundland, Canada, allegedly because of heavy icing on the superstructure.[6] The commander of the *Natsek* was Lt. (jg) Thomas S. LaFarge, Jr. (USCGR), the grandson of the distinguished painter John Lafarge. Lt. LaFarge was also a skilled painter and had submitted several of his works to Coast Guard exhibits. Lt. LaFarge was an experienced yachtsman before he enlisted in the Coast Guard.[7]

Because the U.S. Coast Guard was merged with the U.S. Navy in World

War II, ship and cutter designations overlap. Sometimes Coast Guard cutters are identified as, for example, the USCGC *Modoc* (WPG-46), and are also referred to using the U.S. Navy designation, USS *Modoc*. Because this is a book about the USCG in World War II, the Coast Guard designation is usually given.

The 240-foot CGC *Modoc* performed distinguished duty on the perilous Greenland Patrol. The *Modoc* was built at Union Construction Company in Oakland, California in April 1921, launched in October, and commissioned in January 1922. The *Modoc* served on International Ice Patrols in the North Atlantic before and after World War II. On 24 May 1941, while on North Atlantic patrol, the *Modoc* observed, and nearly became a casualty in, the battle between British naval vessels and aircraft and the gigantic German battleship *Bismarck*. In June 1941 the *Modoc* was assigned to the U.S. Navy and sailed convoy escort, transport, antisubmarine, and search and rescue duty on the Greenland Patrol from 1941 to 1945. The *Modoc* wartime crew complement generally included 10 officers, 2 warrant officers, and 110 enlisted men. Armament and equipment included radio communications, radar, sonar, 5" and 23" guns, 50 caliber machine guns, K and Y guns, and related depth charges.[8]

Maurice Steinberg was a Radio Man Third Class (RM3) petty officer on the CGC *Modoc*. Steinberg's compelling autobiography[9] described the hardships and dangers involved in stormy Arctic seas escorting convoys of merchant vessels, U.S. Army troop ships, and commercial and U.S. Navy fuel tankers between Boston Harbor, Newfoundland, and Greenland in the winter of 1944–1945. RM3 Steinberg, the son of Jewish immigrants, proudly served in the Coast Guard. After the war, "Moe" Steinberg returned to civilian life, got married, and used the GI Bill to complete his education and secure a teaching position in the New York City public school system.

RM3 Steinberg enlisted in the Coast Guard in 1943, went through boot camp and attended the rigorous radio operator school in Atlantic City, New Jersey. Steinberg learned typing, Morse Code, German U-boat radio transmission techniques, and the operation of complex antisubmarine direction finding equipment. Petty Officer Steinberg was assigned to the CGC *Modoc*. In sailing the stormy, ice-clogged seas of the Greenland Patrol, Steinberg recalled "the on-going routines of standing watch during the frigid winter months and the turbulent North Atlantic seas with the ever present fear of capsizing." Steinberg described how in one "severe storm we took a fifty-seven degree roll sending the ship virtually on its side." A "rogue wave righted the ship again, but not without serious damage on the deck."[10]

Steinberg intended his book "to be a tribute to the many brave seamen of the U.S. Coast Guard and Merchant Marine who went down with their ships in the icy waters during the time we plodded along the North Atlantic convoy routes escorting troop ships, merchant vessels and gasoline tankers."[11] He himself performed a variety of duties on and off the *Modoc*, including serving as the radio talker transmitting orders to crew members from the cutter commander and executive officer, acting as the movie projectionist, and performing Shore Patrol (military police) duties when ashore in Boston and Newfoundland, Canada.[12] Steinberg concluded that the *Modoc* skipper, Lt. Commander Mark A. Whalen (USCG), "is quite competent as are most of the officers" and "the gunnery crews were very proficient."[13] Most of the enlisted deck, engine room, commissary, and medical staff (a ship's physician and a Chief Pharmacist Mate) crews were competent and conscientious; but a few of Steinberg's shipmates received punishment (extra watch duties), court martial, and even discharge from the Service for a variety of infractions and failures to adhere to military regulations. Several crewmembers were tough, seasoned sailors who had been New England commercial fishermen before they enlisted in the Coast Guard.[14]

Responding to sonar contacts, general quarters and battle station drills, and around the clock duty in often-inclement weather took a toll on the Coast Guard mariners. Delicious hot meals when weather conditions permitted were an important morale booster, as was mail call when ships and shore stations could acquire and distribute it. Duty in the Combat Information Center (CIC) for radar, sonar, and radio operators required levels of acuity and accuracy that were as essential as they were tedious and exacting.[15]

In the foreword to *Life and Death on the Greenland Patrol*, Vice Admiral Thomas R. Sargent III (USCG, Ret.) described the CGC *Modoc* and RM3 Steinberg: "The living conditions on the *Modoc* were deplorable. The excessive motions of the ship made life on board uncomfortable and extremely dangerous. Maurice Steinberg withstood it all. Although he never fired a gun at anyone, never killed an enemy, he is a hero; a man of honor and integrity." In that statement, Adm. Sargent paid tribute to Petty Officer Steinberg, the CGC *Modoc*, and the other cutters and U.S. Navy vessels that served on the Greenland Patrol. Admiral Thomas Sargent knew what World War II mariners endured. Early in his Coast Guard career, then Ensign Sargent was serving on the *Modoc* "during the nearly fatal encounter with the German Battleship *Bismarck* and the British Fleet off the coast of Greenland on May 24, 1941."[16]

Captain Charles W. Thomas (USCG) chronicled his icebreaking knowledge and experience on the Greenland Patrol in his book, *Ice Is Where You Find It* (1951). Capt. Thomas dedicated this book to "three outstanding Ice Admirals: Rear Adm. Richard E. Byrd (USN), Adm. Edward H. Smith (USCG), and Rear Adm. Richard Cruzen (USN). In his foreword to *Ice* famed Polar explorer Adm. Richard Byrd wrote, "Captain Thomas had a notable career in the Service of the Coast Guard and the Navy.... Experienced ice navigators are rare.... It takes considerable experience ... to achieve the fullest capabilities of modern icebreakers. Captain Thomas had that experience." Adm. Byrd credited Capt. Thomas with successfully completing the mission "to convoy three naval supply and command ships with thin unprotected hulls through 500 miles of ice ... backed by the courage of Rear Admiral Richard Cruzen (USN)."[17]

In his discussion of the origins of the Greenland Patrol, Capt. Thomas credited President Franklin Roosevelt with recognizing the strategic significance of Greenland following the Nazi invasion of Denmark. The Coast Guard was directed to assume the mission of patrolling the region and assisting in the establishment of military stations on the ice-capped island. On 1 May 1940 the American press informed the public that a provisional U.S. consulate was being established at Godthaab, Greenland. The following week the Coast Guard ice-breaker *Comanche* (WPG-76) left New York headed for Greenland loaded with Red Cross supplies and carrying federal officials to the new consulate.

Within three months, the Coast Guard cutters *Campbell* (WPG-32/WAGC-32) *Cayuga* (WPG-CG-54), *Northland* (WPG-49), and *Duane* (WPG-33/WAGC-6) were patrolling Greenland area waters providing supplies, medical aid, technical, construction, and infrastructural support, and carrying mail. The experienced Coast Guard Bering Sea Patrol had transferred to Greenland.[18]

The sparse and extreme climatic and topographic conditions on Greenland necessitated the close cooperation of Coast Guard, Navy, and Army officials in security and defense matters, communications, surveying, building, and transportation activities. Resident Danish and Inuit citizens, independent of German-occupied Denmark, established the Greenland Provisional Government. The Greenland administration signed a defense pact with the United States on 9 April 1941. Cmdr. Edward H. "Iceberg" Smith (USCG), the skipper of the CGC *Northland*, and Cmdr. C.C. Von Paulsen (USCG), the commander of the CGC *Cayuga,* were charged with seeking military base sites and conducting hydrographic surveys of Greenland's coastal waters and major fjords. At the direction of President Roosevelt, Adm. Harold R. Stark, Chief of Naval Operations, established the Greenland Patrol as a subdivision of the Atlantic Fleet. Initially the CGC *Northland,* CGC *North Star* (WPG-59), and the USS *Bear* were placed under the command of Cmdr. Smith (USCG).

On 11 September 1941, three months prior to the Pearl Harbor attack, President Roosevelt issued his "shoot-on-sight" orders against enemy aircraft and naval vessels, putting American military forces into the war against Germany. The day after Roosevelt's order, the CGC *Northland*, then commanded by Cmdr. Von Paulsen, captured the Danish ship *Buskoe*, with German operatives on board. Lt. Leroy McCluskey (USCG) then led an on-land reconnaissance, spotted a concealed building, and, supported by his Coast Guard commando team, captured three German radiomen who were assigned the task of relaying messages from the German Naval Command to the U-boats that were patrolling North Atlantic waters. Less than 12 weeks later, the United States would be at war with Germany.

In response to Cmdr. Smith's request for aid, Vice Adm. R.R. Waesche, the U.S. Coast Guard commandant, secured 10 wooden trawlers that had served as fishing vessels and sent those cutters with specially trained crews to Greenland. The wooden ships and courageous crews served their missions well. Within a year, updated, steel-hulled Coast Guard gunboats and larger cutters replaced the wooden cutters.[19]

The summer 1943 expedition to Sabine Island off northeast Greenland found Capt. Charles Thomas in command of the CGC *Northland* in a task force consisting of the CGC *North Star* and a U.S. Army chartered sealer called the *Polar Bjorn*. The task force sailed out of Reykjavik, Iceland, toward northeast Greenland. Task force commander Captain C.C. Von Paulsen (USCG) was onboard the *Northland*. A veteran ice mariner, Capt. Von Paulsen provided valuable advice in hazardous situations to the younger and less experienced Captain Thomas,

Compact fields of ice alternated with fragments of ice called *brash*. Openings between ice fields are called *leads* and *channels*. Huge compact areas of polar ice (*storis*) break up into *floebergs* and *icebergs*. *Close pack* refers to ice that covers 70 percent or more of the surface water area. A *compact field* means more than one square mile of unbroken ice. A *growler* is a small iceberg. The ice fields change constantly, and ships can become trapped in them.

In one instance, Capt. Thomas found the *Northland* wedged in the ice and tilted at an angle that almost caused the disastrous loss of the propeller. Upon the advice of Capt. Von Paulsen, dynamite was used to free the *Northland*, and the cutter's floatplane, a single engine Grumman J2F-5 flown by Ensign Paul Hershey (USCG), took off from a sufficiently long lead on a reconnaissance mission to provide information for navigation adjustments enroute to Sabine Island.[20]

Surprises loomed out of the Arctic mist. On one occasion, when pulling up the ice anchors which had been secured to an ice field, the *Northland* crew was surprised by a lumbering polar bear and hurriedly escaped up the ladder to the deck with just yards to spare as the junior officer of the deck (Lt. jg Dorris Bell) leveled a machine gun at the pesky predator.[21]

The CGC *Northland* arrived at Sabine Island with an onboard team of rugged and well-trained officers and enlisted personnel from the Greenland Army. Coast Guard, Navy and Greenland Army personnel and a U.S. Army platoon had been organized to complete the mission. After a boat landing, the team trekked overland until they found a German observation post and a camouflaged tent. The German soldiers had vanished, leaving behind supplies and equipment.[22]

While the military mission was carried out on Sabine Island, the shifting Arctic ice patterns required Lt. Reginald F. Butcher (USCG), the *Northland* executive officer, to steam out to open water to avoid entrapment. Lt. Butcher returned to the icy island shoreline in time to get the troops and sailors aboard in late evening before the commencement of the next phase of the mission site—Walrus Island. An additional passenger was escorted by the returning troops: German Navy physician and Gestapo agent Dr. Rudolph Sensse, who chose capture over starvation. Dr. Sensse was brought aboard the *Northland* and confined to quarters.[23]

Captain Thomas nearly lost his life in early August of 1943 when, rowing alone in a small skiff returning from shore to the CGC *Northland*, a sudden squall enveloped and overturned the small boat. Capt. Thomas was dumped into the frigid sea. Unable to climb onto the capsized skiff because of the bulge on his CO2 inflated life jacket, Thomas concluded the estimated 10 minute survival time in Arctic waters had sealed his doom. Fortunately, alert officers and enlisted personnel on the bridge of the *Northland* had observed and anticipated the situation and launched a surfboat into the storm. A Coast Guard crew rescued their grateful skipper from drowning.[24]

A November 1942 mission illustrated the diversity of Greenland Patrol responsibilities. Captain Charles W. Thomas (USCG) was tasked with the establishment of a high frequency direction finder (HF/DF) radio station on the Norwegian island of Jan Mayen located north of Iceland. The skilled *Northland* commander transported 41 officers and men and 30 tons of equipment and supplies to the geographically isolated site in inclement weather and heavy seas.[25]

A German radio and weather station was discovered on the east coast of Greenland in the spring of 1943. A Danish Army commando was killed in a confrontation with German troops from the station. One of the soldiers captured a German soldier, and, after a dangerous trek over treacherous ice fields, turned the Nazi over to U.S. defense forces. Coast Guard bombers and the crews of the cutters *North Star* and *Northland*, joined by three Danish troops and a 40-dog sledge team, returned to the designated area to search for the missing German military personnel. The Allied team, as previously noted, captured German physician and intelligence agent, Dr. Rudolph Sennse, who was subsequently imprisoned and interrogated on the CGC *Northland*.[26]

U.S. Coast Guard Patrol Bombing Squadron Six was a special aviation unit created to support the maritime Greenland Patrol. On 5 October 1943 Squadron Six was commissioned at Argentia, Newfoundland, Canada, and stationed at Narsarssuak, Greenland under the command of legendary seaplane aviator and tactician Cmdr. D.B. MacDiarmid (USCG).

Squadron Six provided convoy air support, flare and smoke signals to indicate ice pathways to icebreaking cutters, mail delivery, antisubmarine surveillance, search and rescue, and radio communications between naval vessels, ground units, and stranded or adrift troops and sailors. Coast Guard aviators flew Navy and Coast Guard aircraft. Aviators flew out of Argentia, Narsarssuak, Arctic Canada, and Reykjavik. By April 1944 Squadron Six administered 12 operational amphibious *PBY-5A Catalina aircraft*, and more than 180 officers, aviators, and enlisted personnel. The skilled and courageous commissioned and warrant officer and enlisted crews coped with isolated land and sea routes, ice cap conditions, winds up to 185 miles per hour, and challenging landing sites.[27]

In the autumn of 1943 the Greenland Patrol seacraft included the Coast Guard manned U.S. Navy vessels *Bluebird* and *Albatross*, and the submarine-chasing (SC) patrol craft *527, 528, 688, 689, 704,* and *709.*[28] On 21 November 1943 Commodore Earl G. Rose (USCG) assumed command of the Greenland Patrol. The following week a U.S. military aircraft was reported missing. Cmdr. D.B. MacDiarmid (USCG), the leader of Bombing Squadron Six, began a two-day search over a 6,000 square mile area that resulted in the discovery of the wrecked AT-7 aircraft on the edge of the ice cap. Several search aircraft dropped marker flags and provisions to the survivors. On 5 January 1944, a USCG PBY-5A directed a rescue party over the final 10 miles to assist the survivors.

On 15-16 December 1943, after a seven-hour search, CGC *Comanche* (WPG-76) under the command of Lt. Langford Anderson (USCG) rescued 29 men and one dog from the abandoned U.S. Army freighter USAT *Nevada.* The 1685-ton freighter succumbed to 60-mile per hour gale force winds, snow squalls, and high seas 200 miles southwest of Greenland. Searching for and rescuing the survivors in dispersed lifeboats in heavy seas resulted in injuries to several Coast Guard rescuers who entered the water in rubber suits secured to lines extending from the *Comanche.* Upon the recommendations and commendations of Lt. Anderson, three Coastguardsmen (Storekeeper First Class William G. Mitchell; Carpenter's Mate First Class Arthur Nickerson; and Fireman First Class Robert C. Vile) later received the Navy and Marine Corps Medal, and Fireman First Class Philip Feldman earned the Meritorious Conduct award.[29]

The Coast Guard Weather Patrol was a significant element of the Greenland Patrol. Weather patrol vessels sent periodic communications to various agencies and military units night and day. The strategically placed cutters watched for storms, enemy air and seacraft, and ships and aircraft in distress. The weather station cutters kept in constant radio contact with civilian and military aircraft.[30] The Coast Guard cutters on the Greenland Patrol monitored German land and sea activities and tried to prevent the permanent establishment of enemy stations in Greenland.

Between July and October 1944 the 216-foot CGC *Northland* (WPG-49), the 230-foot CGC *Storis* (WAGL-38), and the newly commissioned (1944) 269-foot icebreakers *Eastwind* (WAG-279) and *Southwind* (WAG-280) captured 60 Germans, attacked three enemy trawlers, and put two German weather/radio stations out of commission.[31] On 4 October 1944 the *Eastwind* crew destroyed a German weather station in eastern Greenland and captured 12 prisoners. On 15 October the cutter crew commandeered the German trawler *Externsteine* and took 17 Germans captive. The CGC *Southwind* participated in the trawler and prisoner captures.[32] The captured German trawler *Externsteine* was commandeered by the Coast Guard, renamed the CGC *East Breeze*, and placed under the command of Lt. Curtis Howard (USCG) and a 32-person crew.[33] The USCGC WIX *East Breeze* steamed into Boston Harbor on 14 December 1944. The U.S. Navy then took control of the CGC *East Breeze* and on 24 January 1945 commissioned the vessel the USS *Callao*.[34]

In the autumn of 1944, after the capture of the German trawler *Externsteine,* Greenland Patrol combat gradually came to an end. The attempt to establish German bases in Greenland had been thwarted and the threat of German U-boat attacks in the North Atlantic was greatly diminished.

World War II Coast Guard historian Malcolm F. Willoughby cogently synthesized the significance of the U.S. Coast Guard, Army, Navy and the Danish Army in the Greenland theater of operations: "In short, the men who kept Greenland free not only protected America from invasion, but denied the enemy vital weather and shipping information. The Greenland Patrol was a positive factor in winning the Battle of the Atlantic."[35]

10

The Atlantic War

American military operations in the Atlantic Ocean began before the United States was officially involved in World War II (1939–1945). The Atlantic theater encompassed an enormous area stretching from Arctic Greenland to the Eastern Seaboard of Canada and the United States, and from the Western Hemisphere to the western and northern coasts of Europe and Africa. The transatlantic area of operations posed significant tactical and logistical challenges in an oceanic region that presented the full range of climatic and sea conditions.

Within that vast hydrographic realm, the U.S. Coast Guard and U.S. Navy escorted troop and supply convoys, conducted antisubmarine patrols, and performed search and rescue missions. U.S. Navy gunners served on transport vessels manned by the civilian mariners of the U.S. Merchant Marine (USMM). Merchant ship gunners engaged in combat and USMM sailors suffered injuries and death in stormy seas when intrepid German U-boats torpedoed their ships. The frigid route from the North Atlantic to the Arctic waters of the Soviet Union was especially dangerous.

The Atlantic naval and merchant marine missions were predicated upon similar scenarios during World War I (1914–1918). The United States entered World War I belatedly (in 1917) as it did World War II (1941). Provoked by German belligerence, President Woodrow Wilson departed from his initial noninterventionist policy and ordered non-neutral prewar trade and convoy escorts prior to the U.S. entry into World War I. President Franklin Roosevelt followed a similar path early in World War II.

Wilson and Roosevelt each challenged and provoked Germany: Wilson and Germany and the Central powers in World War I, and Roosevelt and Germany and the Axis powers in World War II. Both presidents perceived their objectives as defensive deterrents. But during each American prewar period, the German leaders (Kaiser Wilhelm in World War I and Chancellor Adolf Hitler in World War II) were provoked into attacking civilian and naval vessels. Those responses were declared by the United States to be provocative acts that required sanctions and military responses.

President Roosevelt used German U-boat tactics as justification for his prewar Newfoundland war planning with Britain, Lend-Lease supply aid to the

United Kingdom, his "shoot on sight" orders, the occupation of Danish Greenland by U.S. military forces, and the initiation of the Greenland Patrol by the U.S. Coast Guard.

The significance and peril of the World War II Atlantic convoy missions were prefaced by similar American naval experiences in World War I. The Coast Guard mission in what was then called the Great War was thoroughly covered in Alex R. Larzelere's book, *The Coast Guard in World War I*. Captain Larzelere (USCG, Ret.), a cutter commander in American waters and in Vietnam, credited Coast Guard Commandant Ellsworth P. Bertholf with successfully transitioning the U.S. Revenue Cutter Service into the Coast Guard and skillfully administering the Service during and immediately after the war.

Captain Larzelere surveyed the temporary transfer of the Coast Guard into the U.S. Navy in April 1917, its return to the Treasury Department in 1919, the wartime missions of domestic port security and coastal patrols, search and rescue, convoy escort duty, antisubmarine warfare, aids to navigation; and the courageous contributions of the surfmen of the former U.S. Life-Saving Service.[1]

Larzelere described the sinking of the cutter USS *Tampa* in the English Channel by *U-91* in the evening of 26 September 1918 with the loss of 131 crewmembers. United States Navy and British patrol vessels searched in vain for the vessel and any survivors. The *Tampa* tragedy constituted the highest naval casualty count in a single combat incident in that war. The CGC *Tampa* was sailing from British Gibraltar, Spain, to Wales, Great Britain. In addition to the Coast Guard complement of commissioned and noncommissioned officers and enlisted personnel, the passenger list included 16 British military and civilian personnel, two U.S. Navy watch officers, a USN medical officer, and a USN pharmacist mate.[2]

The knowledge gained from the American naval experiences of World War I contributed to President Roosevelt's war policies and tactics in World War II. As the assistant secretary of the U.S. Navy in the Wilson administration, Franklin D. Roosevelt (FDR) was keenly interested and well versed in naval history and maritime affairs. Historian Doris Kearns Goodwin traced FDR's transition from noninterventionism to interventionism in the World War II era, while the president prepared a neo-isolationist Congress and public for war against the expansionist Axis nations of Germany, Italy, and Japan.

In an 11 September 1941 speech three months before the 7 December Japanese attack on the U.S. military base at Pearl Harbor, FDR used the recent U-boat attack on the Navy destroyer USS *Greer* to persuade Congress to amend the Neutrality Acts of 1935–1939. FDR downplayed the fact that the USS *Greer* had been tracking the U-boat in the Atlantic and reporting its location to the British Navy. The U-boat torpedoes and *Greer* depth charges missed their respective targets, but FDR gained congressional support for his new "shoot on sight" policy toward Axis submarines in the defensive zone of American waters that now extended to Iceland in the North Atlantic.[3]

An American merchant ship was sunk off the Greenland coast on 19 September 1941. The destroyer USS *Kearney* was torpedoed and damaged on 17 October while attacking a German submarine off Iceland, with a loss of 11 lives. Two weeks later, while on convoy escort duty, the Navy destroyer USS *Reuben James* was torpedoed, with a loss of 96 officers and enlisted personnel. With that incident FDR persuaded Congress to amend the Neutrality Acts and allow the arming of U.S. merchant vessels which sailed into combat zones and belligerent ports.[4]

From August 9 to 12 (1941), President Roosevelt met secretly with British prime minister Winston Churchill, whose nation had been at war with Germany since 1939. The war and postwar policy planning sessions took place off the Newfoundland coast of Canada on the USS cruiser *Augustus* and the HMS *Prince of Wales.* The cooperative British and U.S. policy formulations, along with the previous passage by Congress of the Selective Service Act of 1940 that mandated the conscription (draft) of American citizens into the Armed Forces further prepared the nation for entry into World War II.[5]

At Roosevelt's urging, Congress had passed the Lend-Lease Act in March 1941 The act further trimmed the sails of American neutrality by allowing the federal government to sell, transfer, exchange, or lease food, military equipment, vehicles, and ships, including Coast Guard cutters, to Britain in an economic war against the Axis nations. American naval escort vessels began to protect U.S. and British Commonwealth merchant ships from U-boat attacks in the sea-lanes between the Western Hemisphere and Europe, despite the fact that 50 percent of the American people expressed opposition to the policy.[6]

Lend-Lease production lines stimulated the American economy and put civilians to work to protect the United States by building military ships, boats, aircraft, and other supplies, and aiding our Allies.[7] Ironically, Lend-Lease and World War II may have contributed as much, or more, to ending the economic Depression as Roosevelt's New Deal program.

Although the general public may not be aware of the extensive global role the Coast Guard played in World War II, military historians generally give the Service its due. Some naval historians confine their references to the U.S. Navy, either not perceiving the need for differentiating between the combined wartime Sea Services, or, in some cases, not realizing that the Coast Guard was part of the Navy in World War II.

Many past and contemporary World War II historians give the Coast Guard its due. In his splendid *Atlas of American Military History* (2005), Stuart Murray includes a photograph and narrative of Atlantic combat action, as "crewmen of a Coast Guard destroyer look astern to see the effects of their depth charge. Antisubmarine operations (sonar, radar and tactics) improved over the course of the Battle of the Atlantic and hunter-killer convoy escorts led to crippling U-boat losses."[8] Murray later described "Hitting the Beach," and featured a photograph of D-Day (June 6, 1944) showing "American soldiers disembarking from a Coast Guard landing craft to make the long journey under heavy enemy fire onto the Normandy shore" in the Allied invasion of France on the way to Germany.[9]

The Allied invasion of Nazi occupied Europe commenced before the Normandy invasions, however. In Operation Torch (November 1942), British and America forces invaded French, German, and Italian controlled North Africa and the formidable Sahara Desert. Murray's *Atlas* contains an action photograph of U.S. troops embarking from a Coast Guard "Sea Horse" landing craft in the military operation. The North African campaign led to the defeat of German General Erwin Rommel and his mechanized tank and troop divisions and preceded the Allied liberation of Sicily, Italy, and Greece in southern Europe.[10]

The contributions of the Coast Guard in World War II were well summarized by President Roosevelt's secretary of war, Frank Knox: "As part of the Navy ... since November 1941 ... the Coast Guard fought hard and effectively in the Battle of the Atlantic (with heavy losses) of ships and men." The evidence of that fight, Knox contended, "lies at the bottom of the sea in the battered hulls of German U-boats." Secretary Knox credited the contributions of Coast Guard surfmen as coxswains of landing craft in beach landings, the role the Service played in landing U.S. Marines in the Solomon Islands, and supporting "U.S. Navy task forces in North Africa, Europe, and the Pacific islands."[11]

The war secretary did not neglect the contributions of the Coast Guard on the home front, and commended USCG operations in "the security of our all important ports, the protection of our thousands of miles of coastline, the manning of many of our troop transports, the rescue of mariners at sea, the testing and regulation of lifesaving equipment aboard our merchant ships, and the maintenance of aids to navigation.... All of these are functions and responsibilities of the Coast Guard."[12]

World War II *Time* magazine Navy correspondent Reg Ingraham interviewed Coast Guard officers, enlisted personnel, and the commandant, Vice Admiral Russell R. Waesche, at Coast Guard Headquarters in Washington, D.C., before the war ended. Given the global operations of the Service in often extreme geographic and combat conditions, Ingraham quoted the legendary Coastguardsman who said, "I'd like to meet the guy who named the Coast Guard, and find out just what coast he had in mind!"[13]

The U.S. Atlantic coast was almost unguarded early in the war when the U.S. Navy was fighting for survival in the Pacific. The nucleus of the naval coastal defense force consisted of a U.S. Navy destroyer and a few 327-foot Hamilton Class Coast Guard cutters assigned to convoy escort duty to guard vulnerable transatlantic supply lines.[14]

On 22 February 1943 Commander James A. Hirshfield (USCGC *Camp-bell, WPG-32/WAGC-32)* dodged a U-boat torpedo attack in heavy North Atlantic weather after a rescue operation involving the crewmembers of a sunken freighter. Cmdr. Hirshfield rammed and sank the attacking *U-606* and ignored the possible danger of exploding TNT-loaded submarine torpedoes. The *Campbell* suffered hull and engine room damage in the attack. The Polish destroyer *Burza* protected the cutter while damage control crews made the essential repairs to keep the ship afloat. Cmdr. Hirshfield then went below decks where medics tended to the shrapnel wounds the commander had suffered in the deck gun battle between the U-boat and the cutter.[15]

On 9 May 1942, the 165-foot USCGC *Icarus* (WPC-110), skippered by Lt. Cmdr. Maurice D. Jester, sank *U-352* off the North Carolina coast. Lt. Cmdr. Jester and his skilled helmsman, Lt. (jg) Gabriel Pehaim, a former enlisted quartermaster, attacked the U-boat with depth charges, deck machine guns, and "K" guns. The crew of the *Icarus* rescued more than 30 of the survivors, including the U-boat skipper, Kapitan-Leutnant Helmutt Rathke. The prisoners of war were brought to Charleston, South Carolina, Navy Yard and transferred to POW camps in the United States. Lt. Cmdr. Jester earned the Navy Cross for his actions.[16]

On 21 February 1943, the 327-foot USCGC *Spencer* (WPG-36/WAGC-36), under Cmdr. Harold S. Berdine, sank *U-225*. On 17 April 1943, the CGC *Spencer* sank *U-175* with the loss of one Coast Guard enlisted man in the gunfire exchange. Despite the loss of their comrade, the Coast Guard crew rescued the surviving submariners. The German POWs were initially reluctant to eat the food the cutter crew offered them for fear of being poisoned. However, the aroma of corn beef and cabbage gradually weakened enemy discipline, and they dined on cuisine no doubt remembered from their homeland.

The combat action of the CGC *Spencer* was recorded by Chief Boatswain's Mate Jess W. January. CPO January was a former St. Louis, Missouri, newspaper photographer. The *Spencer* story was also ably chronicled by *Time* magazine correspondent William Walton, a civilian passenger on the cutter on his way to England.[17]

Cutter patrol in combat zones was dangerous duty. The convoy escorts that protected other vessels from U-boat attacks sometimes became the targets and victims of U-boats, heavy seas and stormy weather. Ingraham acquired information from Coast Guard Headquarters in Washington about the sinking of cutters, but wartime security needs limited the information that could be published. Reg Ingraham listed the following cutters that fell victim to German U-boats and heavy weather: the *Alexander Hamilton, Escanaba, Muskeget,* and *Natsek* in the Atlantic, and the *Acacia* in the Caribbean.[18]

Postwar information revealed more detail about the tragic cutter losses reported by Reg Ingraham. The 327-foot USCGC *Alexander Hamilton* (WPG-34) was torpedoed 17 miles from Reykjavik on 29 January 1942 by *U-132,* with

The 327-foot USCGC *Spencer* (WPG-36) depth charged and sank *U-175* in the North Atlantic on 17 April 1943.

the immediate loss of 20 crewmembers. Six survivors later died of burns suffered in the attack.[19] The 165-foot CGC *Escanaba* (WPG-77), a Great Lakes icebreaker, was sunk in the North Atlantic on 13 June 1943 with the loss of 101 crewmembers and 2 survivors.[20] The 250-foot *Muskeget* (WAG-48) was sunk at the cutter's assigned North Atlantic weather station (52 degrees North, 42 degrees West) on or about 9 September, with the loss of all 121 crewmembers. It was later ascertained from the log of *U-755* that the *Muskeget* was sunk by that submarine.[21] The 116-foot CGC *Natsek* (WYP-170), stationed at Boston, Massachusetts, was assigned to the Greenland Patrol. On the return voyage to Boston, the *Natsek* was last reported seen in heavy seas and a snowstorm off Belle Island, Newfoundland. It is believed the *Natsek* capsized because of excess icing on the ship's superstructure that made the cutter top-heavy. The vessel foundered on 17 December 1942.[22]

The 172-foot CGC *Acacia* (WAGL-200), built by the Fabricated Shipbuilding Corporation and Coddington Engineering Company in Milwaukee, Wisconsin, was commissioned in 1920. The *Acacia* was stationed at San Juan, Puerto Rico and used in ATN duty.[23] Coast Guard historian Robert Erwin Johnson wrote, "The only Coast Guard submarine victim in southern waters was the 172-foot buoy tender *Acacia*, shelled and sunk in the Caribbean by the *U-161* without loss of life on 15 March 1942."[24] Johnson said the *CGC Acacia* "was one of only two tenders lost during the war; the other, the 42-year old *CGC Magnolia*, sunk in a collision off Mobile Bay [adjacent to the Gulf of

Chief Quarter Master Woodrow Wilson (USCG) taking navigation sightings on the CGC *Escanaba* in the North Atlantic in 1942.

Mexico in southwest Alabama] on 25 August 1945, with the death of one man."[25]

In World War II Coast Guard and Navy, medical officers had MD and DDS degrees as physicians and dentists. Medically trained enlisted personnel were called pharmacist mates. The outstanding service provided by medical and dental officers and pharmacist mates must be acknowledged in any complete account of World War II. The medical officers generally came to the Coast Guard from the U.S. Public Health Service (USPHS) and provided medical aid and comfort to injured military personnel and civilians on shore, at sea, and on merchant vessels. The medical complement went into combat zones. Medics suffered injury and death by accident, drowning, and combat action on the landing beaches, ashore, and at sea.

Some 460 medical officers (physicians and dentists) served with the USCG ashore and afloat in the Pacific from Alaska and the Aleutian Islands to the tropical South Pacific, in the Atlantic as far north as Greenland, and throughout the United States. At the time of the writing of his book before the end of the war, Reg Ingraham reported that two USPHS doctors had perished on cutter duty and one died in an airplane crash.

The medical arm of the Coast Guard provided exemplary support services under extraordinary conditions. A pharmacist mate removed a sailor's appendix on a U.S. submarine in Japanese controlled Pacific waters. Dr. Edward

USCGC *Escanaba* (WPG-77). The 165-foot cutter was built in Bay City, Michigan, launched in 1932, and stationed at Grand Haven, Michigan. Assigned to escort and SAR duty off Greenland, the cutter was sunk by enemy action on 13 June 1944 with the loss of 101 crewmembers and only 2 survivors.

B. Gall performed surgery on an injured sailor in a rolling cutter in heavy seas off the Greenland coast. USPHS physician Dr. Paul W. Lucas performed surgery on Ensign Kenneth B. Nelson. Lt. (jg) Lucas accomplished the medical procedure on a pitching cutter in 100-mile per hour North Atlantic winds. A warrant officer machinist, a first class electrician's mate, and a chief pharmacist's mate assisted Dr. Lucas in surgery while all were lashed to secure structures. In heavy weather conditions, creative Coast Guard personnel rigged up stable platforms and lashed patients and medical personnel to their stations to enhance stability and safety.

U.S. Public Health Service medical officers took direct part in rescue efforts at sea. Assistant Surgeon Dr. Ralph Nix went over the side of the USCGC *Escanaba* with a line tied around his waist into rolling North Atlantic seas to help rescue the surviving crew members of a torpedoed transport ship. Four months later, in June 1943, the CGC *Escanaba* was torpedoed and sunk with the loss of 101 Coastguardsmen and the survival of only 2 men who were fortunately rescued by responding ships in the vicinity.

In combat action against a U-boat, the USCGC *Spencer* suffered 24 crew casualties. The *Spencer* medical officer, Dr. John J. Davies, worked on the wounded for 72 hours doing abdominal surgery beneath the pounding 5-inch deck guns of the cutter.[26]

Coast Guard medical officers and pharmacist mates operated in the dangerous amphibious combat zones of the Pacific and the Mediterranean under challenging conditions. Coast Guard landing craft brought troops to combat shores and transported wounded Armed Forces personnel back to the large U.S. Navy and Coast Guard ships further out to sea. Medical personnel from all of the military services, including physicians, dentists, female nurses, pharmacist mates, and corpsmen, tended to the wounded as the ships transported the sick, injured and deceased back to land facilities.

U.S. Public Health Service medical officers and enlisted medics performed their duties under enemy fire. One physician had his landing craft medical facilities destroyed under enemy fire. The adaptive medical officer then moved the remnants of his sick bay ashore and waited until another medically equipped landing craft came to his location.

Coast Guard medical personnel and the physicians and dentists of the U.S. Public Health Service who served in the World War II USCG certainly lived up to and enhanced the U.S. Coast Guard motto "Semper Paratus."[27]

Two years after Pearl Harbor, the Coast Guard was in the middle of World War II chronologically and geographically. The June 1943 edition of *Coast Guard Magazine* proudly and graphically illustrated the situation with a print titled "Around the Globe with the U.S. Coast Guard." Biplanes, single wing float (sea) planes, and large, amphibious PBY aircraft were featured because Coast Guard aviators flew them. Cutters on convoy duty, landing craft, and other vessels were pictured, as was the Corsair sailboat craft that patrolled silently off America's coasts in search of U-boats. The geographic distribution of Coast Guard activities was illustrated with depictions of the Arctic, Iceland, Atlantic, Pacific (Guadalcanal and Singapore), Mediterranean, North Africa, and Alaska.[28]

11

Guarding the Convoys

With the entry of the United States into World War II, German submarine torpedoes and mines targeted domestic and foreign civilian commercial and military shipping along the U.S. coastline while the U.S. Navy was fully occupied in combat in the Pacific against the Japanese Imperial Navy and Army.

It fell to the U.S. Coast Guard to organize antisubmarine warfare and convoy escort patrols required to secure the essential ship convoy routes to Europe and the Mediterranean. Oceangoing Coast Guard cutters were assisted by the few Navy destroyer escorts that could be spared, and Royal Canadian Navy and Royal British Navy warships. Smaller Coast Guard patrol boats were on the alert close to American shores and in the largest and busiest U.S. harbors under the authority of Coast Guard Captains of the Port.

Protective antisubmarine nets were placed outside strategic U.S. harbors, and mines were planted to deter enemy submarines (U-boats). Coast Guard personnel were trained to carry out port security, convoy escort, air and sea patrols, antisubmarine warfare, and defensive and offensive mine operations. Antisubmarine warfare operations were facilitated by the use of sonar, radar, and depth charge technology gradually installed on Coast Guard cutters at American civilian, Navy, and Coast Guard shipyards. Radio and LORAN technology were essential elements of naval operations and communication between Coast Guard and Navy air and seacraft and shore and air stations.

To train naval personnel for their missions, Rear Admiral Odale Dabney Waters, Jr. (USN) established and directed the first U.S. Navy Mine Disposal School at the Washington Navy Yard from 1941 to 1943.[1] Mine disposal students were trained to recover and deactivate enemy mines. Rear Adm. Waters expressed respect for his Navy and Coast Guard students and said, "We had a small core of Coast Guard men that were to be trained and work with the Navy. The first groups were awfully good men, especially the enlisted men [who] were old time petty officers: first class and chiefs, who were in the mine warfare business [and] knew a great deal about it to begin with."[2] Anxious for a sea assignment, Adm. Waters trained his "own relief" to take charge of the Mine Disposal School and said his replacement was "an excellent Coast Guard officer who had been a graduate of our first class in the training school."[3]

Convoy protection and naval support operations extended from the

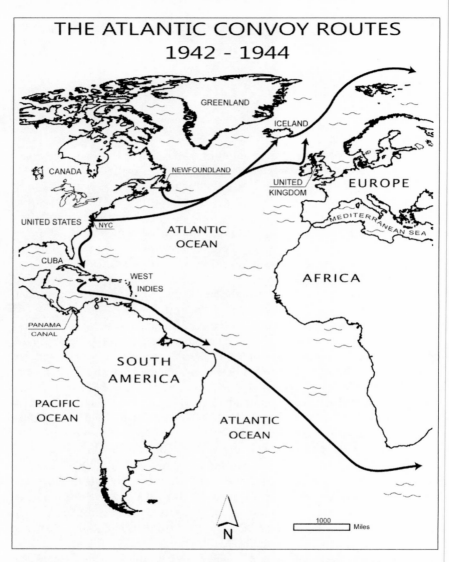

THE ATLANTIC CONVOY ROUTES
1942 - 1944

GREENLAND

ICELAND

CANADA

NEWFOUNDLAND

UNITED KINGDOM

EUROPE

UNITED STATES

NYC

ATLANTIC OCEAN

MEDITERRANEAN SEA

CUBA

WEST INDIES

AFRICA

PANAMA CANAL

SOUTH AMERICA

PACIFIC OCEAN

ATLANTIC OCEAN

1000 Miles

N

Atlantic Ocean to the Mediterranean Sea and the Pacific Ocean. Naval convoy and amphibious operations in the Mediterranean extended from North Africa to southern Europe. Extensive training programs were established to prepare military personnel to operate in a vast and challenging maritime environment on complex missions that posed unique and enormous tactical and logistical challenges.

In 1942, Admiral Ken H. Hewitt (USN) was placed in command of the Amphibious Force of the Atlantic Fleet. Adm. Hewitt directed the training of

U.S. Army, Navy, and Coast Guard personnel in preparation for the amphibious missions to come. The military personnel were trained to operate the amphibious landing craft and ships (LSTs, LCTs, and LCILs) then under construction. Adm. Hewitt stated his high regard for the Coast Guard instructors who trained the troops to operate the landing craft and carry out the transportation, loading and unloading of personnel, supplies, and heavy equipment, and take command of shore parties as beach masters. He described his frustration over the U.S. Army taking "some of our best Coast Guard officers who had been instructing our crews and over the protests of Amphibious Force commanders."

Captain Phil H. Bucklew (USN) joined the Navy after Pearl Harbor. To get in physical shape Bucklew joined a physical training program organized by famed heavyweight boxer Gene Tunney.[4] Ironically, Tunney's nemesis in the ring had been heavyweight boxing champion Jack Dempsey. While Tunney was getting Navy sailors in shape for service, Lt. Jack Dempsey (USCGR) was the director of physical education at the Coast Guard Training Station in Brooklyn, New York. After promotion in rank, Lt. Cmdr. Dempsey requested active duty. Advanced in rank again, Cmdr. Dempsey was assigned to the Coast Guard–manned USS *Wakefield* (AP-21) in 1944. In 1945, he was on the attack transport USS *Arthur Middleton* (APA-25) in the Okinawa invasion.[5]

After getting into physical shape under Tunney's tutelage, Bucklew volunteered for amphibious commando training and was commissioned as an officer in 1943. Ensign Phil H. Bucklew was then assigned to the Mediterranean theater where he trained in landing craft and assault operations in preparation for the invasion of Sicily (1943) and then the Normandy invasion (June 1944) in Europe.[6] Captain Bucklew recalled his initial amphibious boat training, as naval historian John T. Mason described it, "under the direction of four Coast Guard chiefs who were tough, knowledgeable and good." Bucklew said, "It was the best training I ever had in the navy. If you smashed up a boat or an engine quit, all the chief said was: 'Fix it!'"

The U.S. Navy was slow to participate in the American coastal patrol and Atlantic convoy escort duty against German U-boats in 1942 because, officials asserted, the Navy preferred doing antisubmarine warfare patrols with its destroyers, battle ships and carriers further out in the Atlantic, and the USN was busy in the Pacific theater after Pearl Harbor. The Navy lacked the smaller coastal escort vessels of the Coast Guard, and therefore convoy escort patrol responsibilities in the Eastern (Atlantic) Sea Frontier (ESF) went to the USCG. In the heavily traveled sea-lanes between North Carolina and Canada in the first quarter of 1943, the approximately 12 U-boats in the ESF sank 514 thousand tons and 87 ships against an American force of about 100 cutters and naval destroyers and 200 U.S. Army, Coast Guard and Navy land and carrier based aircraft, including floatplanes. The April 1942 U-boat toll of 23 vessels forced naval tactical changes.[7]

Coast Guard cutters on weather station duty furnished essential information to convoy escort commanders. Weather patrol cutters were vulnerable to storms, high winds and seas, ship traffic, and U-boats. Master Chief Boatswain Mate Robert Hammond (USCG), an African American, recalled his tour of duty on the USS/CGC *Sea Cloud* (WPG-284). The armed, 316-foot weather patrol vessel out of Boston patrolled the ESF. The *Sea Cloud* crew complement was integrated, an innovative Coast Guard policy in the days when the U.S. Armed Forces was racially segregated. BMCM Hammond remembered initial racial tensions, but cold Atlantic seas, rescue missions, and the danger in U-boat infested waters served to unite the crew under the benevolent command of Lt., later Cmdr., Carlton Skinner. Hammond began his career as a steward, climbed through the enlisted rates, and retired in 1963 as a Master Chief Petty Officer.[8]

Search and Rescue duty in the Atlantic posed the dual threats of U-boats and seasonal storms. Responding to the 12 September 1944 torpedo attack on a U.S. merchant ship off Cape Hatteras, North Carolina, the Coast Guard cutters *Jackson* and *Bedloe* were lost when struck by the category 4 Great Atlantic Hurricane. Forty-eight Coastguardsmen lost their lives when the cutters rolled and sank in heavy seas. The 124-foot Vineyard Sound and Woods Hole, Massachusetts, lightship LS-73 and all 12 crew members were also lost in the storm.[9]

The 125-foot CGC *Bedloe* (WSC-128), out of Staten Island, New York, and its sister-ship CGC *Jackson* (WSC-142), stationed at Norfolk, Virginia, were patrolling the Eastern Sea Frontier when the hurricane hit.[10] Fireman First Class William Ruhl (USCG) and his fellow survivors were adrift in a raft on initially stormy, and then calm, shark-infested waters for three days and two nights. EM1 Ruhl expressed his gratitude to aviator Joseph Webber (USN), who spotted the survivors and landed his Navy seaplane to monitor them and radio for assistance. A transport ship eventually came alongside and took the Coastguardsmen to shore, where they had physical check-ups and hot food at a hospital in Elizabeth City, New Jersey.[11]

As of 2006, Ruhl, a retired public school administrator, continued to march in the annual Lewisburg, Pennsylvania, Fourth of July parades, William Ruhl "learned to love the Coast Guard," while still remembering how the two cutters were tossed by "waves like mountains" as they sank into the sea carrying the trapped crew members with them.[12]

The 132-foot Coast Guard patrol craft *Wilcox* (WYP-333) foundered in high winds and heavy seas in the Atlantic on 30 September 1943, after courageous but futile stabilization efforts by the 38 crew members. One man was washed overboard before the cutter sank.[13] The official designation of the cutter was the EM *Wilcox*. The "EM" designation stood for "Emergency Manning." The WYPs were former whalers, trawlers, and fishing boats that had been requisitioned by the Coast Guard on an emergency basis. Prior to the sinking 94 miles off the North Carolina coast, the CGC *Wilcox* had been assigned to the Caribbean Sea Frontier (CARIBSEAFRON), and home-ported in San Juan, Puerto Rico.[14]

The maritime skills and leadership of *Wilcox* skipper Lt. Elliott P. Smyzer (USCG) saved the crew on the ship, and later in the water. Lt. Smyzer's command presence had been honed by his previous service in the U.S. Merchant Marine and U.S. Navy. After being spotted by the crew of a lighter than air Navy dirigible (blimp), the commander and crew were rescued by another ship after enduring 17 hours in the cold Atlantic waters.[15]

The Coast Guard–manned USS *Leopold* (DE-319) was sunk by a U-boat torpedo in the North Atlantic on 9 March 1944. Of the 199-crew complement, only 28 enlisted personnel survived. The *Leopold*, commissioned only five months previously, was skippered by Cmdr. Kenneth Phillips (USCG). One of the few survivors of the convoy destroyer escort was Seaman First Class Lucas Bobbitt (USCG), who had fortuitously dressed in foul weather gear for his battle station watch by a deck gun. SN1 Bobbitt was thinking about the coming liberty time scheduled in Ireland when disaster struck.

Responding to General Quarters, Bobbitt fired six shells at a surfaced U-boat off the port side of the *Leopold*. The U-boat's deck gun shells ripped apart the deck grates on the torpedoed *Leopold* and, as Bobbitt later recalled in an oral interview with Lt. (jg) Burton Benjamin (USCGR), shrapnel ripped into an ammunition handler and blew "the whole side of his face off."[16]

The damage to the USS *Leopold* caused Cmdr. Phillips to issue an abandon ship order, after which he shouted out to his scrambling crew members, "Don't worry men, you'll be picked up soon. God Bless you all."[17] In the cold Atlantic water some crew members became frozen to the life nets on the side of the ship and could not escape. SN1 Bobbitt was thrown into the oily sea and got sick while swimming to escape the suction and propellers of the sinking ship, prowling U-boats, and the potential of exploding depth charges as the USS *Leopold* submerged.

Bobbitt somehow made it to a crowded raft with approximately 20 occupants being tossed about and out in 20 to 40 foot seas. In the terror and cold, Bobbitt asserted, some men became delusional and swam away from the raft to their doom. U-boat periscopes were observed in the area of operations. Enemy submarines drove off the destroyer escorts that tried to rescue the survivors.

A British patrol aircraft dropped flares over the two observable life rafts in the area, but could not drop depth charges on the U-boats because of their proximity to the rafts. A destroyer escort ship finally got close enough to the survivors to allow those that had the strength to struggle up the extended safety nets and collapse on deck. The destroyer crew assisted other survivors too weak to climb the nets. Warm food and coffee in the comfortable galley were welcomed treats, Bobbitt reported, but the gratitude of the survivors could not dispel the sadness over the loss of their shipmates, or the feelings of remorse which occurred as they watched the destroyer which had rescued them fire into the bobbing bow of the USS *Leopold* to sink the floating hulk that had become a hazard to navigation.[18]

Petty Officer John Philo (USN) was one of the more than 100,000 members of the Navy Armed Guard assigned to battle stations on armed American and Allied merchant vessels during World War II. Combat action and stormy seas resulted in the estimated deaths of more than 2,000 Navy Armed Guard personnel. BM2 Philo traced the origins of the Navy Armed Guard (NAG) to the defense and strategic needs of the United States following the sinking of the U.S. merchant vessel SS *Robin Moore* in the Atlantic in May 1941 by *U-69*. Using the German attack on the *Robin Moore*, President Roosevelt eventually convinced Congress to amend the Neutrality Act. "Finally," Philo asserted, "on 14 November 1941, the Neutrality Act was modified to allow defensive weapons aboard the ships of our merchant fleet, less than one month before Pearl Harbor."[19]

The training and stationing of NAG personnel on American and other Allied merchant vessels was stalled, Philo contended, because modern weapons were in short supply. Philo said, "All the Navy had for immediate use were the left over relics from World War I. Trained Navy gunnery students were quickly taken by the U.S. Fleet, and some of the top Navy brass thought the arming of merchant vessels was merely paying lip service to the Merchant Seaman's Union and had little tactical merit." However, as much as merchant ship companies might desire naval protection, some representatives of the seafarer's unions reported that many of their members did not want to be trained to fire ship weaponry.

"Nonetheless, the training of U.S. Navy crews eventually commenced under the supervision of Cmdr. Edward C. Van Cleve (USN)," Philo explained, and Armed Guard gunnery schools were established in Virginia, Mississippi, and at the U.S. Navy Base on Treasure Island, California. "By June of 1942," Philo asserted, "1,064 commercial ships were armed and had trained Navy crews to man the weapons." Philo was selected for gunnery school. After training, he was assigned to merchant vessels that sailed the Atlantic, Caribbean, Mediterranean and Pacific. BM2 John Philo sailed on the SS *Will B. Otwell* and the SS *George Uhler*. Liberty ships generally had crews of 40 or more merchant seamen and officers, 15 to 20 Naval Armed Guards, and were armed with one or two 3" to 5" guns on the bow and stern of the vessels, and from two to six machine guns.

U.S. Navy and Coast Guard ships escorted ship convoys that sailed with and without NAG personnel. The cargo vessels brought essential supplies and equipment to global U.S. and Allied bases. GM Philo did not mind sailing in heavy seas, "because the storms kept German U-boats from surfacing and effectively firing their deck guns and torpedoes." On one petty officer deck watch, PO Philo observed "the incongruous sight of a German U-boat in the neutral Portuguese Azores taking on fuel from an American Standard Oil facility."[20]

British military historian John Keegan attributed the Allied successes and eventual victory over the U-boats in the Atlantic to Western technology and human and electronic intelligence assets. Knowledge of where enemy submarine groups ("Wolf Packs") were and having the means to intercept and destroy them tilted the advantage to Allied naval forces and diminished the toll taken by U-boats on Allied merchant and military vessels.

Without the successful convoy escort patrols conducted by U.S. Coast Guard cutters, U.S. Navy warships, the slightly smaller Canadian corvettes, and British combat vessels and aircraft, Keegan contends, the United Kingdom might have lost the war, and the United States would have been cut off from Nazi-occupied Europe. The convoy system, Keegan concluded, prevented the subjugation and starvation of the United Kingdom and shortened the time frame of the brutal global war.[21]

Britain began World War II with 180 destroyers, 60 of which were World War I era vintage. Most of the smaller British combat ships were not well adapted to transoceanic antisubmarine patrols and heavy seas, and they consumed excessive amounts of fuel. Prime Minister Winston Churchill requested smaller but more seaworthy vessels that could carry more depth charges and powerful guns.

The Roosevelt administration loaned the British fifty destroyer-class ships, including 10 Coast Guard cutters. British Navy officials preferred the "Coast Guard cutters, which were roomy vessels with excellent sea keeping qualities … small destroyers possessing enough speed to outrun [overtake] U-boats, and economic in fuel consumption."[22]

Convoy escort groups were designated by the letters A (American), B (British), and C (Canadian). Convoy screening and attack techniques improved significantly with the use of sonar, radar, depth charges, ramming, and deck gun barrages upon emerged U-boats that were in torpedo firing modes. After the first torpedo salvos, U-boats generally sought safety under the sea, which allowed targeted convoys to steam out of range.[23]

By 1943, U-boat craft and crew losses were so extensive and costly that the German Admiralty made plans for the gradual withdrawal of its submarines from Atlantic waters to safer European coastal locations. The U-boats were the victims of skillful coded message interceptions by Allied cryptographers, and radio communication triangulation and location techniques developed by Allied radio operators. Ship sinking rates diminished as merchant sea captains gradually subordinated their maritime autonomy to the instructions and decisions of convoy naval commanders.

Depth charge attacks upon U-boats were quicker and more accurate with the use of the "Y" and "K" explosive devices that could be propelled forward and to the sides of pursuing destroyers. Allied merchant sailors did suffer casualties in the thousands, as did U-boat crews. After the loss of hundreds of U-boats and their crews, the German Admiralty finally decided to remove the submarines from the transatlantic in May 1943.[24]

The challenge, costs, and successes of the U.S. Navy and Coast Guard in combat against the U-boat menace in the Atlantic is chronicled in Homer Hickam's classic history, *Torpedo Junction.* Homer H. Hickam, Jr., a decorated U.S. Army officer, credited several people for contributing to his book about the Coast Guard in the U-boat war. Among the contributors is Major Harold "Swede" Larson, a retired Marine Corps officer and former radio operator on the USCGC *Dione.*

Hickam acquired an interest in the Coast Guard Atlantic war from his diving experiences among World War II shipwrecks off the North Carolina coast in the "Graveyard of the Atlantic." Rear Adm. James Alger, Jr., contributed his wartime experience to *Torpedo Junction.* As a young officer, Lt. James Alger, Jr., "maneuvered" the *Dione* in high winds and heavy seas, "stalking the [U-boat] killers on what had become an incredible sea of death." Hickam dedicated his book to the *Dione* for "serving her country well."

"And while the U.S. Navy failed to react," Hickam writes, "a handful of Coast Guard sailors scrambled to the front lines. Outgunned and out-maneuvered, they heroically battled the deadliest fleet of submarines ever launched. Never was Germany closer to winning the war. When the U-boats arrived off Cape Hatteras in January 1942, there was only one large antisubmarine ship there to oppose them ... the United States Coast Guard Cutter *Dione.*"[25]

The 165-foot *Dione* (WPC-107) was built by the Manitowoc, Wisconsin, Shipbuilding Corporation. The cutter's keel was laid in 1933 and the submarine chaser was launched in 1934. The cutter served on the Eastern Sea Frontier out of Norfolk, Virginia, on Air-Sea Rescue and ASW duties from 1941 to 1945.[26] The CGC *Dione* completed support missions with the U.S. Navy destroyer *Ellis* in May 1942. The two naval combat vessels responded to Coast Guard aircraft reports and steamed to the locations of two allegedly damaged and submerged U-boats 50 miles off the New Jersey coast and dropped depth charges on the targets.[27]

The CGC *Dione* crew escorted fuel tankers and witnessed the horrible fires and carnage visited upon merchant vessels and crews struck by U-boat torpedoes and deck guns. The rescues of survivors and the burned bodies of merchant sailors who survived flaming ships and burning waters were etched in the minds of *Dione* crew members. In several encounters, the *Dione* closed in, depth charged, and drove off attacking U-boats. The *Dione* also became the target of several U-boat attacks and avoided disaster because of alert spotters, orders issued by competent officers and enlisted personnel, and skillful seamanship.[28]

Radioman Harold "Swede" Larson (USCG) recalled receiving frequent merchant ship radio signals and the frustration of sometimes being unable to get to all of the vessels that reported U-boats sightings, and then help (SOS) requests after being torpedoed.[29]

Although the U.S. Navy was slow to participate in the Atlantic ESF patrols, USN patrol boats did participate in convoy escort and ASW missions with the Coast Guard. In the late evening of June 1942, in proximity to the CGC *Dione*, the small patrol boat YP-*389*, under the command of Lt. R.J. Phillips (USN), was guiding merchant ships away from the defensive minefields off Cape Hatteras, North Carolina when the Navy craft was attacked by *U-701.*

After an hour of evasive action, return fire, and being struck by the shells of the U-boat's powerful guns, Lt. Phillips ordered his crew to abandon the boat. He then applied full throttle to the heavily damaged patrol boat to draw the U-boat away from the crew members now afloat, and then joined his colleagues in the water. At dawn a Coast Guard lifeboat found the Navy sailors, took them aboard, treated the wounded, and brought them to a naval shore station. The brave men of YP-*389* had been sent to sea in a small vessel without sound gear or adequate armament.[30]

After the 7 December 1941 attack on Pearl Harbor, Admiral Ernest Joseph King (USN) was appointed commander in chief of the United States Fleet. In March 1942 Adm. King received a second command as Chief of Naval Operations (CNO).[31] Under Adm. King, Rear Admiral Adolphus Andrews (USN) was given command of the Eastern Sea Frontier, which extended from the Canadian border to southern Florida.

Admiral Andrews was ordered to direct the antisubmarine war against German U-boats and to protect merchant vessels with military escort ships and air patrols. Under Adm. Andrews, the ESF had insufficient ships and aircraft to adequately suppress the U-boat attacks, but by August 1942 enemy submarines inside the ESF sank no more commercial vessels.[32] ESF commanders administered offshore defense tactics, onshore and offshore aircraft, blimp, and water patrols, and the land-based patrol planes of the U.S. Navy, Coast Guard, and Army. The Canadian Atlantic coast established similar military command structures and cooperative policies with the United States.[33]

Admiral Andrews gradually persuaded Adm. King to assign more Navy destroyers to the ESF. By 1 April 1942, Adm. Andrews had a surface fleet under his command consisting of 23 large (90 feet in length or more) and 42 small (75- to 83-foot) Coast Guard cutters, 3 Navy patrol craft, converted yachts skippered by civilians and Coast Guard Reservists in the "Hooligan Navy" (or "Bucket Patrol"), 14 armed British trawlers crewed by rugged sailors, and approximately 170 Army and Navy aircraft at air stations stretching from Maine to Florida ready for ASW patrol and convoy escort duty. Add to that the civilian Civil Air Patrol consisting of eager, experienced pilots whose surveillance flights directed air- and watercraft to rescue sites, and frightened many a U-boat commander into diving beneath the sea out of range of merchant convoys.[34]

Admiral Andrews gradually convinced an initially reluctant Adm. King of the need for more destroyer-type U.S. Navy and Coast Guard cutters for ESF patrol duty, which King thought would constrain his ability to fight the Pacific War. But U-boat tolls on merchant vessels got too high to ignore. Adm. Andrews also convinced recalcitrant military, political, and business leaders to support the extinguishing ("black out") of civilian night lights along the Atlantic coast to lessen the urban illumination that helped U-boat commanders target their victims.[35]

A staff officer in Adm. Andrew's command presented him with a naval study that proved the success of Navy and Coast Guard convoy escort vessels in decreasing the toll of U-boat attacks on merchant vessels in World War I. The report was forwarded to Adm. King.[36] The incident that finally convinced U.S. Navy leaders to increase the number of patrol craft for convoy escort duty in the ESF was the sinking of the destroyer escort *Jacob Jones*, which was under the command of Lt. Cmdr. Hugh David Black (USN). The USS *Jones* was sunk in the early hours of 28 February 1942 by a torpedo from *U-578*. The *Jones* exploded when the ammunition hold was hit. Only 11 members of the 200-man crew survived in the oily, burning waters of the Atlantic.

As the destroyer sank, its depth charges detonated beneath the waves, sending concussion pressures to the surface that injured or killed several crew members, some of whom were blown out of life rafts. The Coast Guard patrol boat *Eagle* later rescued the survivors in heavy seas. The sinking of the *Jones* convinced Adm. King that Rear Adm. Andrews was correct in his assertion that in 1942 the Atlantic coast of the United States was not controlled by the U.S. Navy, and an enhanced convoy-escort system was necessary to defeat the Nazi maritime threat to American sovereignty and shipping in the Eastern Sea Frontier.

More naval escort vessels would soon accompany the USCGC *Dione* on convoy and ASW duty. The 165-foot *Dione* crew complement of 70 continued its 16-knot patrols powered by two diesel engines, twin 3-blade screws and armed with four deck guns, and two Y-gun and two Mousetrap depth charge systems, prepared for convoy escort, lifesaving search and rescue, or ASW combat missions.[37]

Captain John M. Waters, Jr. (USCG), witnessed the Atlantic war against the U-boats as a young watch officer on the bridge of the USCGC *Ingham* (WPG-35). The 1942 U.S. Coast Guard Academy graduate was soon placed in the middle of the 1942–1943 war on convoy escort duty and participated in battles that lasted for days at a time. "The enemy," Capt. Waters later wrote in his book, *Bloody Winter*, "was seldom seen, though his presence was often evidenced by burning ships, a shadow in the night, a small blip on the radar scope, a returning beep on the ASDIC detection gear, or the high pitched chirp of his radio transmissions."[38]

The winter victories over the U-boats, Waters contends, were due to the combined operations of the Royal Canadian Navy (RCN), the Britain's Royal Navy (RN), and the U.S. Navy and Coast Guard. The Coast Guard patrol craft consisted of a few cutters of World War I vintage and the six modern "Hamilton Class" cutters assigned to the North Atlantic (*Ingham, Hamilton, Bibb, Duane, Campbell, and Spencer*).[39] Capt. Waters dedicated his book "To those who fought in the Battle of the Atlantic, on, over, and beneath the sea," and included in his narrative, postwar interviews with former World War II German submarine commanders.

In the 1942–1943 Atlantic war, the 327-foot *Ingham* rescued more than 50 survivors from six-torpedoed merchant vessels and on 15 December 1942 sank *U-626*. The *Ingham* later served in combat zones in the Mediterranean and Pacific.[40] The CGC *Alexander Hamilton* (WPG-34) was sunk by an enemy torpedo off the coast of Iceland in early 1942.[41] Captain Waters described the *Ingham* "rolling up to 50 degrees in mountainous seas" with waves hitting the bridge "35 feet above the waterline," screws coming out of the water, and wet, cold crew members threatened with being washed overboard on icy decks in 50–100 knot winds.[42]

In such stormy seas and ice, snow, squall or gale conditions, vessels were in danger of foundering, convoy ships were lost and had to make port on their own, and vessels were damaged in collisions.[43] Coastguardsmen risked their lives in lowering and accessing lifeboats to carry out rescues in such sea conditions. The task of recovering the bodies of dead sailors and cold and burned survivors was an arduous and horrifying task which was carried out with the ever-present risk of attack by the predator U-boats.[44]

Successful convoy protection missions by destroyer escorts required effective organization and communications and experienced ship lookouts. Merchant vessels carrying strategic supplies to Europe had to be protected. Troop ships carrying the soldiers, sailors and Marines who would direct and participate in military operations had to be protected and brought safely to their destinations.

Convoys varied in size from two to three to more than one hundred merchant vessels. The convoy cargo ships sailed in columns spaced one-half mile (one-thousand yards) apart, with each ship maintaining 500 yards distance from the stern of the ship in front of it. An average sized convoy of 50 ships in columns of five or six merchant vessels would cover an area of four miles in width and three to four miles in length. The naval escort vessels that flanked the merchant fleet would expand the armada to about 36 square miles. Each convoy was led by a civilian master (commodore) of the merchant ships, and a naval commander of the escort warships. The civilian would ride on one of the merchant vessels in the convoy. The naval commander would ride on one of the naval vessels, thus it would be designated as a flagship.

Radio communications were limited because of the danger of enemy reception. Flag and light signals were the preferred inter-ship communications method. Radio signals and oral communication were used in emergencies, such as distress (SOS) signals in the case of enemy attack, ship collisions, situational awareness, defense, and search and rescue. When radio communication was used the messages and oral terminology would be disguised or in code as much as possible.

A complex but clear standard of alphabetically arranged letters indicated the nationality of the vessel, harbors of departure and arrival, whether the convoy was fast (high nautical speed) or slow, or eastbound or westbound across the Atlantic. Each convoy was assigned a number. Using the charts and communications systems designed for the commodores, commanders, and ship captains, a convoy designation might be HX-112, a designation that identified that particular flotilla as the 112th Halifax to United Kingdom convoy.[45]

The North Atlantic winter of 1943 was especially devastating for ship losses, despite the coordinated actions of the RN, RCN, USN and the USCG. Troop convoys were escorted across the Atlantic to the United Kingdom in preparation for the troop and supply buildups for the coming invasion of the German-occupied European continent.

The U-boat threat was harrowing enough, but ship collisions and fires also took their toll. On 3 September 1942, in Convoy TA (Troop American), a fire broke out on the Coast Guard–manned transport USS *Wakefield* (AP-21). Three U.S. Navy vessels assisted in the rescue of all of the 1500 civilian construction workers and crew from the *Wakefield* and from the several rafts that had put out to sea. The Coast Guard–manned transport was towed to Halifax (Nova Scotia, Canada), then Boston, Massachusetts, for repairs and subsequently returned to duty.[46]

In the evening of 27 August 1942, the U.S. Army troop transport USAT *Chatham* was torpedoed 25 miles off the Canadian coast. Most of the 560 crew and Canadian and American soldiers from the sunken vessel were saved by the USCGC *Mojave* (WPG-47).[47] The 240-foot CGC *Mojave* rescued the 293 survivors of the *Chatham* sinking.[48]

On the evening of 3 February 1943, the USAT *Dorchester* was sunk 46 miles south of Greenland by *U-456*, with the loss of 677 crew members and American soldiers. In the chaos of the "Abandon Ship" order and rush to get to the lifeboats, several passengers were without life jackets. The four ship chaplains (Lt. C.V. Poling and G.L. Fox, Protestant ministers; Lt. A.D. Goode, a rabbi; and Lt. J.P. Washington, a Roman Catholic priest) gave their life-vests to others, joined arms, and went down with the ship.[49] The 165-foot CGC *Comanche* (WPG-76), assisted by the 327-foot CGC *Duane* (WPG-33), rescued 97 survivors.[50]

Most of the Allied troop ships got safely across the Atlantic to Britain escorted by U.S. Coast Guard and Navy warships. The troop transports were gradually replaced by the gigantic, fast European passenger liners, which could outrun the German submarines and their torpedoes,[51] and when the U-boat menace was gradually being subdued by the superior tactics and technology of British, Canadian, and American escort vessels and their skilled and well trained crews.

David Fairbank White, a historian of the Battle of the Atlantic, observed that the vast ocean contains the bodies of World War II sailors, merchant mariners, and U-boat crews at rest with no grave markers to commemorate their sacrifice. Thirty-six thousand Allied troops, aircrews, and sailors, men and women, died in the Atlantic Ocean in World War II, along with the 36,000 merchant seamen. Many of the maritime victims died of weather exposure, drowning, and malnutrition in lifeboats and rafts or afloat in life vests.

More than 660 of the nearly 1,200 German U-boats that engaged in the Atlantic war sank and 33.000 German officers and enlisted personnel perished in the Atlantic between 1939 and 1945. The Battle of the Atlantic and the protection of the military personnel and supply lines that traversed the ocean between North America and Europe were essential elements of the victory that prevented the conquest of Great Britain by Nazi Germany. White credits the victorious outcome to British and Canadian naval forces and the U.S. Coast Guard, U.S. Navy, U.S. Merchant Marine, and the industrial productivity and technology of the American people and civilian workers. [52]

The U.S. Treasury Class Coast Guard cutters, named after U.S. Treasury Secretaries, were sturdy 327-foot oceangoing warships. Five of these 22-knot cutters, the *Bibb, Duane, Campbell, Spencer,* and *Ingham,* sank three U-boats and shared in the destruction of a fourth submarine. The CGC *Ingham* sank *U-626* on 15 December 1942. In the same winter the CGC *Spencer* sank *U-225* in February 1943 and *U-175* in April. The CGC *Campbell* teamed up with the Polish warship *Burza* to sink *U-606* in February. 1943.[53]

The naval alliance between the United Kingdom and the United States in World War II is commemorated at the American Memorial in Cambridge, England. The names of the 1,371 members of the U.S. Navy and the 201 members of the U.S. Coast Guard who sacrificed their lives in the Battle of the Atlantic are etched on the wall of the Memorial adjacent to the American Military Cemetery.[54]

12

The Mediterranean: North Africa, Sicily, Italy

During the course of World War II, the U.S. Coast Guard manned 351 U.S. Navy ships and craft that ranged in size from a converted transatlantic passenger ship with a crew complement of 934 to amphibious landing craft with two-man crews. It is estimated that by the end of 1945, approximately 3,300 Coast Guard officers and 45,200 enlisted men manned, or were crewmates of, Navy personnel on U.S. Navy ships and boats,[1] excluding the hundreds of autonomous Coast Guard craft under U.S. Navy control.

The first Allied naval and troop invasion into the Axis held territories around the Mediterranean Sea from North Africa into Southern Europe occurred in 1942 and 1943 and extended through the end of World War II in 1945. The major geographic invasion sites were the French colonies of Morocco, Algeria, and Tunisia in North Africa, the Mediterranean island of Sicily owned by Italy, and the Italian peninsula of southern Europe. The Allied naval and military forces of Britain and the United States led the attack against the pro-German Vichy French forces in North Africa and the Axis naval and military forces of Germany and Italy in North Africa, Sicily, and Italy. General Dwight David Eisenhower (U.S. Army) was the commander of Allied forces. General Bernard L. Montgomery led the British combat troops against the German commander, Field Marshal Erwin Rommel and his Afrika Korps. General George S. Patton (U.S. Army) led American combat forces in the amphibious attacks in the Mediterranean combat theater.

U.S. Coast Guard landing craft, Coast Guard–manned U.S. Navy ships, U.S. Navy ships, and British Royal Navy craft and crews transported Allied troops and equipment ashore against enemy air, land and naval forces. The Allied and Axis forces suffered heavy casualties, but the Allies inevitably prevailed along the 1,000 mile North African coast and in Sicily and Italy. Among the key North African ports of assault were Casablanca, Morocco, Oran and Algiers, Algeria, and Bizerte and Tunis, Tunisia.

American naval crews trained for Operation Torch in U.S. coastal waters around Norfolk, Virginia, and then sailed the ships and Army troops across the Atlantic and into the Mediterranean. The North African cam-

THE MEDITERRANEAN THEATER
(1942 - 1944)

paign and the experience gained led the way for the Allied invasion of Sicily and Italy.[2]

The Anglo-American invasion of Sicily commenced on the evening of 9 July 1943. The amphibious invasion consisted of 3,000 ships with landing craft aboard, 60,000 troops, and 14,000 vehicles including trucks, jeeps, bulldozers, and 600 tanks. Allied bombers, fighter aircraft, and warships softened up enemy defenses as Axis naval and military forces retaliated. The Allied naval and troop amphibious assault was the largest military operation to that date in World War II and provided the experience necessary to more effectively plan the 1944 Normandy invasion in northwestern Europe.[3]

The AP and APA hull designations indicated the identity of a transport ship for cargo, personnel, and troop landing craft. APs ranged from 522 to 622 feet in length. APAs were attack transports that possessed defensive and offensive deck guns powerful enough to challenge enemy submarines and aircraft. Several Coast Guard–manned attack transports performed multiple missions and served as the flagships for U.S. Navy commanders in the Mediterranean and Pacific campaigns. The Coast Guard–manned attack transports included the *Leonard Wood* (APA-12), *Joseph T. Dickman* (APA-13), and *Samuel Chase* (APA-26).[4]

The North African invasion was called Operation Torch. The invasions of Sicily and regions of Italy were identified as Operations Husky, Avalanche, and Shingle. Operation Torch involved the landing of U.S. and British troops by U.S. Navy and Royal Navy ships and landing craft. The American naval armada consisted of more than 100 USN and USCG vessels under the command of Rear Admiral H. Kent Hewitt (USN).[5]

The U.S. Navy element of the Anglo-American Sicily invasion was identified as the Western Naval Task Force (WNTF) under the command of Adm. Hewitt (USN). The British Royal Navy was responsible for the Eastern Naval Task Force. The WNTF consisted of 500 ships and three types of amphibious landing craft and vehicles: the 1500-ton Landing Ship Tank (LST), the 200-ton Landing Craft Infantry (LCI), and the DUKW amphibious truck. The troop transports successfully landed 24,000 soldiers in a storm and high surf on the evening of 9 July 1943.

His dynamic tactics, naval gunfire upon enemy positions, and skillful amphibious troop landings facilitated General Patton's rapid advance across Sicily. The U.S. Navy and U.S. Army assaults on the Italian mainland were carried out in two different regions of the west coast in September 1943 and January 1944. Several sites were hit, but the most significant targets were the ports of Salerno, Naples, and Anzio. The fighting was ferocious and casualties on the Allied and Axis sides were high. The Germans carried the fight to the Allies because the Italian government surrendered soon after the Allied invasion of Sicily in July of 1943.[6]

Prior to Operation Torch, in early 1942, the Amphibious Force Atlantic Fleet (AFAF), under the command of Rear Adm. Henry Kent Hewitt (USN), was active. Headquartered at Norfolk, Virginia, the AFAF developed the six-division "Transports Atlantic Fleet" and trained several thousand Coast Guard and Navy personnel in landing craft seamanship. The training centers were located on the appropriately named Solomons Island, Maryland (in Chesapeake Bay), and at Little Creek, Virginia. Amphibious attacks would later be conducted in the Solomon Islands in the Pacific. Captain W.P.O. Clarke (USN) directed the training operations. The U.S. Army trained its landing craft personnel at Fort Bragg, North Carolina.[7]

The Center Attack Group in the North African amphibious assault was directed by Capt. R.M. Emmett (USN) from the Coast Guard manned flagship *Leonard Wood*, under the command of Cmdr. Merlin O'Neill (USCG). The attack groups assigned to Operation Torch that had trained in the United States left Hampton Roads, Virginia, for North Africa on 23 October 1943. The Coast Guard–manned USN transport *Joseph T. Dickman*, skippered by Cmdr. C.W. Harwood (USCG), led the attack force to sea.

Two British Naval Forces sailed to the Mediterranean from the United Kingdom on 22 and 26 October 1942. The Coast Guard–manned attack transport *Samuel Chase*, under the command of Cmdr. Roger C. Heimer (USCG), was part of this Royal Navy fleet. The *Samuel Chase* was the flagship of Capt. Campbell D. Edgar (USN). Several Coast Guard landing craft crews participated in the invasion while serving on seven different U.S. Navy warships run by USN crews.

Two former Coast Guard cutters, the *Pontchartrain* and the *Sebago*, were part of the Torch invasion fleet of the Royal Navy. The cutters had been transferred to the RN through President Roosevelt's Lend-Lease program. The *Pontchartrain* was renamed HMS *Hartland*. The *Sebago* became the HMS *Walney*.[8]

To facilitate the landing craft operations in darkness, scout patrol boats went ahead to mark the beaches. Weapons support was provided by small landing craft LCSSs (Landing Craft Support, Small) which carried rocket launching racks on each gunwale to fire on enemy machine gun, small arms, and mortar positions after the warships further out at sea suppressed their fire to avoid hitting the beached amphibious teams. Flashlights and flares were used by the scout boats to show coxswains where to land. The landing craft crews deposited troops and treated and carried back the wounded, and transported the dead, soldiers and sailors, including Coast Guard casualties.[9]

The enormity of the loads and the significance of the missions of the APA transport ships are well illustrated by the mission and activities of the Coast Guard–manned *Leonard Wood* (APA-12) in the North African invasions. Onboard were Major General J.W. Anderson (USA) and his staff, the landing groups and supporting units of the infantry division, and 3,000 tons of equipment, supplies and vehicles. The military contingents onboard the *Leonard Wood* consisted of 92 officers and 1,693 enlisted men of the U.S. Army; 28 officers and 122 enlisted men of the U.S. Navy; and 41 officers and 541 enlisted men of the U.S. Coast Guard, for a total of 2,517 military personnel.[10]

From the transport ships, an armada of landing craft sailed for the darkened beaches, with some vessels remaining fast on the beach or crashing amidst hidden rocks, forcing soldiers ashore minus some equipment. In one landing over the evening and subsequent daylight hours, 21 of the 32 boats of the *Leonard Wood* were wrecked on the rocks or disabled in landing attempts in heavy surf. Some ships were torpedoed and enemy aircraft disabled several landing craft, forcing the *Leonard Wood* and sister ships to dodge torpedoes and rescue several hundred soldiers and sailors in that and future missions in November 1942.[11]

The USN and USCG officers and enlisted men of the USS *Joseph T. Dickman* (APA-13) exhibited similar courage, skill and success in the North African landings. After taking a position off the port of Fedhala, Morocco, with more than 1,500 U.S. Army and Navy personnel, and a bountiful cargo of supplies, equipment, and ammunition, the *Dickman* managed to land most of her landing craft and troops while under enemy fire. Heroic action by Navy and Coast Guard crews got wounded personnel out of boats, off the beach, and back to Navy destroyers. Several sailors earned commendations and medals for their combat actions and rescues.

Ensign Harry A. Storts (USCGR) and a complement of 9 Navy and Coast Guard personnel and 32 Army troops were dug in on a beach and under siege by Vichy French troops, armored vehicles, and enemy aircraft. The American servicemen took a toll on the enemy, but they suffered casualties. The survivors experienced several more days of fighting and walking, but finally reached a U.S. Army post. After resting, the intrepid platoon acquired a half-track vehicle, a .75-mm. gun, and a support rescue squad. In an ensuing battle, the group was taken prisoner by French forces but escaped after a U.S. fighter plane strafed their captors. A French priest subsequently escorted the American survivors to Fedhala and safety aboard an Allied ship.[12]

The *Leonard Wood* and the *Joseph T. Dickman* successfully offloaded their cargo at the port of Casablanca (Morocco). On 17 November 1942, the two attack cargo ships sailed back across the Atlantic to Norfolk, Virginia. Captain O'Neil (USCG) and Captain Harwood (USCG), the respective skippers of the *Leonard Wood* and the *Joseph T. Dickman*, later received the Legion of Merit for their courage and leadership in Operation Torch.[13]

The Coast Guard–manned attack transport *Samuel Chase* (APA-26), under Cmdr. Roger C. Heimer (USCG), was the flagship of the 37-vessel Transport Division Eleven. Division Eleven carried U.S. Coast Guard, U.S. Navy, U.S. Army, and British Army and Navy officers and men. Commander Heimer skillfully maneuvered the *Chase* off the Spanish coast to avoid submarine torpedoes. Transport Division Eleven put 72,000 Allied officers and men on North African shores in October 1942.

In combat off the Algerian coast, Cmdr. Heimer avoided submarine torpedo and torpedo plane attacks with skillful seamanship and command decisions that were carried out by his well-trained crew. In a five-day period, the *Samuel Chase* fought off air attacks and shot down three German bombers. The British Admiralty commended the crew of the *Samuel Chase* for exemplary combat action and courageous rescue operations.

The "Lucky *Chase*" was the only Division Eleven attack transport that escaped battle damage in Operation Torch. The *Samuel Chase* and its sister ships, landing craft, and Allied naval and military support led to the liberation of North Africa and Sicily. The successful combat operations secured the seas and paved the way for the eventual Allied victory over the Axis forces in Europe.[14]

On 23 January 1943, Lieutenant General Dwight David Eisenhower received orders from the U.S. Combined Chiefs of Staff of the U.S. Armed Forces to plan an attack on the Italian island of Sicily in the Mediterranean Sea. General Eisenhower was appointed Supreme Commander of Allied Forces. British General Alexander was named deputy commander. Admiral Cunningham (Royal Navy) was appointed the naval commander. British Air Chief Marshall Tedder was ordered to lead the air forces. The Western Naval Task Force was placed under the command of Vice Admiral Henry Kent Hewitt (USN). The Eastern Naval Task Force was to be commanded by Vice Adm. Sir Bertram Ramsay (RN).[15]

American and British Task Forces were trained in Chesapeake Bay, Maryland, and Scotland (the Canadian First Division) and Algeria, where Rear Adm.

Richard L. Conolly (USN) prepared landing craft personnel. The Western Naval Task Force landed the Seventh Army troops of General George S. Patton (USA) on Sicily. After Sicily, the Allied naval and military forces were tasked with invading the Italian peninsula.

The new 328-foot "Landing Ship Tanks" (LSTs) were to be used to off-load tanks, vehicles, guns, supplies and personnel. The new, armed 158-foot "Landing Craft Infantry Large" vessels (LCI-Ls) were built to accommodate 25 crew members and 200 assault troops. The Coast Guard–manned attack transports that had served so well in the North African invasion, the *Samuel Chase, Leonard Wood,* and *Joseph T. Dickman,* participated in the Sicilian campaign. The armed attack transports (APAs) were supported by the 175-foot submarine chasers *PC-545* and *PC-556.* Coast Guard manned landing craft included five LSTs (hull numbers 16, 326, 327, 331, 381); and 24 LCI(L)s with hull numbers 83–96, 319-326, 349 and 350.[16]

Coast Guard vessels were assigned to the different coastal regions of Sicily. LCI(L) Flotilla Four was led by Cmdr. Miles H. Imlay (USCG). The *Samuel Chase,* the flagship of Adm. John L. Hall (USN), performed valiantly again after Operation Torch under the experienced skipper Cmdr. Heimer (USCG), as did the *Joseph T. Dickman* (Cmdr. Harwood, USCG) and *Leonard Wood* (Cmdr. O'Neill), the sister ships of the North African campaign.

Heavy enemy resistance led to high naval and military casualty rates. The *Dickman* landed U.S. Army Rangers, combat engineers, and artillery support troops. *Dickman* boats rescued 92 survivors from an exploding cargo ship that had been struck by artillery while unloading on the beach. The *Leonard Wood* exhibited exemplary seamanship in unloading cargo and 28 landing craft in heavy seas as its scout boats fired smoke bombs to shield vessels and personnel from enemy snipers. The missions, seamanship, enemy attacks and rescues performed by the APAs and landing craft in the Sicily invasion replicated the challenges and successes of the recently completed Torch operations in North Africa. On 11 and 12 July 1943, *LST-331* added to the Coast Guard legacy by shooting down one enemy bomber and two fighter planes.[17]

For his leadership in clearing mines, supporting U.S. Army forces, port security and supply operations while under enemy fire, and the skillful operation of the LCIs under his command, Cmdr. Miles H. Imlay (USCG) earned the Legion of Merit. Captain Harwood (*Joseph T. Dickman*) received the Legion of Merit for his command of the Naval Task Group and landing and supplying assault troops while under enemy fire and bombardment.[18]

On 3 September 1943, Italy signed an armistice with the Allied forces and withdrew from the war. But the Allies still had to conquer the German military machine throughout Italy. On 9 September 1943, American, Canadian, and British forces supported by the USN and RN landed in the Salerno region under heavy attack. Naval supply and support missions continued while German artillery and aircraft attacked the convoys.

In the early morning darkness of 9 September 1943, the new skipper of the *Joseph T. Dickman,* Captain Raymond J. Mauerman (USCG), disembarked an LCS(S) boat piloted by Lt. (jg) Grady R. Galloway (USCG). Lt. Galloway located the beach by sighting in on a medieval stone tower, signaled for the *Dickman* landing craft to come ashore, and suppressed enemy gunfire with his rocket launchers. The *Samuel Chase* under Cmdr. Heimer (USCG) got its boats, troops and cargo ashore under enemy fire, and received casualties and prisoners of war from returning landing craft. The wounded received medical care in sick bay.

Cmdr. Miles Imlay (USCG) received military honors for bringing his landing craft flotilla from Tunisia, North Africa, to the port of Salerno, Italy, under enemy air attack in heavy seas to the appointed landing zones on schedule. Coast Guard–manned transport ships and landing craft performed valiantly under heavy enemy artillery and air attacks in the Anzio assault in January 1943. Naval gunfire suppressed the German attacks enough so Allied troops and supplies could be landed. The casualty count was high. The landing craft completed the mission and either returned to the mother ships or the port of Naples, Italy, for more vehicles and supplies.[19]

The courage, fear, challenges, and skill of combat are uniquely described by primary sources: by the oral and written testimony veterans who were there. Lt. Cmdr. Blair Walliser (USCGR) wrote about his combat experiences while stationed on the attack transport USS *Samuel Chase* (APA-26) during the invasions of North Africa (1942) and Sicily and Italy (1943). The *Chase* was the flagship of the Eighth Amphibious Force. Capt. Roger C. Heimer (USCG), the commanding officer, dodged bombs, torpedoes, and artillery barrages, got troops and supplies ashore, made rescues, and took defensive and offensive combat action throughout the Mediterranean campaigns. Capt. Heimer would earn a Gold Star and the Legion of Merit for his combat leadership.

Lt. Cmdr. Walliser described the work of skilled boat coxswains, troop landings, logistics and tactics, the deactivation of mines while under enemy fire, and the rescue and treatment of U.S. Marine, Army, and Navy casualties onboard landing craft while on the return trips to the larger ships far offshore.

Walliser chronicled how U.S. Navy warships pounded enemy positions prior to the landing craft deployments and endured enemy air attacks and shot down ("crashed" and "splashed") combat aircraft over land and sea. Navy and Coast Guard ship and boat personnel rescued downed Allied and enemy aircrews and the survivors of ship and boat wrecks. Navy and Coast Guard beach masters directed traffic and the unloading of LSTs and often had to dig in and respond to enemy troop, artillery, tank, and air attacks.[20]

Petty Officer Charles P. Giammona (USCGR) narrated his experiences as a crew member on the assault transport USS *Joseph T. Dickman* (APA-13), under the command of Captain R. J. Mauerman (USCG). Coxswain Giammona was wounded by a bullet and shrapnel piece during the invasion of Sicily (July

On 20 April 1944 the Coast Guard crew of the USS *Menges* and a U.S. Navy destroyer escort rescued 230 Navy personnel from the Mediterranean Sea after German aircraft sunk the USS *Landsdale*. The *Menges* gun crew shot down one enemy plane in the engagement.

1943). Then, in September 1943, PO Giammona was on a landing craft heading into Salerno Bay in the invasion of Italy. The LC crew unloaded the combat troops under steady German gun fire, pulled up the bow ramp, and were headed back to the *Joseph T. Dickman* when a German artillery shell made a direct hit on the landing barge. Giammona was thrown to the deck after being struck by shrapnel. His "dog [identification] tags" were blown off and his trousers were torn to bloody shreds.

Giammona said his life jacket and water canteen absorbed much of the shrapnel. His shipmates lifted him off the deck and placed him across the engine cover. A coxswain administered morphine to him. Giammona was transferred to a patrol boat and returned to the USS *Dickman*. A pharmacist's mate administered sulfa drugs to the wounded coxswain. Giamonna was then transferred to a larger transport where a medical officer performed surgery to extract the largest pieces of shrapnel.

Giammona subsequently suffered several more surgeries, but not all of the shrapnel could be removed. The dangers that landing craft crews and troops faced coming to shore under enemy fire are well illustrated by Coxswain Giammona's riveting account of bravery and danger in combat.[21]

The successful Allied assaults on Sicily and Italy forced German military commanders to send massive numbers of guns, troops and tanks into Italy from the European heartland at a heavy cost in equipment and manpower. The victories enabled the Allies to expand their territorial reach and aid the insurgent forces on the European continent that contributed to the eventual defeat of the overextended German empire.

13

D-Day at Normandy

In June 1944, Axis-controlled continental Europe stretched from the Atlantic coast to the western boundaries of the Soviet Union. The Soviet Army was in the process of attacking Germany from the Eastern Front, as the other Allied Nations, primarily the United Kingdom, Canada, and the United States, were poised for the invasion of continental Europe through the French province of Normandy.

The Allied invasion of Normandy was called "Operation Overlord." Anglo-American warships pounded the defenses of the entrenched enemy. Landing craft and assault ships flanked by rescue boats brought the troops ashore in the coordinated operations of the U.S. Navy, U.S. Coast Guard, and British Royal Navy. The Canadian troops of the British Commonwealth fought valiantly in the costly amphibious and paratroop landings.[1]

Invasion ("D") Day and the Normandy Campaign commenced on 6 June 1944, the day after heavy seas and stormy weather had caused a 24-hour postponement. The Normandy campaign from the French shores to the inland breakout through enemy defenses took place in June and July of 1944. The selected fifty-mile Normandy beachfront was divided into the code-named sectors of UTAH, OMAHA, GOLD, JUNO, and SWORD. Allied glider planes whose valiant crews joined airborne troops behind enemy lines supplemented the invading naval vessels. More than 4,000 Allied combat vessels and rescue boats, 5,800 bombers, and 5,000 fighter aircraft assaulted the "Atlantic Wall" defense infrastructure of the Germans. Combat engineers and demolition crews went in first to dismantle steel and concrete barriers in shoal waters and landing craft traps under cover of naval bombardments and in the face of enemy shell fire.[2]

Despite the heavy Allied casualties, and a comparative tally of enemy wounded and killed, the Normandy invasion was a success. By 25 April 1945, Soviet troops were in Berlin and British and American troops were just west of the German capital. On 30 April, the German Führer, Adolf Hitler, committed suicide, two days after his Italian Axis partner, Benito Mussolini, was captured and executed by partisans. German troops in Berlin surrendered on 2 May 1945.[3] The devastating success of the Normandy invasion led to the eventual Allied victory in Europe, and the reallocation of Allied military resources

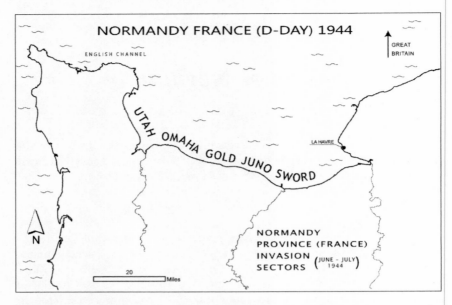

NORMANDY FRANCE (D-DAY) 1944

ENGLISH CHANNEL

GREAT BRITAIN

UTAH OMAHA GOLD JUNO SWORD

LA HAVRE

N

NORMANDY PROVINCE (FRANCE) INVASION SECTORS (JUNE - JULY 1944)

20   Miles

to the Pacific theater for the defeat of Japan, the remaining Axis power. The significance of Normandy requires further examination.

The Allied invasion of France commenced from ports in southern Britain. British and American naval mine sweepers cleared the designated sea-lanes from the United Kingdom, across the English Channel, and to the Normandy coast. Buoys were laid and beach markers placed to guide the Allied naval armada to combat destinations from the initial "Zebra Fleet Assembly Area" to the final navigation site called "the spout."[4]

An overview of D-Day and its aftermath illustrates the significant role the USCG played at Normandy. Coast Guard personnel served as combat photographers and beach masters. The USCG and USN piloted the full array of landing craft, including assault craft (LCAs), LCCs (primary control craft), LCIs (landing craft infantry), LCM (landing craft medium), LCT and LST (landing craft tank and landing ship tank), LCTR (landing craft rocket), and LCVP (landing craft vehicle and personnel).[5] Other landing craft included the "L" at the end of the initials which stood for "Large," and letter designations indicating specialized functions, such as LBE (land barge emergency repair), LCE (landing craft emergency repair), LCG (landing craft gun), and LCH (landing craft headquarters). Headquarters vessels included berthing and command centers for naval flag officers and military commanders.[6]

D-Day historian Stephen Ambrose was told by General Eisenhower (USA) that if Andrew Higgins, the New Orleans, Louisiana, boatbuilder, "had not designed and built those LCVPs, we could never have landed over an open beach. The whole strategy of the war would have been different." Gen. Eisen-

USS LST-21 unloading British tanks and trucks off Normandy on 6 June 1944.

hower credited Higgins (and his "Higgins boats") as having "won the war for us."[7] Andrew Jackson Higgins had previously designed racing boats, the Prohibition-era rumrunning boats of the smugglers, and the patrol boats the Coast Guard used to pursue the rumrunners. The Higgins boats were used by U.S. Coast Guard and U.S. Marines at Guadalcanal in the Pacific. Higgins also influenced the design of the well-armed USN patrol torpedo (PT) boats in the Pacific war.[8]

Most of the LC (landing craft) coxswains were U.S. Coast Guard personnel. Their ranks and rates included African-American personnel, the result of an enlightened Coast Guard and Navy policy decision in the era of the segregated U.S. Armed Forces.[9] In 1944, the USCG and USN, responding to a U.S. Navy Department directive, authorized the enlistment of African-American women. Yeoman Second Class Olivia J. Hooker (USCG) was the first Black woman to become a Coast Guard SPAR. YN2 Hooker recalled, "There were six nurses of my heritage who were ensigns [officers]."[10]

The USCG commanded 97 D-Day vessels and the landing craft that were carried on three attack troop transports. Coast Guard personnel served on other ships with U.S. Navy crews. Lt. Cmdr. Alexander V. Steward (USCGR) commanded the 60 wooden 83-foot Coast Guard cutters that crossed the English Channel with the troop transports as part of the Rescue Flotilla suggested by President Franklin D. Roosevelt. The rescue cutters dodged mines, underwater obstructions, German shore guns, and enemy aircraft. The Rescue Flotilla is credited with saving 1,437 soldiers and sailors and a female nurse.

USCG rescue cutters *20* and *21* were part of an 83-foot boat flotilla that saved lives and property in the Channel crossing and off the beaches of Normandy in June 1944.

The 83-foot cutters navigated in between the flanks of the LSTs and LCs as the larger craft brought tanks, other vehicles, artillery, ammunition, supplies and troops to the beaches and carried troops and naval personnel wounded and killed in action back to the larger ships at sea.

Coast Guard action occurred on the sea and shore. Cmdr. Quentin R. Walsh (USCG) led a heavily armed 16-member U.S. Navy and 50-troop Army commando team into the French port of Cherbourg. The reconnaissance unit killed snipers, freed 50 captured U.S. paratroopers, and took several hundred German prisoners.

At sea, the 492-foot attack transport USS *Bayfield* (APA-33), skippered by Captain Lyndon Spencer (USCG), landed troops on the beach and served as a hospital ship, treating several hundred wounded personnel. The *Bayfield* was the flagship of Rear Admiral Donald P. Moon (USN), the commander of the naval assault force. The *Bayfield* also served as command posts for U.S. Army and U.S. Army Air Force liaison officers. The *Bayfield* was the radio communications center for the invading naval, army, and air force units.

The attack troop transport USS *Joseph T. Dickman* (APA-13), under the command of Capt. Raymond Mauerman (USCG), lost seven landing craft but debarked 1,900 soldiers, 68 vehicles, and a load of explosives. After unloading, the *Dickman* got back to sea with 153 wounded naval and military personnel aboard.

The USS *Samuel Chase* (APA-26), under Capt. Edward E. Fritzche

A Coast Guard–manned LCVP landing craft from the USS *Samuel Chase* brings Army troops ashore on "Omaha Beach" at Normandy.

(USCG), put infantrymen, vehicles, and three Piper Cub scout planes ashore at Omaha Beach. Swamping, gunfire, mines, and creatively designed underwater impediments destroyed six *Chase* landing craft. None of the large 328-foot Coast Guard–manned LSTs stationed at British and American stations were destroyed or sunk, but several suffered battle damage and crew casualties. The LSTs sailed to England with wounded personnel and returned to Normandy with more troops, vehicles and even railroad freight cars. LST-*561* made 53 cross-Channel trips.

Coast Guard fleet commanders assumed enormous leadership responsibilities. Captain Miles H. Imlay (USCG) commanded USCG Flotilla 4, which included twenty-four 158-foot LCI(L)s. Mines and enemy gunfire destroyed four of the LCIs. The Flotilla 4 vessels served the multi-mission tasks of tugboats, firefighting, aids to navigation, channel guides, and transport ferries.[11]

The USS *Bayfield* can serve as a template for the combat missions performed by the attack transports. The 492-foot *Bayfield* was 70 feet in width and displaced 8,300 tons. The former merchant vessel was taken over by the U.S. Navy in 1943 and manned by 600 Coast Guard personnel under the command of Capt. Lyndon Spencer (USCG).

The *Bayfield* sailed across the English Channel from Britain's historic Plymouth Harbor on 5 June 1944 as part of a transport convoy to Utah Beach. The USS *Bayfield* carried more than 12 LCVPs, and sailed from its initial station 11 miles offshore to the beach to unload troops and cargo. The *Bayfield* served as the flagship and information center for Adm. Donald P. Moon (USN), provided logistical support and repairs to landing craft, and gave medical care to wounded Army and Navy personnel. The *Bayfield* also served as a treatment and dissemination center for captured German prisoners of war.[12] On 25 June 1944, the USS *Bayfield* (APA-33) returned to Britain. In the fall of 1944, APA-33 sailed to the Mediterranean as a U.S. Navy flagship and part of Task Force 87 in the invasion of southern France.[13]

The vicious German defense at Normandy exacted a heavy toll on the Allied naval and army forces. By the middle of June (1944), two weeks after D-Day, German mines and gunfire had sunk the U.S. Navy destroyers *Rich, Glennon, Meredith,* and *Corry* and two minesweepers, while damaging 25 other vessels in Adm. Moon's Task Force. Fast German torpedo boats, called "S" boats by the Axis (and "E" boats by the Allies) contributed to the collateral damage exacted on British and American naval vessels and crews. Among the survivors on the USS *Corry* (DD-463) was medical officer Lt. (jg) Howard A. Andersen. Lt. Andersen tended to wounded sailors as the *Corry* sank after German shelling and contact with a mine. He survived immersion into the cold Atlantic waters and was pulled from the water by a rescue boat. Later in the war, Lt. Andersen served with the Sixth Marine Division in the Pacific theater on Okinawa. After the war, Dr. Andersen joined the staff of the Mayo Clinic and was a professor at the Mayo Medical School until his retirement.[14]

Illustrative of the courage of U.S. Armed Forces teams in combat at Normandy, was the crew of Coast Guard patrol boat *CG-16*, commanded by Lt. (jg) R.V. McPhail (USCG). *CG-16* rescued a burning and sinking LCT under enemy fire. The LCT was carrying volatile ammunition, as Coast Guard volunteers went onboard the cargo vessel during the conflagration and rescued all of the wounded. Fifteen *CG-16* crewmembers and Lt. McPhail later received the Navy and Marine Corps Medal for bravery.

The naval component of Operation Overlord was called Operation Neptune. Cmdr. Kenneth Edwards, a British Royal Navy officer, paid tribute to another courageous rescue boat skipper, Lt. (jg) George Clark (USCG). As Cmdr. Edwards (RN) described the action, "Lt. Clarke [sic], of the United States Coast Guard Service ... drove his cutter (*CG-35*) through the flames and rescued the survivors of a British landing craft carrying high-octane petrol to the beach." The British Admiralty decorated Lt. Clark for his valor. Lt. Clark concisely and modestly described the event in his Coast Guard report: "Survivors, rescued five. Corpses, none. Comments, none."[15]

The danger, injuries, death, uncertainty, horror, and emotional strains of combat seem to enhance the levels of spirituality and faith of many battle participants. In those circumstances, commissioned officer chaplains contribute to troop morale. The uniformed clergy support members of the Armed Forces with counseling, prayers, and religious services. Chaplains serve the wounded, dying, and deceased with personal contact and religious rituals. The presence of the rabbis, ministers and priests among military personnel in combat zones is comforting but risky. During this war, chaplains suffered casualties in their own ranks in disproportionate numbers because they were often where the action was on land, sea, and in the air.

Military photographs are vivid testimonials to the good work that chaplains in the U.S. Armed Forces have performed in the past and present. Archival photographs pictured in the *D-Day Encyclopedia* illustrate a religious service aboard a Coast Guard–manned assault transport ship shortly before the Normandy invasion. Once the invasion commenced, chaplains went ashore with sailors and troops. One chaplain reported how he "landed from an LCI in ten feet of water and had to swim fifty yards ... and waded through a hail of death to the shore [where] I spent the first hours ministering to the wounded while we were pinned down on the dune line until enemy resistance was liquidated."[16]

On one fully loaded landing craft just prior to the D-Day invasion at the designated "H" hour, Capt. Fulmer Koon, the chaplain of the Fourth U.S. Army Division's Twelfth Infantry Regiment, was administering an ecumenical service for Protestant, Roman Catholic, and Jewish sailors and soldiers. Gunner's Mate Third Class William Sweeney (USCG) recalled the comforting religious services. From the deck of his Coast Guard cutter, GM3 Sweeney observed that the attack transport USS *Samuel Chase* (APA-26) used its blinker lights to signal: "Mass is going on."[17]

The preinvasion D-Day numbers of military personnel and naval craft are enormous, uncertain, and therefore controversial. The Allied military force, according to one source, consisted of "Free [anti–Vichy]" French, Polish, Belgian, Czech, Dutch, Norwegian, Canadian, British, and American personnel. More than half of the command force of the Allied commander, General Dwight D. Eisenhower (USA), was American, "roughly 1,700,000 soldiers, sailors, airmen and coastguardsmen."[18]

The D-Day Anglo-American invasion force which left the United Kingdom consisted of Coast Guard cutters, U.S. Navy minesweepers and destroyers, buoy tenders, barrage balloons attached to cables to discourage low flying enemy aircraft, fighter aircraft, 350-foot attack transports that carried an estimated 1,500 landing craft, motor vehicles, guns, tanks, supplies and equipment. Not counting small naval vessels and assorted boats, the naval force consisted of an estimated 702 warships. Including all of the landing craft onboard and afloat, and the smallest vessels, the total number of watercraft was calculated by one official U.S. Army military history to be around 5,000. Cmdr. Kenneth Edwards (RN), the eminent British D-Day historian, calculated the total number of Allied watercraft to be approximately 4,500.[19]

Lt. (jg) Francis X. Riley (USCG), in command of an LCI on the way to

Utah Beach, recalled the screams for help from drowning victims who had leaped or were blown off LCs into deep water with their heavy equipment. Some landing craft broached or were hit by enemy gunfire. Several amphibious tanks released from LSTs hit mines or just sank as waves tore apart their unreliable balloon floatation devices. Some soldiers survived by getting to the surface and inflating their personal life vests. LST officers who witnessed the loss of more than 20 tanks out of 50 kept their tanks onboard until their LSTs reached shore. "Wounded and shocked sailors and soldiers," floating amid dead bodies, "pleaded with us to pull them out of the water," Lt. Riley recalled. But the 24-year-old Coast Guard officer's orders were to "disembark the troops on time regardless of casualties."[20] One Navy crew swung their boat toward struggling survivors, but was cut off by a launch. The commander of the police boat yelled to the potential lifesavers over his loudspeaker, "You are not a rescue ship! Get on shore."[21]

As Coastguardsmen were being trained to operate the assorted landing craft ("Higgins boats") for the coming European invasion, Lieutenant General Omar Bradley (USA) expressed doubt that tanks from the LSTs could operate out of the soft beach sands of Normandy. British midget submarines were sent out to navigate between the German mines and structures placed in front of the beaches. A British naval officer spent a night on the beachfront getting core samples that proved the viability of the tank mission to Gen. Bradley's satisfaction. The beach sands were supported by solid bedrock.[22]

On 4 June 1944, General Eisenhower gave the order to send five separate Allied invasion fleets into action across the English Channel after having to postpone the first attempt on 3 June because of extreme weather conditions. Nonetheless, winds and seas were still challenging enough to render thousands of troops and sailors seasick during the Channel crossing.[23]

By 5 June 1944, the 7,000-ship armada was in place at assigned positions several miles offshore, poised to steam to the Normandy shores on 6 June. Fast destroyers patrolled the flanks of the fleet in search of German E-boats, the equivalent of the U.S. torpedo patrol (PT) boats so effective in the Pacific war. German submarines were a threat, as was the dreaded German Luftwaffe (Air Force) that, because of Berlin's logistical and tactical blunders, never materialized to the extent Allied war planners had feared.

Furthest out to sea were the huge battleships, cruisers, and destroyers that would bombard German artillery positions before the landing craft got to the beaches. French resistance groups had placed markers further inland to guide paratroop and glider landings to the most open and accessible locations on the east and west sides of the north-facing invasion front.[24] Sadly, hundreds of paratroop and glider crew casualties occurred when soldiers and fliers crashed in the dark of night into forests and swamps and in fields that had been purposely flooded by the enemy.

That the Normandy invasion took place at all in June of 1944 was a surprise to many observers and a testimonial to Allied communications and planning. In 1942, Admiral Ernest J. King (USN) and General George C. Marshall (USA) had pleaded with the British government to help plan and launch the invasion. The British resisted the pressure and insisted that the shortage of naval personnel, ground forces, aircraft, and sea vessels, especially landing craft, made the amphibious assault impossible to carry out successfully.

The landing craft designs were prepared in Britain and the United States, but most of the vessels would have to be built in U.S. shipyards. While the U.S. Navy was tasked with running the building program, U.S. Navy officers were not enthusiastic about building amphibious barges. The USN hierarchy preferred building and commanding oceangoing warships. Conversely, and not without contradiction, the Pacific theater commanders, Admiral Chester W. Nimitz (USN) and General Douglas MacArthur (USA) and the European Allied commander, General Dwight David "Ike" Eisenhower (USA) and his liaison, Adm. Harold R. Stark (USN), had different perspectives about the priorities, applications, and allocations of the landing craft that later proved so critical in the Normandy invasion and the insular war in the Pacific.

In 1943, the European amphibious invasion had been delayed again. But, in the early months of 1944, due to the organizational skills of British and American military and civilian leaders, the situational assessment was more positive. By the summer of 1944, the numbers of British, Canadian, American, French and Polish troops and Allied naval personnel seemed sufficient.

By General Eisenhower's calculations, Allied military equipment and vehicle inventories had grown significantly. Approximately 15,000 kinds of aircraft (combat, transport, and gliders) were available. The total number of military officers and men able to report for duty was about 2,876,000. An estimated 7,000 naval vessels now existed, ranging from warships to the critical landing craft that represented a plethora of styles, sizes, and functions. The Allied force complement was now considered sufficient for what some military experts predicted was only a 50 percent chance to prevail over the formidable German war machine embedded on the Western Front.[25]

Even the generally optimistic British leader, Prime Minister Winston Churchill, had expressed frustration and uncertainty over the invasion plan, wondering how "the fate of two great nations seems to be determined by some damn things called LSTs and LCIs," but every amphibious operation in the Atlantic and Pacific depended on these versatile and vulnerable craft.[26]

Covering the war was the dangerous job of civilian and military print and electronic (radio) journalists and cameramen. *Los Angeles Times* correspondent Tom Treanor covered the Coast Guard landing craft flotilla at Normandy and was later killed in France soon after his articles were published in June 1944.

Treanor covered the combat operations of USCG Flotilla No. One, under the command of Lt. Cmdr. Alex V. Steward, Jr. (USCGR). Flotilla One consisted of fifty 83-foot wooden rescue boats and their intrepid crews that pulled 1,000 Allied military personnel from the sea during the Normandy invasion. Treanor described the wet, cold conditions and rolling seas he and the 15-man cutter crews endured. "While jauntily flying the American flag and Coast Guard ensign," Treanor wrote, "the unarmed *match boxes* boldly sailed among the invasion fleets, plucking Allied soldiers, sailors, and flyers from the sea."[27]

Treanor sailed on an 83-foot craft, under the command of Lt. (jg) Raymond M. Rosenbloom (USCG), in rough waters from Britain, across the English Channel, and into the coastal waters of Normandy. During the rescue operations, the observant reporter noted how Coast Guard coxswains were trained to dress the wounds of troops, transfer able-bodied soldiers to landing craft headed for shore, and bring the bodies of deceased sailors and soldiers to the large transport and hospital ships several miles offshore.[28]

Boatswain's Mate Second Class Gene Oxley was on LCI(L) 85 under the command of Lt. (jg) Coit T. Hendley, Jr. (USCGR) as part of Flotilla Ten commanded by Capt. Miles H. Imlay (USCG). BM2 Oxley, a landing craft coxswain, earned the Silver Star for bravery in combat. In one instance, BM2 Oxley dove off his craft and held and secured a lifeline to guide heavily equipped soldiers to shore across water of uncertain and varied depths.

Interviewed by a reporter for the prestigious naval journal, *Sea Power* (November 1944), Oxley described how his LCI(L) was blown apart by German artillery and a mine attached to steel stakes the enemy had secured underwater close to shore. Already on shore, BM2 Oxley could not get back to the departing craft, which later capsized. The coxswain dug foxholes along the beach under German gunfire as several amphibious craft sent to rescue him were disabled or destroyed. Racing 100 yards, Oxley reached another LCI just as German artillery struck it and wiped out all onboard except him. A small boat sent out from a Navy destroyer finally got close enough to rescue Petty Officer Oxley.[29]

A.J. Liebling, a war correspondent for the *New Yorker,* exposed himself to danger on rough seas and combat action to report on LCI(L)-*88,* a landing craft under the command of Bronze Star winner Lt. Henry K. Rigg (USCG). Liebling's July 1944 article described the fear, courage, carnage, casualties, and lifesaving feats performed by the four officers and 29 crew members on the 155-foot LCI's trek across the English Channel to Normandy. LCI(L)-*88* was loaded with tanks, other vehicles, supplies, and 140 soldiers. Liebling described the skill of the coxswains who piloted the LCIs through minefields, artillery barrages, and enemy aircraft attacks to the beaches where cargo and troops were discharged and the equally dangerous trips back out to mother ships where casualties were taken for medical treatment or sea burial.

Photographer's Mate Second Class Seth Shepard (USCGR) got a bird's-eye view of the Normandy invasion while filming combat action from the conning tower of LCI(L)-*92.* Shepard was later wounded in action and transported

An LCI(L) convoy crossing the English Channel for the "D-Day" Normandy invasion in June 1944. The barrage balloons tethered to cables discouraged low-flying enemy aircraft attacks.

to England for medical treatment. Pho.M.2c Shepard preserved his account of Normandy on film and in a spirited written account.

Lt. Robert M. Salmon (USCGR), the LCI(L)-*92* skipper, later won a Silver Star for his naval leadership and skill. LCI(L)-*92* had sailed across the Atlantic from Norfolk, Virginia, and participated in the Mediterranean campaigns before steaming to Normandy. At Normandy, the crew of LCI(L)-*92* suffered a casualty count of six and the death of 41 soldiers before reaching shore. Coming into the beach, the LCI-*92* crew witnessed Coast Guard–manned LCI-*91* engulfed in smoke and flames and numerous Higgins boats ripped apart on the wooden and steel traps set by German troops. Petty Officer Shepard and his comrades hit the beach with the troops, took combat photographs, dodged sniper bullets, machine gun and artillery fire, dug foxholes, tended wounded military personnel, and got survivors back to the larger ships at sea.

Coast Guard photographer Shephard chronicled the courage of U.S. Navy, Army, and Coast Guard personnel under enemy fire, and the medical officers and pharmacist's mates onboard the hospital ships and ashore who did their work under primitive and hazardous conditions.[30]

U.S. Coast Guard, Navy, and Army combat reporters, photographers and artists, and their civilian counterparts, recorded the battle action at Normandy and throughout Europe and the Pacific. Lt. Cmdr. Jack Dixon (USCGR) wrote about dangers combat reporters, artists, and photographers faced in his aptly titled narrative, "Picturing the War." The photographs and paintings the combat illustrators provided were used for military analysis, public information, and the historical record.

Cmdr. Dixon related how a Coast Guard photographer at Salerno, Italy, took refuge in a foxhole 75 yards from shore, endured enemy bullets and mortar shells, and survived artillery shrapnel that burned into his life jacket. At Normandy, the same photographer leaped out of a landing craft and into the surf to record the battle action around him. It is no wonder that Coast Guard, Navy, and Army photographers and artists suffered dented helmets and casualties, and won awards and medals while preserving the valor of their comrades.[31]

U.S. Navy and Coast Guard personnel joined each other on mission teams. Ensign Joseph Vaghi (USN) was on the large Coast Guard ship LCI(L)-88, more than 10 miles offshore in heavy seas. LCI(L)-88 had experienced enemy combat fire while taking troops ashore on Sicily and Italy. Now LCI-88 was taking Ensign Vaghi and Company C of Navy Beach Battalion 6 to Omaha Beach. Vaghi was assigned the responsibilities of beach master. The Navy Beach team would use blinkers, flags, and megaphones to get the equipment and men of the Sixteenth Infantry Regiment of the First Infantry Division (USA) safely on shore, and then they would set up emergency medical aid stations.

The flat-bottom, 300-ton LCI-88 barge had a Coast Guard crew complement of 33 and space for 140 other military personnel, including Ensign Vaghi's platoon and a contingent of amphibious engineers. Personnel and troops on LCI(L)-88, and LCs in proximity were alone with their thoughts, some suffering seasickness. "Everywhere you looked," Vaghi recalled, "you saw ships … ships, ships, ships."[32]

Ensign Vaghi's shipmates got to shore safely, crossed more than 250 yards of shale beachhead under enemy fire, and struggled to the sand dune line. Several Coast Guard crew members on the LCI-88 were not so fortunate. A coxswain in swimming trunks and wearing a helmet stepped off his barge holding a guideline for troops to follow: "A shell tore him apart." Then an anti-tank shell destroyed the starboard bow of LCI(L)-88, killing one of the Coast Guard crew that had lowered the ramp, and wounding others.[33]

Coast Guard photographers have immortalized D-Day at the Omaha Beach site of the designated Normandy beachfront sectors. The combat cameramen captured scenes from the front of LCVPs with bow ramps down, and from stations onshore. Photographs of tanks and troops heading to shore under fire have recorded the danger, courage, bloodshed, and victories associated with Normandy. Coastguardsman E.R. Mecher was photographed taking possession of an abandoned German 88mm PaK 43/41 "Scheunentor" gun that

Crewmen and troops on a landing craft heading to a Normandy beach in June 1944.

had been removed from a bunker. The reinforced enemy bunkers were also called casemates, pillboxes, and machine-gun pits.[34]

Landing craft sped to the Normandy shores with bow ramps up, lettered with "No Smoking" warnings in the volatile environment of fuel, enemy ordnance, ammunition, enemy shell fire, and the flames and oil around them in waters congested by damaged or destroyed vessels. LCVPs generally carried one officer and 31 enlisted personnel sitting three abreast in eleven rows. Troops carried rifles, wire cutters, automatic weapons, mortar, and bazookas. Rifles were encased in waterproof plastic wrap that was quickly discarded before the troops disembarked from the landing craft. A second team leader, usually a noncommissioned officer, sat in the back of the barge in case the officer at the front of the LC was wounded or killed in enemy action after the ramp was lowered. Navy and Coast Guard crews and coxswains piloted the barges to shore.[35]

The First Division of the Sixteenth Regimental Combat Team (USA) loaded into an LCVP off the Coast Guard–manned USS *Samuel Chase* (APA-26). The soldiers were loaded onboard the assault transport directly into the landing craft and then lowered by ropes and pulleys into the sea. That method was used because the heavy equipment load carried by each soldier made descending rope ladders over the side of the *Chase*[36] problematic, and, in heavy seas, potentially catastrophic.

The first assault wave on Omaha Beach occurred in the early morning hours between 9530 and 0700. The LSVP from the USS *Samuel Chase*, piloted by Coxswain D. Nivens (USCG), was hit by German machine-gun fire that detonated explosives onboard the landing craft. Nonetheless, the barge beached safely onshore and then got back to the *Chase*. The second and final wave on D-Day by the LCVPs from the USS *Samuel Chase* occurred at approximately 0730.[37]

In the initial chaos of D-Day, some landing craft drifted off course and landed outside the assigned sectors at locations with unexpected depths, sandbars, and enemy concentrations. Company L, Sixteenth Infantry (USA), landed to the far east of their assigned Omaha Beach sector, near an area called Fox Green. With the changing tides at 0800 hours, several LCIs missed the shore markers and drifted off course. At around 1015, landing craft skippers found gaps in the German obstacle course and sped to the beaches.

At 1100 hours, the Coast Guard–manned LCT-*30* crashed through the obstacles to Fox Green beach. Other landing craft coxswains followed. When LCI-*83* (USCG) was unable to land the Twentieth Engineer Battalion at 0830, its troops were transferred to LCVPs that made it to shore. LCI-*83* finally got to shore at 1100 hours, but an artillery shell struck the ship, damaged a ramp, and killed seven crewmembers. While under enemy fire, the intrepid LCT-*30* crew, under the supporting barrage of a U.S. Navy destroyer, responded with its own machine guns and cannons. LCT-*30* made it to the beach, unloaded the troops, and then abandoned the heavily damaged ship. During the beach assault, enemy fire and obstacles destroyed four LCTs, two LCIs, and twenty-two LCVPs.[38]

Skilled Coast Guard and Navy landing craft and landing ship tank crews accomplished successful missions on D-Day and subsequent days. But crew and troop casualties accompanied the successes. Landing craft were destroyed and abandoned because of enemy gunfire, mines, obstacles, high surf and storms. Changing tides prevented some LCs and LSTs from backing off the Normandy beaches.

Lieutenant G.F. Hutchinson (USCGR), the commanding officer of LCI-*83*, could not reach Omaha beach on 6 June at 0830 because of tides and obstacles. Thirty-six troops were placed on a small boat and brought to shore. A German shell hit the LCI, killing three men and wounding thirteen. Lt. Hutchinson tried landing again. A mine blew up, wounding troops and crew members. The uninjured soldiers got to shore. The LCI crew brought the wounded ashore to medical stations. The badly damaged LCI-*83* relied on its pumps to stay afloat. Guided by an escort ship, LCI-*83* got back to England for repairs and future missions.

LCI-*84* damage control crews salvaged several LCs, kept others afloat with repairs and pump systems, fought shipboard fires, and pushed damaged and sinking vessels ashore. LST-*21* (Lt. Charles M. Brookfield, USCGR) served with

British units. Arriving at Normandy from Britain on 6 June 1944 at 1210, LST-*21* unloaded six amphibious vehicles, took on wounded soldiers, survived two bombing attacks, and returned to England. On 10 June, during another air attack, LST-*21* discharged 40 vehicles and 146 troops.

Lt. (jg) Francis X. Riley (USCG), the commanding officer of LCI-*319*, towed two ammunition ships out of mined waters in a storm off Normandy on 10 June 1944. Lt. Riley later received the Bronze Star for his actions. Lt. Cmdr. L.I. Reilly (USCG), in command of LST-*261* while serving British units, made 53 Channel crossings transferring wounded troops to medical units, and loaded and unloaded military equipment and supplies. While commanding LCI-*91*, Lt. (jg) Arend Vyn, Jr. (USCGR) traversed stakes with attached mines to reach Omaha Beach. A crew member entered the water with a guide rope to lead troops to the beach. While backing off the beach, LCI-*91* hit a mine that exploded and killed several men. Lt. Vyn moved his ship 100 yards down shore and unloaded 200 troops. Another explosion caused hull damage and extensive fires that forced the abandonment of LCI-*91*.

Lt. Robert M. Salmon (USCGR) navigated LCI-*92* through mine-laden waters to Omaha Beach. An explosion ignited the ship's fuel and fires spread to the upper deck. While the crew battled the flames and a subsequent explosion, 192 troops were unloaded under German rifle and machine gun fire. When retraction from the beach became impossible, LCI-*92* had to be abandoned. LCI-*93* commander, Lt. (jg) Budd B. Bornholf (USCGR), landed troops on the first trip with little enemy resistance. On the next trip, enemy artillery killed one soldier onboard LCI-*93* and wounded four. The Coast Guard crew suffered five shrapnel casualties. Ten direct enemy shell hits during low tide while the stern of the barge was mired on a sand bar forced the abandonment of LCI-*93*. Small boats came alongside to rescue the wounded first, and then the crew.[39]

The attack transport ship USS *Bayfield* (APA-33), under the command of Capt. Lyndon Spencer (USCG), was the headquarters of Maj. Gen. Raymond O. Barton (USA), the Fourth Infantry Division commander. Troops and sailors crammed the APA. The deputy Division commander, Brig. Gen. Theodore Roosevelt, Jr., the son of former president Theodore Roosevelt, joined his soldiers under enemy fire on the Normandy beaches. Hours into the battle, wounded American and German soldiers were brought back to the *Bayfield* and tended to by U.S. Navy pharmacist's mates and medical officers.[40]

The LCVPs were lowered over the sides of the transport ships with the young coxswains, mostly young Coastguardsmen, many just teenagers, aboard. Once the LCVPs were in the water, the coxswains started their engines and circled the ships as the soldiers descended the rope ladders of the transport vessels.[41]

The LCVPs disembarked American soldiers on the beaches and brought wounded and dead military personnel back to the ships. Despite the fact that

U.S. Coast Guard and U.S. Navy–manned Landing Ship Tanks (LSTs) discharge cargo and vehicles on Normandy beaches.

the U.S. Armed Forces were racially segregated for most of World War II, African-American naval personnel were on deck to lift the wounded in wire baskets from the LCVPs to the ship. A Coast Guardsman tried to steady one of the baskets on the way up to the ship and literally received a blood bath over his helmet, face, and clothing. An officer yelled down to the landing craft crew ordering them to take the dead soldiers back to the beach for burial. The landing craft coxswain refused to obey the ridiculous order.[42]

For his skillful and courageous combat command of the USS *Bayfield*, the flagship of Adm. Donald P. Moon (USN), Capt. Lyndon Spencer (USCG) later received the Legion of Merit.[43]

The Normandy assault forces were estimated to comprise sixty 83-foot Coast Guard rescue cutters, 1,089 LCVPs, 229 LSTs, 480 LCMs, 911 LCTs which were smaller that LSTs), and 245 LCIs. To protect the landing craft and LSTs by bombarding entrenched onshore enemy strongholds, warships further out to sea included two gunboats, 73 destroyers, six battleships, and 23 cruisers. American and British air support capacity lined up on English airfields included more than 5,400 fighter planes and 5,000 medium and heavy bombers.[44]

As LCI-*85* headed toward the Normandy coast, Seaman First Class Robert A. Giguere (USN) of Sixth Beach Battalion described a mine explosion that killed and wounded several sailors. "Medical men of the Sixteenth Infantry

(USA)," SN1 Giguere explained, were "helping with the casualties and the Coast Guard started putting the fire out."[45] Winds and currents made landing craft trips to predetermined shore sites problematic. Five-foot waves made even the strongest and most experienced Coast Guard and Navy coxswains unable to prevent drifting off target. The slow landing craft made good targets for German gun crews. LCI-*85* grounded on enemy obstructions and gunfire started fires on the vessel. The Coast Guard reservist running LCI-*85* saw that his crew placed the wounded on another vessel before the LCI-*85* sank.[46]

On 5 June 1944, Motor Machinist Mate First Class Clifford Lewis (USCG) wrote in his diary (on 5 June 1944) that the skipper on his LCI-(L)-*94* called the crew into mess quarters and put maps and photographs of the enemy strength and obstacles they were about to face on the tables. MMM1 Lewis recalled how the commanding officer "wished us the best of luck ... and checked over all our names for correct serial numbers and beneficiaries."[47]

In the entire Normandy operation, Coast Guard crews ran 99 vessels. The largest naval contingent run by the Coast Guard in one sector was Assault Group O-1 at Omaha Beach under the command of Captain Edward H. Fritzsche (USCG). Capt. Fritzsche was the skipper of the USS *Samuel Chase* (APA-26), he also commanded two transport ships, six LSTs, six large LCIs, and 97 other vessels. In addition, there were Coast Guard LSTs at Juno, Gold, and Sword beaches in the Canadian and British combat sectors.[48]

The U.S. Coast Guard and U.S. Navy paid a heavy price as part of the Allied successes at Omaha Beach on 6 June 1944. It has been estimated that U.S. naval demolition units, beach battalions, landing craft crews, and other shore parties suffered a total casualty count of 539 personnel killed, wounded, and missing in action on that fateful day. More casualties would come on subsequent days and missions.[49]

14

The Aleutians and the Bering Sea

The World War II combat theaters in the Pacific Ocean encompassed a vast maritime region stretching from the Bering Sea and Alaska's Aleutian Islands in the cold Northern Hemisphere to the warm waters of the South Pacific and the Philippines, Dutch East Indies, New Guinea, Australia, New Zealand, and the smaller islands and atolls across the Pacific.

The Pacific Ocean manifests weather and climate patterns which range from Arctic and Polar frigidity to the heat, monsoons, and typhoons of the tropics. The differences in temperatures, winds, and currents give rise to tempestuous seas that belie the literal meaning of the word "pacific," which denotes calm.

The Pacific theater posed enormous logistical and tactical problems for Allied and Japanese military and naval forces. The Allied armed forces suffered high casualties in the Pacific war because of the fanatical and suicidal Japanese resistance on desolate islands, and the logistical and tactical challenges of waging amphibious warfare in the insular Pacific across barrier reefs, changing tides, and steamy jungles.

The U.S. Army and Army Air Force, and the U.S. Navy, Marines and Coast Guard faced Japanese aircraft, ships, boats, submarines, and troops from the South Pacific to the inhospitable Aleutian Island chain that ran in a south-southwest direction from its geologic connection to Alaska, then a territory of the United States. Alaska shares its eastern border with Canada, a U.S. ally and member of the British Commonwealth. Canadian air, naval, and military forces joined U.S. Armed Forces in the Aleutian campaign as part of the Allied Pacific Offensive of 1942–1945.

The following dates indicate the start of Allied offensive military operations against Japanese occupying forces in the Aleutians. The Japanese bombed the port of Dutch Harbor in June 1942. The military campaign involved the islands of Kiska (August 1943) and Attu (May 1943). Japanese land and sea forces attacked the Aleutians (June 1942) in an unsuccessful attempt to divert U.S. forces from attacking Midway Island in the Central Pacific in the same month.[1]

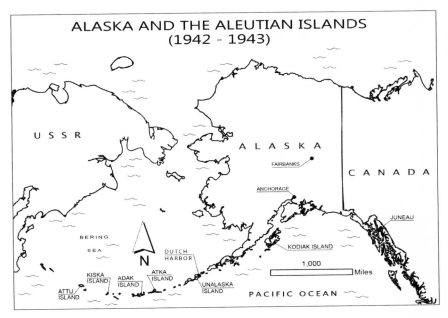

ALASKA AND THE ALEUTIAN ISLANDS
(1942 - 1943)

Admiral Samuel Eliot Morison (USNR), the noted Harvard historian, chronicled the history of U.S. Navy and Coast Guard operations in World War II. Morison asserted that American naval and military forces in the Alaskan theater had insufficient personnel and resources to quickly expel the Japanese from the Aleutians, but just enough to keep the enemy pinned down, isolated, and deprived of supplies from Japan.

American policy makers chose to concentrate their attention and provisions on the war in the Central and South Pacific. U.S. Army, Marine, and Navy commanders in the Aleutians "felt neglected," Morison claimed, especially Rear Adm. Robert A. Theobald (USN), commander, North Pacific Force. Admiral Theobald's flag headquarters was ashore on Kodiak Island. Rear Adm. William W. Smith (USN) commanded Adm. Theobald's few cruisers, destroyers, submarines, and, Morison noted, "flock of Coast Guard cutters and other small craft."

Although neglected, and historically unheralded, U.S. and Canadian naval and military forces fought bravely in horrendous climatic and sea conditions. The Allies eventually forced the Japanese retreat from the islands onto waiting transports under blankets of fog.

One example will suffice to illustrate Japanese tenacity, Allied aggressiveness, and combat casualties. In the final assault on Attu Island (19–29 May 1943), Colonel Yamazaki's Japanese troops clashed with American forces under the command of Colonel Wayne C. Zimmerman (USA). The Japanese attack commenced at 0330 on 29 May. One thousand screaming Japanese soldiers armed with guns and bayonets overran two military posts and entered a medical station, where they killed Lt. Col. James Fish (USA) and stabbed patients and medical personnel. The enemy was driven off by a U.S. Army engineer detachment. Over the next two days the remaining Japanese forces were killed in battle or committed suicide. Five hundred Japanese killed themselves with their own hand grenades. The human cost of recapturing Attu was 2351 Japanese killed and 28 captured. Out of an amphibious landing force of 11,000 Americans, 1200 were wounded and 600 died.

Attu was only the third amphibious operation of World War II. Admiral Morison described the sacrifices and courage of brave military personnel and the eventual success of the mission. Professor Morison also concluded that military commanders learned important lessons from ineffective naval bombardments, inefficient landing craft and transport operations, and examples of inadequate training and leadership.[2] Those lessons were later applied to the amphibious campaigns in the Atlantic and Pacific.

In the spring and summer of 1943 troop and fleet operations occurred in the Aleutians and north to the Bering Sea. The combat theater would include the Aleutians, and the Komandorski Islands located between Attu and the Kamchatka peninsula in the USSR. A group of islands stretching south of the Kamchatka peninsula provided the invaders with a base at Paramushiro in the Kurile Islands of Japan.

Professor and naval historian Admiral Samuel Eliot Morison (USNR) wrote that the military operations in the Aleutian region of "almost perpetual mist and snow" accomplished nothing "of importance or had any appreciable effect on the outcome of the war. Both sides (American and Japanese) would have done well," Morison asserted, "to leave the Aleutians to the few Aleuts unfortunate enough to live there."[3] Coast Guard historian Malcolm F. Willoughby partially agreed with Morison; he wrote that after the Aleutian combat zone quieted down, "the Aleutians ceased to be of military or historical significance for the rest of the war." But Willoughby found a positive outcome in the Aleutian war between America and Japan: "Nevertheless, the campaign furnished bases which added measurably to the security of Alaska and the west coasts of Canada and the United States, and gave Americans the initiative in the North Pacific."[4]

"Finally," Professor Morison writes, "on 26 March 1943, a really interesting event broke: The Battle of the Komandorski Islands."[5] A small naval task force commanded by Rear Adm. Charles H. McMorris (USN) fought a much larger Japanese naval force in a three-hour daytime battle inside an 8 to 12 mile shooting range. Adm. McMorris was on the flagship USS *Richmond* (Capt. T.W. Waldschmidt, USN), and was joined by the cruiser USS *Salt Lake City* (Capt. Bertram J. Rodgers, USN) and four destroyers under Capt. Ralph S. Riggs (USN). This U.S. Navy task force group intercepted the Japanese Northern Area Force of four cruisers and four destroyers commanded by Vice Adm.

Hosogaya of the Imperial Japanese Navy (IJN). The battle zone was located between the Aleutian island of Attu and the Kamchatka Peninsula of the Soviet Union.

In concentrated battle action the *Salt Lake City* suffered three hits by IJN warships that flooded the engine room and stopped the heavy cruiser dead in the water. The *Salt Lake City* was then concealed by a protective smoke screen from the USS *Richmond*, and Adm. McMorris ordered three of his destroyers to close in on the advancing enemy naval force and hit the Japanese vessels with torpedoes.

Under fire from the U.S. destroyers, and fearing the arrival of U.S. bombers from Dutch Harbor, Adm. Hosogaya broke off the action and headed west toward the insular port of Paramushiro, south of the Kamchatka Peninsula. Adm. Hosogaya thus deprived himself of a potential naval victory and suffered recrimination upon his return to Japan.[6]

After the outbreak of the war in Europe (1939), and the attack on Pearl Harbor (1941), the U.S. Army and Navy expanded their presence in Alaska. The Army and Navy cooperated closely with the Coast Guard, given the experience the USCG and its predecessor, the U.S. Revenue Cutter Service, had in Alaskan and Bering Sea waters since 1867. Coast Guard expertise in patrolling, search and rescue, law enforcement, aids to navigation, and the transportation of supplies, military personnel, and American officials to Alaska gave the Service regional credibility with the other U.S. Armed Forces, just as the Coast Guard benefited from U.S. Army, Navy and Marine platforms, personnel, and expertise.

In 1942, the United States and Canada cooperated through their mutual defense agreements, and expanded bases and radio communications throughout the region. The U.S. Army constructed and expanded infrastructure at strategic sites and completed the Alaskan-Canadian (ALCAN) Highway. The U.S. Navy expanded its base at Dutch Harbor in the Aleutians and set up submarine and air bases at Sitka and Kodiak. The United States and Canada had limited contacts with the Soviet Union. Soviet boundaries extended from the Bering Sea and down the Pacific Rim to Japan, although the USSR honored its nonaggression pact with Tokyo.

To meet the commercial and military needs of that vast and volatile maritime realm, the Coast Guard upgraded and expanded the aids to navigation systems, including lighthouses, buoys, and beacons. U.S. Navy PBY amphibious aircraft expanded the boundaries of the reconnaissance patrol areas in anticipation of an expected Japanese attack.

In May 1942, Capt. Ralph C. Parker (USNR), the Alaskan Sector commander, had the responsibility of defending against Japanese air and naval attacks. Captain Parker initially had at his disposal only two old U.S. Navy destroyers, three Coast Guard cutters, several converted fishing trawlers, and ten PBY Catalina aircraft. The Coast Guard would lose none of its cutters in the coming battle, but several naval landing craft would be destroyed in the shoal waters and surf and on beaches.

Rear Admiral Robert A. Theobald (USN), the North Pacific Force commander, had a few cruisers, destroyers, submarines, Coast Guard cutters, and small boats in his task force. Brigadier General William O. Butler, the Eleventh U.S. Army Air Force commander, had a few medium bombers, PBYs, and fighter aircraft at his disposal. Major General S.B. Buckner (USA), the Alaskan Sector commander, had a garrison at Fort Morrow on the Alaskan peninsula.[7]

In May 1942, Japanese naval forces attacked Midway Island to the south, and sent another task force north to the Aleutians. The Aleutian task force consisted of Japanese submarines, two carriers transporting fighter-bombers, two heavy cruisers, and several destroyers.

U.S. Coast Guard cutters were part of Admiral Theobald's task force. The 165-foot CGC *Onondaga* (WPG-79), under Lt. Cmdr. Stewart B. Mehlman (USCG), was the only cutter in Dutch Harbor. Other cutters in the area were the 125-foot CGC *Bonham* commanded by Lt. (jg) William C. Gill (USCG), the 240-foot CGC *Haida* (Cmdr. Norman H. Leslie, USCG), and the 165-foot Coast Guard cutters *Cyane* (Lt. Cmdr. Leslie B. Tollaksen, USCG) and *Aurora* (*Lt.* (jg) Frank M. McCabe, USCG).

Dutch Harbor was not up to full strength when the Japanese attacked. The military complement included two U.S. Army units, a few U.S. Marines, half a dozen U.S. Navy ships, and the USCGC *Onondaga*. At dawn on 3 June 1942, crew members on the *Onondaga* and the USS *Gillis* (Lt. Cmdr. Norman Garton, USN) observed 17 Japanese carrier fighter aircraft reconnaissance and attack planes coming through the mist and flying over Dutch Harbor. The *Onondaga* gunners fired several hundred rounds of ammunition at the enemy aircraft and drove several off. Other Japanese airplanes were shot down by naval gunfire. No Coastguardsmen were wounded or killed in the action, but buildings burned, two USN PBYs were unaccounted for, and 25 sailors and soldiers died. Several Japanese aircraft were shot down or damaged, and many were believed not to have gotten back to their carriers. PBY pilot Lt. L.D. Campbell (USN) was shot down by a Japanese Zero fighter plane, but he was later rescued by the 125-foot USCGC *Nemaha* (WSC-148).[8]

A Royal Canadian Air Force (RCAF) plane flying from a base near Ketchikan, Alaska, sighted and damaged a Japanese submarine on 8 July 1942. The 125-foot USCGC *McLane* (Lt. Ralph Burns, USCG) and the Coast Guard–crewed U.S. Navy *YP-251* (Lt. Neils P. Thomsen, USCG) searched for the enemy submarine. On 9 July the CGC *McLane* (WSC-146) dropped a depth charge at a likely site, found an electronic contact a few hours later, and dropped four additional depth charges. *YP-251* and the *McLane* evaded a submarine torpedo assumed to have come from the stricken enemy vessel. In a subsequent search pattern, *YP-251* actually made physical contact with the submerged submarine, and the two American naval vessels dropped more depth charges. On 10

July, floating debris indicated the submarine *(RO-32)* had broken apart. The Legion of Merit was awarded the two American naval officers for their intrepid and skillful seamanship. Earlier in the month (on 4 July 1942), U.S. Navy submarines had sunk three IJN destroyers; and on 31 August the surviving sailors from a torpedoed IJN submarine were captured as prisoners of war.[9]

The IJN submarine fleet was not finished yet. Between 27 August and 16 December, *RO-61* torpedoed the USS *Casco*, inflicting 25 casualties on the Navy seaplane tender. A Navy PBY warplane depth-bombed the submarine. The USS *Reid* forced the *RO-61* to the surface with two depth charges and the destroyer gun crew destroyed the vessel.

On 12 January 1943, more than 2,000 American troops landed on Amchitka Island after the U.S. Army Air Force carried out a bombing support mission. The USS *Arthur Middleton* (APA-25), commanded by Capt. Paul K. Perry (USCG), was one of the transports that supplied the landing craft that carried troops, equipment, supplies, and vehicles ashore. A gale-force wind ("williwaw") struck the invading naval force and capsized, sunk, destroyed or broached several landing craft, which crews then had to unload by hand in near-freezing water.

The destroyer *Worden* (Lt. Cmdr. William G. Pogue, USN) was driven by the gale into rocks near the harbor. Fourteen sailors drowned abandoning the warship. A landing craft from the *Arthur Middleton* (Lt. Cmdr. R.R. Smith, USCG) and rescue boats from the USS *Dewey* succeeded in rescuing 169 enlisted men and six officers from the USS *Worden*. Five Coastguardsmen later received the Navy and Marine Corps Medal for their actions in the treacherous seas.

The USS *Arthur Middleton* was later driven aground by the storm, and used its deck guns to fight off armed Japanese float planes based on Kiska Island. The *Middleton* was refloated three months later and repaired at Dutch Harbor and Bremerton, Washington.[10]

After the Komandorski Islands campaign, the 2400 enemy troops on the mountainous island of Attu were cut off from Japanese supplies and reinforcements. American forces began their air and sea attack upon Attu on 11 May 1943. Coastguardsmen joined the U.S. Navy crews of five transport ships, participated in landing operations during the attack, and took wounded military personnel back to the transports.

The number of Allied and enemy forces involved in the Aleutian campaign was significant. By July 1943 there were about 1,900 U.S. Navy and 15,000 U.S. Army personnel on just the island of Kiska. Rear Adm. M. Kimura had evacuated more than 5,000 Japanese troops from Kiska under cover of fog on 28 July. On 10 July aircraft took off from the new base on Attu and bombed the IJN naval base at Paramushiro in the Japanese Kurile islands.

Aleutian waters were still dangerous in August 1943. The USS *Abner Read* (Cmdr. Thomas Burrowes, USN) hit a Japanese mine and lost its stern. Forty-seven crew members were wounded, and 70 were killed or missing in action.[11]

Canadian military forces aided United States troops in the Aleutian campaign. In the summer of 1943, the First Special Service Force of 35,000 American and Canadian commandos invaded Kiska Island to find that the 6,000 Japanese troops had already evacuated. Twenty-one military personnel lost their lives to the "friendly fire" of their comrades in arms. A destroyer and seventy sailors were lost when the ship hit a Japanese mine. The Royal Canadian Air Force (RCAF) and the Royal Canadian Navy (RCN) took part in military operations in the Gulf of Alaska and the Aleutians.[12]

Some historians have argued that the Aleutian campaign, while achieving some tactical and strategic successes, was largely unnecessary and unproductive. But James F. Dunnigan and Albert A. Nofi contend that by ridding the islands of Japanese bases, the United States gained an efficient route over which to fly 6.000 Lend-Lease aircraft to the USSR.[13] Malcolm F. Willoughby argues that the Aleutian campaign gave the United States "an unbroken string of naval and air bases stretching from Ketchikan to Attu. There were no Japanese left in the Aleutians, and they never returned."[14] Although critical of the Aleutian campaign, Samuel Eliot Morison seemed to support Willoughby's premise with this statement: "Ironically, one of the main reasons for these efforts in the Aleutians was the desire of the [United States military] Joint Chiefs of Staff to expedite aid to Russia in the expected event of her going to war with Japan."[15]

The University of Alabama maritime historian Robert Erwin Johnson is the author of several articles and books on U.S. Coast Guard and U.S. Navy history. Professor Johnson was a Quarter Master Third Class (QM3) on the 240-foot CGC *Haida* (WPG-45) from July 1941 to March 1944. The *Haida* was assigned escort and weather patrol duty in the Alaska Sector, which covered the Aleutian Islands and Bering Sea. Professor Johnson's compelling autobiography of his World War II experiences provides a more complete understanding of the diversity of naval operations in the North Pacific combat theater.[16]

Johnson was assigned to the Northwestern Sea Frontier (NSF) on the CGC *Haida*. Other cutters assigned to the Alaska Sector of the NSF included the 165-foot antisubmarine and escort patrol cutters *Onondaga* (WPG-79), *Atalanta* (WPC-102), *Aurora* (WPC-103), and *Cyane* (WPC-105).[17] The CGC *Onondaga* was attacked by Japanese aircraft carrier planes at Dutch Harbor, Alaska, on 3 June 1942. No Coast Guard casualties were suffered.[18] Petty Officer Johnson wrote about one of the first *Haida* missions he participated in: the rescue of the crew of the *YP-86*, a storm damaged patrol boat that nearly sank. The *Haida* escorted *YP-86* to Dutch Harbor.[19]

While the *Haida* was generally 70 to 100 miles from enemy ships and island troops, the crew stood constant watch because submarines could always be close by. The *Haida was* out to sea when Japanese carrier planes bombed Dutch Harbor. The attack cost the lives of 43 American military personnel. On

USCGC *Haida* (WPG-45). The 240-foot cutter carried out escort and weather patrol missions on the Bering Sea Patrol and Northwestern (Pacific) Sea Frontier from 1941 to 1945. The *Haida* was stationed at Juneau, Alaska.

12 June 1942, the crew of the CGC *Haida* returned to Dutch Harbor to inspect the damage at the U.S. Navy base, the U.S. Army base at Ft. Mears, and the nearly completed aircraft hanger.

Johnson's skipper on the *Haida*, Commander Robert C. Sarratt, was a by-the-book taskmaster who ordered on deck exercises to keep his sailors fit. Cmdr. Sarratt preferred to respond to suspect enemy submarine contacts with four single barrel K-guns that tossed 300-pound charges off the port and starboard sides of the cutter. The deck K-guns became Cmdr. Surratt's weapon of choice after an earlier incident in which a released 600-pound depth charge off the fantail exploded too close to the cutter and caused a leak in the steering engine room. A "double mousetrap" weapon forward of the main mast launched rocket propelled antisubmarine charges ahead of the cutter.[20]

The Aleutian–Bering Sea patrols afforded cutter crews a variety of challenging weather conditions. Professor Johnson chronicled the plight of the large attack transport USS *Arthur Middleton* (APA-25). After rescuing crews from other storm-wrecked naval vessels in a March 1943 storm, the *Middleton was* blown aground. A "williwaw" gale struck the Coast Guard–manned U.S. Navy ship in Amchitka Harbor. The *Arthur Middleton*, under the command of Lt. Cmdr. R.R. Smith (USCG), was eventually towed to safe harbor and repaired; it went on to participate in several of the most significant amphibious assaults in the Pacific island campaigns.[21]

QM3 Johnson was also on North Pacific weather patrols in the Alaskan-Bering Sea region. The drifting CGC *Haida* crew manned battle stations, ever on the alert for Japanese submarines and air attacks. Radio silence had to be periodically broken to transmit weather information to naval vessels and military stations ashore. The weather station missions required refueling at sea by USN tankers ("oilers"), the release of tethered helium balloons and battery powered electronic equipment, and the expertise of the U.S. Navy aerographer's mate assigned to the *Haida*. Some patrols were conducted out of the port of Seattle, Washington. The December-January (1943–1944) weather patrol period exposed the *Haida* to high seas, gales, and snowstorms.[22]

After the war, the USCGC *Haida* met the fate of many other old naval vessels. While doing historical research at U.S. Coast Guard Headquarters in Washington, D.C., in 1983, Professor Robert Erwin Johnson discovered the following information in a 1953 Coast Guard Bulletin: "The 30 year old cutter Haida, veteran of 10 Bering Sea patrols, was recently reduced to scrap metal at the Puget Sound Bridge and Dredging Company." A retired Coast Guard crew member who observed the destruction said it was "like watching an autopsy on an old friend."[23]

Before we leave the Aleutian-Alaskan-Bering Sea theater of operations, mention must be made of a classified mission not revealed until after the war. The secret training mission in the Aleutian Islands was intended to prepare the naval forces of the United States and the Soviet Union for the contemplated invasion of Japan. United States Army and Marine Corps personnel also contributed to the mission. The Soviet-American program was called "Project Hula."

Before the end of World War II, United States Navy and United States Coast Guard personnel secretly trained 12,000 Russian officers and enlisted men to operate the amphibious vessels scheduled for transfer to the Soviet Union under the American Lend-Lease program.[24]

Richard A. Russell was a U.S. Army Specialist Five, and then became a lieutenant in the Army National Guard. Russell earned undergraduate and graduate degrees in American diplomatic and military history at Pennsylvania State University and studied Russian history at Georgetown University. Russell utilized that academic and military background to research and publish *Project Hula*. Between 1993 and 1996, Russell participated in the Soviet Naval Archives Project and did research at the Russian Central Naval Archives in Gatchina.[25]

Between 1905 and 1939, Tsarist Russia and its political successor, the Union of Soviet Socialist Republics (USSR), experienced several naval and military engagements against Japan. The Soviets signed a nonaggression pact with Japan in April 1941 to protect its Eastern Empire from attack.

Soviet dictator Joseph Stalin was anxious to preserve the Japanese neutrality treaty after Germany, Japan's Axis partner, invaded the Soviet Union in

June 1941. After the German invasion of the Soviet Union, British prime minister Winston Churchill and U.S. president Franklin Roosevelt sent military equipment and supplies to Stalin, temporarily ending the adversarial relationship that had existed between the USSR and the West since the Communist takeover of Russia in the 1917 Bolshevik Revolution.

As early as 1942, Roosevelt and Churchill encouraged Stalin's participation in the war against Japan. The two Allied leaders speculated that the Japanese might invade the Soviet Union on its Asian perimeter, suggested the establishment of Allied bomber bases in Siberia would be strategically advantageous, and said the 1942 Japanese invasion of the Aleutian Islands might require military cooperation between the Anglo-Americans and Russia.

The 1943 recapture of the Aleutians by American and Canadian forces did not completely diminish the Japanese threat in the North Pacific. In October 1943, the Soviets informed U.S. secretary of state Cordell Hull that Stalin would commence the war against Japan after Germany was defeated. In November and December 1943, Soviet officials reiterated their intention to declare war on Japan after Germany's defeat, and they promised to provide intelligence information about Japan to the Allies.[26]

In mid–January 1945, Admiral Ernest J. King (USN) informed Vice Admiral Frank Fletcher (USN), the commander of the North Pacific Force (NPF), that 250 American naval vessels were going to be transferred to the USSR between April and December 1945. Admiral Fletcher was also notified about the projected arrival of an initial contingent of 2,500 Soviet naval personnel to the Aleutian Islands to train on and then sail donated American naval craft back to the Soviet Union. Official estimates predicted that by the end of the project, up to 15,000 members of the Soviet navy would have been trained to operate the U.S. Navy vessels, including frigates, mine sweepers, armed infantry landing craft, submarine chaser patrol boats, and floating repair platforms.

Admiral King suggested Dutch Harbor as the site for personnel accommodations and training. Admiral Fletcher advised against Dutch Harbor and suggested Cold Bay, located at the southwest terminus of the Alaskan peninsula. A U.S. Army post (Ft. Randall) and a Navy auxiliary facility, both located at Cold Bay, would provide suitable housing, food, and training facilities after quickly being brought up to standards by U.S. Navy Construction Battalion (CB) teams. Cold Bay offered protected waters, isolation from civilian populations, and other logistical and security advantages.[27]

Commander William S. Maxwell (USN), a veteran seagoing engineering officer, was appointed to lead Project Hula. Captain Boris V. Nikitin (USSR) took command of the Soviet naval detachment then headed for the Aleutians. By the time he got to Cold Bay, Cmdr. Maxwell was promoted to captain. Captain Maxwell worked well with Capt. Nikitin and Rear Adm. Boris D. Popov and other Soviet naval officers. Capt. Maxwell established close professional and personal relations with Cmdr. John J. Hutson, Jr. (USCG), Lt. Cmdr.

George V. Stepanoff (USCG), Lt. F.H. Burt, Jr. (USCGR), and the other Coast Guard and Navy officers who brought administrative, seafaring, and technical expertise to the secret Hula project.

Captain Maxwell commandeered the U.S. naval officers and enlisted men whose ships were being transferred to the Soviet navy. Coast Guard and Navy instructors were selected by Capt. Maxwell to update the Russians on radio technology and communications, radar, sonar, gunnery, ordnance, damage control, engineering, and ship and landing craft operation. Several of the Soviet naval officers spoke English. Soviet officers and enlisted personnel generally got along well with their U.S. Coast Guard, Navy, Army, and Marine Corps counterparts.[28]

On August 6 and 9 (1945), the U.S. Army Air Force dropped the two nuclear bombs on Japan that ended the Pacific war and the rationale for Project Hula. British and American military and naval forces stopped their operations against Japan on 15 August. On 8 August, Soviet dictator Joseph Stalin declared war on Japan. The Red Army immediately attacked Japanese troops in the Manchurian region of China. Soviet naval personnel and their "Hula" craft engaged Japanese forces in the disputed Kuril Islands between the Soviet Union and Japan, in Korea, and on Sakhalin Island (USSR). Stalin ended Soviet military operations against the Japanese in late August.

Admiral Boris D. Popov informed Captain William Stewart Maxwell about the successes of his American trained Soviet Navy and the Hula vessels, but he did not mention the heavy Soviet casualties. With the end of the war, the flow of Lend-Lease ship transfers to the USSR was terminated. The Soviet Union later returned some of the Hula vessels to the United States.[29] At the end of September 1945, as Richard A. Russell concisely described, Capt. William S. Maxwell "closed his books, disposed of equipment, decommissioned the base, and began to ship his men home." In less than five months, U.S. "Navy Detachment 3294 had transferred 149 ships to the Soviet Navy."[30]

The cooperation between Soviet and American military personnel in Project Hula, and on other fronts during World War II, led some of the more optimistic observers of diplomatic affairs to believe positive Russo-American relationships would continue in the postwar years. But, as Richard A. Russell concluded, "Project Hula proved to be the end rather than the beginning of Soviet-American military cooperation." Within one year of the termination of Hula, "The former Allies had become bitter antagonists."[31] The Cold War had begun.

15

The Pacific Campaign

The Armed Forces of the United States was involved in the Pacific theater of World War II from the time of the attack upon the U.S. military base at Pearl Harbor by the Imperial Japanese Navy (IJN) on 7 December 1941, until August 1945, and subsequently in a peacetime role.

Fortuitously, the United States Coast Guard had been transferred from the Treasury Department to the War Department five weeks before the Pearl Harbor attack. On 1 November 1941, as per Executive Order 8929, President Franklin Roosevelt placed the Coast Guard under the jurisdiction of the United States Navy.[1]

The U.S. Navy, Marines, Coast Guard, Army (and U.S. Army Air Force) responded to the attack in separate and combined terrestrial and insular campaigns across the Pacific from December 1941 until the capitulation of Japan in August 1945. The naval war on the high seas and the amphibious assaults on the enemy controlled Pacific islands were masterful operations. The combat missions required the personnel, skills, and platforms of each of the U.S. Armed Forces in integrated military operations in the air, on the high seas, and in land-sea amphibious assaults across the vast Pacific. America's British Commonwealth Allies (United Kingdom, Australia, and New Zealand) contributed essential naval and military forces to the Pacific theater and suffered significant casualties.

Weather and sea conditions varied from warm and calm to cold and stormy. The island and archipelago topography varied from shifting volcanic sands to mountainous terrain and tropical rain forest. U.S. Navy, Marine and Army crews carried out the air war from land bases and aircraft carriers. The transportation of troops, equipment, and supplies was accomplished by Coast Guard, Navy, Marine, and Army crews in a heterogeneity of air- and seacraft. In retrospect, the combat and supply missions were unbelievably complex and masterful in their logistical and tactical coordination.

The geographic regions and the chronological order and commencement of the central and south Pacific island campaigns included Guadalcanal and New Guinea (August 1942), Tarawa (November 1943), Guam (July 1944), Kwajalein (January 1944), Saipan (June 1944), Iwo Jima (February 1945), Okinawa (April 1945), and the Philippines (October 1944–April 1945). The Southwest

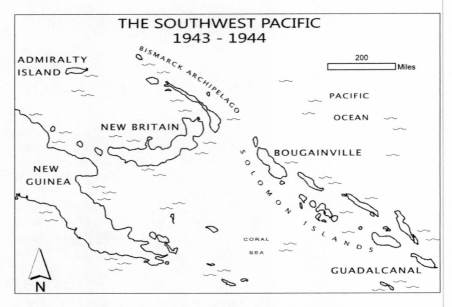

Pacific theater of operations (1942–1945) included the waters off northern and eastern Australia, New Guinea, the Coral and Bismarck seas, and the Solomon Islands. Wake Island, 2,000 miles west of Hawaii, had a small U.S. Navy and Marine and Army garrison that protected civilian construction workers and the Pan American Airlines base. Civilian and military personnel gallantly opposed the initial Japanese invasion of Wake Island, but enemy forces eventually prevailed (December 1941). Japanese forces struck Midway (June 1942) and launched a diversionary strike in the Aleutian island chain of Alaska that same month to draw in and isolate American military forces.[2]

The Battle of Midway in the Central Pacific took place from June 3 to June 6, 1942. The Japanese hoped to defeat the U.S. Pacific Fleet there and use Midway for the conquest of Hawaii. Admiral Isoroku Yamamoto hoped to crush the U.S. Pacific Fleet with 200 Japanese Imperial Navy vessels. United States Navy code breakers had warned Admiral Chester Nimitz of the pending attack, so Nimitz had his destroyers, carriers, and aircraft ready. The battle ended with the USS *Yorktown* damaged on 4 June and sunk on 7 June. Japanese bombers destroyed most the land-based U.S. torpedo planes, but the IJN lost four carriers, and the balance of Pacific naval power shifted to the United States Navy.[3]

Chief of Naval Operations Admiral Mike Mullen (USN) assessed the significance of the Battle of Midway in a June 2007 naval journal article. Adm. Mullen concluded that the courage and skill of American sailors made the difference at Midway and contributed significantly to postwar naval traditions and power. "Midway was a great turning point," Mullin wrote, but the significance of the battle was not immediate. "Even Pacific Fleet commander Admiral Chester Nimitz hadn't fully grasped the impact," Mullen concluded, and "the war would rage on for three more years; more ships would sink; more islands would change hands; more Sailors, Marines, Coastguardsmen, and Soldiers ... Japanese and Americans alike ... would die. The end was clearly not in sight in June 1942."[4]

At Pearl Harbor, the gun crews of the 327-foot USCGC *Taney* (WPG-37/WAGC-37) fired on Japanese aircraft, and subsequently engaged in combat across the Pacific. During the battle of Okinawa (1945) the *Taney* shot down five Japanese aircraft. The venerable cutter would later provide meteorological, communications, and search and rescue support on ocean station duty in the Korean War (1950–1953) and monitor enemy activities and provide gun fire support for American and South Vietnamese forces in Vietnam (1969).[5] In April 1945, the *Taney* served as the Combat Information Center (CIC) for Okinawa naval operations.[6] The *Taney* CIC was manned solely by Coast Guard crew members responsible for radar and air coverage, and the reception, transmission, and evaluation of enemy and Allied combat activities.[7]

The Coast Guard–manned U.S. Navy attack transport *Hunter Liggett* (APA-14) carried U.S. Marines in the Guadalcanal invasion of 7 August 1942. The USS *Hunter Liggett* joined 22 other attack transports at Guadalcanal, eighteen of which had mixed crews of Navy and Coast Guard personnel. Coast Guard gunners on the *Liggett* shot down several Japanese aircraft and picked up the survivors of one Australian and three American naval cruisers sunk in combat.[8]

U.S. Navy and Coast Guard crews suffered significant casualty (killed and wounded) rates from enemy air attacks and ground fire. Coast Guard Petty Officer Douglas A. Munro was in the landing party the *Hunter Liggett* skipper, Lt. Cmdr. Dwight H. Dexter (USCG), led ashore to set up a Guadalcanal landing site. On 27 September 1942, Signalman First Class Munro volunteered to lead several landing craft in a rescue mission. The 500 U.S. Marines of the First Battalion, Seventh Marine Division, that Munro and other LCVP landing craft coxswains and crews had previously landed came under withering Japanese fire. Munro placed his boat between the Japanese troops and the Marines and fired light weapons at the enemy. Munro was killed in action as the other boats completed the evacuation. Petty Officer Munro was posthumously awarded the Medal of Honor.[9]

Private First Class Ed Poppendick (USMC) recalled his unit being pinned down and taking heavy casualties in the Japanese offensive prior to the return of the rescue landing craft. The USS *Monssen* (DD-436) fired a barrage of gunfire in to create an escape path back to the shoreline. Signalman First Class Munro and his close friend, Petty Officer First Class Raymond Evans, Jr., had volunteered to return to the combat zone. From their landing craft, Munro and Evans provided cover fire. In an oral interview after his retirement from the Coast Guard, Cmdr. Raymond Evans recalled, as their landing craft embarked from the beach, he noticed "a line of machine gun bullets coming across the water," and one of the bullets hit Munro in the neck. PO Munro's last words, Evans recalled, were, "Did they [the surviving Marines] get off?" For his actions in combat, Evans earned a battlefield promotion to the rate of Chief Petty Officer and a Navy Cross.[10]

Petty Officer Douglas A. Munro (USCG) had previously rescued the two crew members of a downed U.S. Navy dive-bomber before his fatal mission to rescue 500 U.S. Marines. PO Munro's portrait was later hung in honor in the enlisted barracks of Munro Hall at the U.S. Coast Guard Academy in New London, Connecticut. The World War II hero is the namesake of the USCGC *Munro* (WHEC-724).[11]

Douglas Munro's commanding officer, Lt. Cmdr. Dwight H. Dexter (USCG), submitted a citation for the Medal of Honor in Petty Officer Munro's name. Cmdr. Dexter later received the Silver Star for gallantry in the Guadalcanal campaign. Douglas Munro's mother subsequently joined the Coast Guard to further honor her son. Lieutenant Edith Munro (USCG) served with distinction in the Women's Reserve of the United States Coast Guard.[12]

The variety of Navy and Army ships and boats and Coast Guard cutters run by USCG crews in World War II speaks volumes about the training and seafaring skills of Service personnel. The diversity of seacraft and missions is illustrated by the USCGC *Balsam* (WAGL-62/WLB-62). Zenith Dredge Company of Duluth, Minnesota, launched the 180-foot Great Lakes icebreaker and buoy tender on Lake Superior in April 1942. The *Balsam* served LORAN stations in the Pacific and missions in the Okinawa region and assisted in the suppression of a fire onboard the USS *Rawlins* after a Japanese kamikaze pilot struck the Navy ship.[13]

While convoying a U.S. Navy munitions ship, the CGC *Balsam* sank a Japanese submarine with depth charges and rocket fire. The *Balsam* crew prepared to ram the enemy craft with the cutter's reinforced icebreaker bow, but that action proved unnecessary.[14] The *Balsam* (under Lt. Cmdr. L.P. Toolin, USCG) served in the South Pacific for two years laying down channel markers and buoys to guide Allied warships, transports, and landing craft to their stations. The *Balsam* missions were chronicled by onboard war correspondent Petty Officer Donald D. Morgan (USCG). PO Morgan reported that the CGC *Balsam* performed ATN and SAR missions, and rescued downed U.S. aircraft aviators in treacherous reef and heavy seas situations.[15]

Coast Guard crews manned more than fifty 83-foot rescue vessels in the Philippines and around other Pacific islands. The dangers posed by mines, Japanese sea and aircraft, shore fire, and shipboard fires and explosions were ever present. While loading depth charges off Guadalcanal (29 June 1945), the Coast Guard–manned ammunition cargo ship USS *Serpens* (AK-97) exploded.

The disaster constituted the greatest single lethal incident involving Coast Guard personnel in the entire war: 196 Coastguardsmen, U.S. Public Health Service medical officer Dr. Harry M. Levin, and 57 Army personnel were killed. A Coast Guard–manned fuel tanker avoided a similar fate when its crew abandoned the grounded vessel in a June storm off Iwo Jima in 1945.

Coast Guard crews manned the FS (freight supply) ships of the Army Transportation Corps. The vessels included a variety of transports and tankers, repair ships, and tugboats. The Coast Guard manned 200 such vessels. By the end of 1944, seven thousand Coast Guard officers and enlisted personnel were running Army transport ships. Captain Frank T. Kenner (USCG) administered the Coast Guard/Army contingent that controlled the vessels. The 180-foot FS cargo vessels were called "Island Hoppers."

The Army ships carried military personnel, mail, and supplies, and sometimes returned from ports of call with the bodies of combat personnel whose remains would be buried in temporary graves as topographic characteristics permitted. Several FS vessels sank in typhoons and other storms in heavy seas, or from grounding in poorly charted waters. Japanese warships, aircraft, and submarines attacked FS vessels. *FS-255* lost four crewmembers in an enemy torpedo attack.[16]

The Gilbert Islands are approximately 1,200 miles northeast of Guadalcanal in the Solomon Islands. The Gilberts were part of the ferocious 1943–1944 insular war in the Central Pacific that paved the way for the invasions of Eniwetok, Saipan, and the Philippines. Americans learned the names of the Marshall, Caroline, and Marianas archipelagos, and individual islands like Tarawa, Bougainville, Guam, Iwo Jima, Okinawa, and the other strategic stepping-stones to Japan.

More than 200 naval vessels prepared to invade the Japanese-held Gilbert Islands. The vessels carried 30,000 Allied troops, 100,000 tons of cargo, and 6,000 vehicles. The Coast Guard–manned vessels included the USS *Arthur Middleton* (APA-25), USS *Leonard Wood* (APA-12), and 5 Coast Guard LSTs. The attack commenced in the early morning hours of 20 November 1944. Battleships and carrier aircraft bombarded entrenched Japanese positions before the arrival on the beaches of vehicle and troop-laden landing craft. The *Leonard Wood* landed 1,700 officers and enlisted personnel.

Coral reefs caused landing craft pileups and confusion. Many troops were forced to wade more than 200 yards to shore carrying heavy equipment through waist-deep water. At Tarawa, Coast Guard coxswains and boat crews unloaded landing craft under fire from Japanese gunners and snipers. The *Arthur Middleton* disembarked the 1,400 officers and enlisted men of the Second Marine Division into smaller, shallow draft landing craft brought to the dangerous coral reefs by large LST attack cargo ships. The *Arthur Middleton* placed a landing party ashore of 46 officers and enlisted personnel that directed boat landings and unloading for five days under the ever-present danger of enemy attack.

The U.S. Marines had to contain and liquidate Japanese troops who waged ferocious combat, and preferred death in battle or suicide to surrender.[17]

The variety and versatility of Coast Guard craft and missions is illustrated by the 180-foot USCGC *Ironwood* (WAGL-297). The tender was launched at Coast Guard Yard in Curtis Bay, Maryland, on 16 March 1943. The cutter served in the South Pacific positioning and serving mooring buoys and anti-torpedo nets, and performing SAR operations. From August 1945 through July 1946 the *Ironwood* performed ATN duty in the Philippines. In January 1945 the *Ironwood* was engaged in a most unusual mission.[18] On that date, the crew discovered and recovered a sunken "midget" Japanese I-boat (submarine) off the island of Guadalcanal.[19]

In the fall of 1943, the USCG fought alongside the U.S. Army, Navy, Marines, and British Commonwealth forces in the South and Central Pacific campaigns. In February 1944, the Marshall Island archipelago attacks commenced on Majuro, Eniwetok, and Kwajalein, with the 300 vessels and 85,000 military personnel of the Joint Expeditionary Force. One of the task force flagships was the Coast Guard–manned attack transport *Cambria* (APA-36). Four other Coast Guard–crewed attack transports supported the Marshall campaign. U.S. Navy battleships, cruisers and Coast Guard–manned destroyer-type frigates provided combat support and delivered devastating gunfire upon entrenched Japanese forces.

The immensity of the Pacific theater is illustrated by the fact that Eniwetok is located more than 300 miles from its Marshall Islands neighbor Kwajalein. The Eniwetok assault was supported by 89 vessels, including the flagship *Cambria*, and the Coast Guard–manned, or mixed, USCG-USN ships and crews of the *Leonard Wood (APA-12)*, *Centaurus* (AKA-17), *Electra* (AKA-4), *Arthur Middleton (APA-25)*, *Heywood* (AP-12), and *President Monroe* (AP-104). The large attack transports and LSTs supported amphibious operations and served as medical stations where Coast Guard and Navy personnel treated and fed the wounded U.S. Marines brought back to the naval vessels from combat.

The invasion of the Marianas archipelago involved the Japanese-held islands of Saipan, Tinian, and Guam. The 400-mile Marianis chain was 1200 miles south of the Japanese capital city of Tokyo, and an equal distance east of the Philippine Islands. The Marianas invasion commenced with Saipan on 15 June 1944, when 8,000 Marines were put ashore on more than 700 landing craft and armored vehicles. Coast Guard teams joined the Marines on the beaches.[20]

In the Saipan landings, Japanese troops concentrated their gunfire on a strategic lagoon, inflicting significant casualties on American forces. Undeterred by enemy bullets and shells, Lt. (jg) Clifford L. Bensen (USCG) and Lt. (jg) Truman C. Hardin (USCG) searched for and found an alternative channel through the coral reef into a lagoon which sheltered the pier of a sugar refinery. Skilled coxswains and naval crews guided troops and supplies through

U.S. Marines salute the Coast Guard for putting them ashore in the 1944 invasion of the Pacific island of Guam.

the confined access route. The small, shallow-draft craft negotiated the channel with inches to spare to bring critical ammunition and medical supplies to the besieged Marines. When the Japanese concentrated their fire on this secondary channel, coxswains were forced to crouch down to steer their craft between quick stand-up glances over the confined water route. The supplies enabled the Marines to repel an enemy counterattack, and secure the refinery and strategic front.[21]

The largest and most significant island in the Marianas chain was the island of Guam that was thirty-five miles in length and seven to nine miles wide, U.S. combat ships approached the island on 20 July 1944. Seven U.S. Navy ships with Navy–Coast Guard crews were joined by the Coast Guard–manned transports *Cor Caroli* (AK-91), *Aquarius* (AKA-16), *Centaurus* (AKA-17), and *Sterope* (AK-96); LSTs 24, 70, 71, and 207; and the 180-foot buoy tender *Tupelo*.[22] The USCGC *Tupelo* (WAGL-303) was launched by Zenith Dredge Company in Duluth, Minnesota, in November 1942. The *Tupelo* served in the South Pacific in 1944–1945. The *Tupelo* crew saw combat action at Eniwetok and Guam, and performed general ATN missions in that area of operations for most of 1945.[23]

The USS *Arthur Middleton* (APA-25) made a diversionary landing to the north of the intended attack, and sent waves of landing craft to shore, and then the flotilla retreated. As in the other amphibious assaults, the landing craft transferred troops and supplies over the reefs to the beach. Japanese resistance continued for several months after the July assault.

The task force assigned to attack Tinian commenced naval and air attacks on Japanese forces on 11 June 1944. Two hundred ships and their landing craft struck Tinian, three miles south of Saipan. The naval flagship USS *Cavalier* (APA-37) and the USS *Cambria* (APA-36) landed troops on Tinian on 24 July. The *Cambria* recovered 293 wounded Marines from the beachfront through heavy surf.

On 21 April 1944, American amphibious forces, the attack cargo ship *Etamin* (AK-93), and 20 other Coast Guard–manned naval vessels with the Eastern Attack Group task force occupied Hollandia. In the evening of 27 April, a Japanese torpedo bomber attacked the *Etamin*. Gas fumes ignited the flames that destroyed the engine room. Firefighters were unable to extinguish the fires before the vessel started to sink. The ship complement of 150 Army troops and 200 Coast Guardsmen abandoned ship with the loss of two personnel.

On 17 May 1944, American and Australian ships bombed Wake Island, 115 miles west of Hollandia. Then Coast Guard and Navy LSTs carried cargo and combat personnel toward the beaches. Upon reaching the coral reefs, the large 400-foot LSTs off-loaded men, supplies, and equipment into smaller, shallow draft LCI (land craft, infantry) boats. The Coast Guard manned patrol frigates *El Paso* (PF-41), *San Pedro* (PF-37), and *Orange* (PF-43) protected ships, crews, and soldiers from enemy aircraft and submarines with concentrated fire support and coordinated patrol maneuvers.

In the last two weeks of July 1944, General Douglas A. MacArthur (USA) ordered an amphibious expeditionary force to attack Japanese-held New Guinea, immediately north of Australia. From there, Gen. MacArthur planned to liberate the American Philippines from its Japanese conquerors. The New Guinea assault was achieved with the coordinated efforts of Navy destroyers and cruisers, 11 Coast Guard LSTs, aircraft bombardments, and 17,000 U.S. Army troops.

The Coast Guard–manned USN LST-*831* in the invasion of Japanese-held Okinawa in the spring of 1945. U.S. naval forces faced kamikaze attacks, a devastating typhoon, and one of the bloodiest campaigns of the Pacific war.

In September 1944, the U.S. Armed Forces shelled, bombed, and occupied the Palau Islands in the Western Caroline chain. The Peleliu assault in the Palau Islands included 800 vessels and 48,000 Army soldiers and Marines. There were two hundred American casualties at the beachhead in the ferocity of the Japanese response. But, with the conquest of the Carolines, the U.S. Armed Forces were ready to advance on the Philippines.[24]

"D-Day" for the American occupation of Iwo Jima was 19 February 1945. The four-mile long, two-mile wide island was to be used as an airfield for fighter aircraft support for American bombers on missions over Japan, and damaged aircraft on the return flights. The American Fifth Fleet task forces consisted of 900 vessels, 74,000 Marine and Navy personnel, and 30,000 specialized troops assigned to attack the estimated 20,000 embedded Japanese garrison forces.

Coast Guard–manned invasion fleet naval craft were the USS *Bayfield,* USS *Callaway,* the submarine chaser patrol boat *PC-469,* 14 LSTs, and a plethora of smaller, shallow draft LCTs, LCMs, LCVPs, and LVTs. High winds subjected the vessels and troops to challenging surf conditions that caused small craft to broach, land sideways, and clutter the beach. Coxswains had to back their landing craft into the waves and wind to prevent onshore grounding. Concentrated Japanese gunfire forced beach masters and support personnel to take cover off the beach as coxswains assumed the responsibility of landing, unloading troops and supplies, and then backing off the beach for the return run to the mother ships. Tugboat crews came in under enemy fire to tow away beached and damaged vessels and clear the beaches. U.S. Navy and Coast Guard vessels landed Marine divisions, vehicles, food, water, arms and ordnance, and other combat gear.

American and Japanese military personnel suffered high casualty rates. The enemy targeted the bright Red Cross icons on the helmets of the medics and the medical supply belts worn by medical personnel. U.S. Marine Corpsman Leonard Jansen (USN) recalled orders to conceal the Red Cross icons and medical supply bags to discourage enemy sniper targeting. Jansen was severely wounded while tending to Marine casualties, and he eventually was transported to a Navy hospital in Hawaii.[25]

The subsequent photographs of U.S. Marines and a Navy pharmacist's mate raising the colors in the two flag raising ceremonies on Mt. Suribachi inspired America. Crew members of the Coast Guard–manned LST-758 and LST-779 furnished the flags and poles to the Marine Corps unit on the venerable mountaintop. The flags were raised to the cheers of the combat personnel who observed the ceremonies. But the Battle of Iwo Jima was not yet over. More U.S. casualties were to come.

The 1 April 1945 invasion of Okinawa was the last major operation after the Philippines in the Pacific campaign and World War II. The Philippine campaign preceded Okinawa, and is considered in a separate chapter of this book.

Naval warships blasted the Japanese positions on Okinawa for one week prior to the land invasion. Coast Guard personnel manned or joined U.S. Navy crews on 59 ships and boats in the invasion fleet. The flag ships, cargo and transport vessels, and landing craft in the entire naval attack force totaled the more than 1,400 ships and boats which supported 550,000 U.S. Marines, Army, Navy, and Coast Guard personnel.

The attack force was immediately targeted by Japanese suicide aircraft, one of which hit the Coast Guard–manned LST-884. The kamikaze pilot struck the ammunition cargo. The commanding officer of LST-884 ordered "Abandon Ship" in the inferno of flames and explosions that cost twenty-four lives. Japanese torpedo boats and aircraft took advantage of the unloading challenges in the high and low tides to aggressively strafe and bomb the vessels and personnel of the invasion force, until the enemy was eventually defeated.[26]

Distinguished Pacific War historian John Costello described the significance of the maritime campaign, the battles of which "were fought across one-third of the Earth's surface" in a "massive campaign that ultimately brought about the defeat of Japan despite deep divisions in the Allied command." Despite the preliminary Japanese victories in the Pacific, Allied unity and ingenuity ultimately "enabled the U.S. Navy to mount the largest amphibious operation in history, projecting American forces across the Pacific Island stepping stones to the very shores of Japan."[27]

16

Pacific Reminiscences

The recollections of Coast Guard personnel who served in the Pacific combat theater in World War II have been recorded in autobiographies, diaries, oral interviews, and the narratives of professional historians. The reminiscences of those who served in the Pacific realm have clarified the complex events of the war and recorded the significance of the maritime campaign for future generations.

Quarter Master Robert L. Resnick (USCG) was beached on Iwo Jima on *LST-758* during the February-March 1945 battle. "We were scared," Resnick recalled, "but we were committed.... We were young and impassioned." A U.S. Marine approached the Coastguardsman on the 329-foot combat transport ship and requested a flag. QM Resnick supplied the Marine with a flag and a 150-pound, 21-foot steamfitter's pipe to use as the flagpole. Five Marines and a U.S. Navy corpsman later raised that flag on Mt. Suribachi in the historic event immortalized by Associated Press photographer Joe Rosenthal. Four days before the 23 February flag incident, QM Resnick was struck by a bullet and suffered a facial wound. Resnick recalled that a Marine major onboard told Resnick he was entitled to a Purple Heart for the wound. "But, we were fighting a war," said Resnick, and he did not file a Purple Heart request report.[1]

Boatswain's Mate First Class Robert W. Schindler (USCG) served for one month in the crew of the USS *Little* on supply runs off Tulagi in the Solomon Islands. BM1 Schindler was unloading hand grenades on Guadalcanal when Japanese aircraft sank the transport vessel USS *Calhoun*. *Calhoun* survivors were rescued by barges (landing craft) from the *Little*. On 5 September 1942, the USS *Little* dropped antisubmarine depth charges while maneuvering to avoid bombing and I-boat (submarine) attacks. An enemy shell lighted the sky around the USS *Little* at around 1:00 AM, as three Japanese Imperial Navy destroyers closed in to shell the U.S. Marines on Guadalcanal. Enemy gunfire hit the *Little's* ammunition hold. The resulting explosions blew Schindler into burning ocean waters where sharks attacked wounded sailors and Japanese naval gunners targeted survivors with searchlights.

BM1 Schindler was picked up by a life raft from the USS *Gregory*. A U.S. Marine aircraft spotted them at dawn and reported their position. Later that day small boats appeared and took survivors to a transport vessel. Medical

USS *Hunter Liggett* (APA-14), a large Coast Guard–manned USN attack transport, participated in the Guadalcanal invasion. The *Hunter Liggett* served as a command post and carried 35 landing craft, 51 officers, and 634 crewmembers. *Liggett* gunners downed four Japanese bombers on 8 August 1942.

officers informed the wounded Coastguardsman that the ocean saltwater probably saved him from gangrene infection. Robert W. Schindler returned to San Diego, California, and endured 60 surgical operations that removed most of the shrapnel from his body. BM1 Schindler received the Purple Heart.[2]

The USS *Hunter Liggett* (APA-14), under the command of Captain Roderick S. Patch (USCG), was in the thick of the Solomon Islands battle at Bougainville. Robert B. Pero, Radioman Second Class wrote of his experiences on the *Liggett* on 1 November 1943. In that battle, the 12 destroyers and cruisers of the attacking Japanese naval force lost four destroyers and one cruiser sunk, and four other IJN vessels were damaged.

The *Hunter Liggett* was the flagship of the amphibious attack force. RM2 Pero described how the USS *Liggett* and its landing craft carried military personnel, supplies and equipment to shore, after U.S. aircraft and warships suppressed much of the enemy artillery and machine gun fire. The *Liggett* moved into shoal waters firing its 3-inch and 20mm guns, downed one enemy bomber, and drove off other aircraft. Nonetheless, several barges were lost or damaged by heavy surf and Japanese guns.[3]

The 15 March 1944 invasion of Manus Island in the Admiralty campaign was one more step in the Allied naval voyage to the Japanese homeland. *LST-67,* under the command of Lt. (jg) William D. Hemeon (USCGR), was the amphibious force flag (command) ship, and headquarters of Brigadier General Mudge (USA), the commander of the Second Cavalry Brigade. B-25 bombers and U.S. Navy destroyers initiated a barrage on Japanese positions before *LST-67* discharged its landing craft and soldiers for the island assault. Bulldozers and tanks disembarked from the large LSTs, paved the way for advancing Army troops that inflicted high casualty rates upon the enemy defenders. U.S. Navy, Army, Marine Corps and Coast Guard casualties were fortunately relatively light.[4]

Chief Specialist William A. Haffert, Jr., (USCGR) earned a Meritorious Achievement commendation for actions he performed in the invasion of Saipan. Chief Sp. Haffert served aboard the USS *Callaway* (APA-35) under Capt. Donald C. McNeil (USCG). The *Callaway* took part in the invasions of the Philippines (Leyte and Luzon), Iwo Jima, and Okinawa. A Japanese suicide aircraft struck the *Callaway* off the island of Luzon and caused 50 casualties.[5]

Lt. Matthew P. Cantillon (USCGR) described the crucial role of naval beach master traffic cops in the landing and unloading process of troops and supplies from landing craft under enemy gunfire. Lt. Cantillon dodged enemy bullets, landing craft and assorted vehicles in several Pacific landings, including New Guinea and the Philippines. Lt. Cantillon was an LST navigation officer at sea, but on the beaches he guided U.S. Navy "Seabees" and Army and Marine assault troops on and off the beaches. USN and USCG beach masters worked together out of foxholes packed with maps and communications gear. Beach crews consisted of 20 or more personnel who were boat repair, hydrographic, communications, and medical specialists. The beach personnel quickly put up navigation aids consisting of colored triangles and poles to guide LST and landing craft coxswains to assigned landing sites. Beach masters and support crews were susceptible to snakes and insects, enemy sniper fire and troop attacks, aircraft strafing, and the vicissitudes of vehicle traffic, rain, high winds and surf, and storms.[6]

Chief Specialist Stuart L. Parker (USCGR) served on the USS *Bayfield* (APA-33), under the command of Capt. Walter R. Richard (USCG). Chief Petty Officer Parker participated in the invasion of Iwo Jima where U.S. Navy and Coast Guard–manned landing craft brought U.S. Marines ashore. More than 2,000 Americans died in the assault that commenced on 19 February 1945. The Coast Guard crews were veterans of the Normandy invasion in 1944. Landing craft crews and Marines braved Japanese fire going into the beaches, and Navy and Coast Guard crews remained stationary targets as they loaded wounded and dead U.S. Marines onboard for the return trip to hospital ships. One attack transport captain discovered his dying Marine Corps son among the wounded.[7]

Chief Specialist John G. Cole (USCGR) chronicled the role of courageous Coast Guard and Navy chaplains who counseled soldiers, marines, and sailors on ships and ashore. Chaplains comforted the wounded. Several dedicated clerics became casualties of war themselves on ships, landing craft, and the beaches and islands of the Pacific.[8]

Cmdr. Arch A. Mercey (USCGR) and Chief Petty Officer Lee Grove (USCGR) wrote a perceptive editorial epilogue in their magnificently edited wartime chronicle of the U.S. Coast Guard in World War II combat zones. In *Sea, Surf and Hell* (1945), Mercey and Grove traced naval combat from the Atlantic to the Pacific, from Pearl Harbor to the Aleutians, from Normandy in Europe to Iwo Jima and the Philippines, and ultimately to the Japanese home islands. The editors used primary sources written by combat participants and journalists.

In their summation of the Coast Guard at war, Mercey and Grove paid tribute to Coast Guard aids to navigation units ranging from buoy tender patrols to "the LORAN units on lonely but strategically located islands ... Coast Guard manned frigates on weather stations ... manned attack transports and attack cargo vessels" and LSTs and LCIs and port security and cargo loading units "in Pacific ports" and "in the Caribbean Sea" and the Mediterranean. The demobilization of the Coast Guard after World War II from a peak of nearly 200,000 personnel, included, Mercey and Grove continued, "10,000 members of the Women's Reserve, in addition to the Temporary Reserve of 34,000 volunteers on part-time home (front) duty." With the surrender of Japan, the USCG was transferred from the Department of the Navy back to the Treasury Department, "which meant the Service, which had taken life in battle, could return to devote itself wholly to the saving of life and the enforcement of maritime regulations ... and ... new duties brought about by the war, such as air-sea rescue."[9]

Given the transoceanic missions in the storms and variable climate zones of the Pacific and Atlantic combat theaters in which the Coast Guard operated in World War II. Lt. Scott Wilson (USCGR), a veteran of the Saipan invasion, pondered a question he shared with a musical Coast Guard colleague. The query led to the song and lyrics written in 1943 by Specialist First Class Chris Yacich (USCGR). The Eighth Naval District Coast Guard Band first performed the song on a New Orleans radio station. The composer queried: "I'd like to find the guy that named the Coast Guard, and find that bit of coast he had in mind.... The coast we were shelling on a South Pacific shore.... With LCIs and LSTs galore.... [or off the Atlantic shore where] ... I'm dodging enemy torpedoes.... Or, on the beach at Attu.... Or, on polar waters ... in the Greenland icy night.... Oh, I'd like to find the guy who named the Coast Guard and find that bit of coast he had in mind."[10]

Colonel Joseph H. Alexander (USMC, Ret.) surveyed the Central Pacific amphibious battles in his book, *Storm Landings*. Col. Alexander quoted combat correspondent Robert Sherrod's assessment that the United States won the Pacific War with its steel production and the steel "in the hearts of the men who stormed the beaches at Tarawa, Saipan, Taiwan, Iwo Jima, Okinawa," and other landing sites. With 29 years of experience as an amphibious assault officer, Colonel Alexander added his well informed conclusion: "And each of those soldiers, sailors, airmen, Coastguardsmen, and Marines who did so on our behalf left us a national heritage and legacy of salt water, coral sand, and young blood."[11]

The storming of the Central Pacific islands of Guam, Tarawa, Tinian, Saipan, Peleliu, Okinawa and Iwo Jima resulted in 74,805 Navy, Marine and Coast Guard casualties. Army and offshore Navy unit losses increased the total casualty count to almost 100,000 military personnel.[12]

After Lt. (jg) Jules J. Fern (USCGR) passed away, Juliana Fern Patten discovered her father's wartime correspondence, news clippings, photographs, documents, other memorabilia, and letters to his mother in an attic box. Julia Fern Patten, who holds a master's degree in English, organized the primary sources and edited and published her father's story in *Another Side of World War II: A Coast Guard Lieutenant in the South Pacific*.

After graduation from the U.S. Coast Guard Academy in 1943, J.J. Fern was assigned to the South Pacific on *LST-169*. Lt. Fern participated in the 1944 invasions of Saipan, and the Philippines in Leyte Gulf. After those amphibious campaigns, Lt. Fern sailed on a gasoline tanker and then a weather patrol frigate. After discharge from active duty, Fern taught English courses at the University of Cincinnati. Commander Jules Fern retired from the USCGR in 1973.[13]

In his 1944–1945 letters home, Lt. (jg) Fern described LST and landing craft beach landings and the process of unloading guns, ammunition, vehicles, provisions, medical supplies, and troops under Japanese sniper and artillery fire and enemy air attacks, while under the much appreciated protection of "the anti-aircraft fire that our naval convoys put up."[14] Lt. Fern writes of his experiences on Saipan, of going ashore "with drawn pistols," observing Japanese troops, the danger of enemy-detonated "pre-arranged charges," "piles of dead Japanese," medics treating the wounded, bringing combat casualties back to landing craft for transfer to LSTs and other large ships at sea for medical treatment on board, and the sadness of burials on land and at sea. On a lighter note, Lt. Fern recollected the acquisition of Japanese rifles, flags, swords, food, and alcoholic beverages, which he and other military personnel shared with Coast Guard, Navy, Army, and Marine colleagues ashore and afloat. Among the much-appreciated gratifications Lt. Fern discussed were the church services and counsel of dedicated chaplains and letters from home.[15]

In November 1944, *LST-169* headed into the Leyte Gulf for the invasion of the Japanese-held Philippine Islands. Lt. Fern wrote that the naval armada around him consisted of "hundreds of ships: battleships, cruisers, destroyers, LSTs, LSDs, LCMs, LCVPs, LSRs, LCIs, LCTs, transports, cargo ships, oilers, tugs, freighters, aircraft carriers, tenders, lighters—everything the Navy has." The beaching formations were assumed, Fern asserted, and "the soldiers aboard

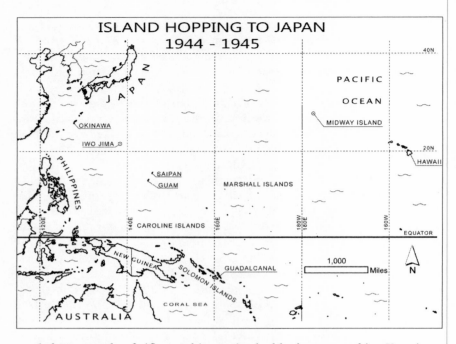

carried 50 pounds of rifles, carbines, pistols, blankets, mess kits, K-rations, ammunition, knives, hatchets, and shovels. They had had steak and eggs for breakfast … and when they climbed into their amphibious tanks, each one was given a sandwich and two apples."[16]

Going ashore in an amphibious DUKW to meet up with a U.S. Army Infantry unit and distribute essential supplies, Lt. Fern experienced limited sniper and mortar fire, returned to *LST-169* in the evening, and put out to sea contemplating the battle hazards the disembarked American troops would again have to endure.

The second day of the invasion found the American naval convoy under withering Japanese air attacks. *LST-169* gun crews splashed two enemy aircraft and hit two others. Enemy shells hit a shoreside ammunition dump, forcing *LST-169* to withdraw to sea to escape the horrific explosions and shrapnel. "Hundreds of soldiers bivouacked nearby," Lt. Fern recalled, "were killed. The next day, several who survived came aboard for treatment and clothing." The wounded were taken to safe ports. Underway, the LSTs and other naval craft plucked exhausted, cold, and wounded officers and men from the sea whose ships had been destroyed in peripheral combat with the Japanese Imperial Navy.[17]

The variable weather, cyclonic winds, typhoons, and heavy sea conditions of the Pacific Ocean posed periodic challenges to the commanders and crews of naval vessels. Larry Thornberry reviewed the 2007 book *Halsey's Typhoon,* by Bob Drury and Ted Clavin. Thornberry and the authors vividly described the December 1944 typhoon which interrupted the Philippine invasion, threatened the career of the Western Pacific Fleet commander Admiral William F. Halsey (USN), damaged dozens of naval vessels and sunk three destroyers in the 170-ship armada, and drowned hundreds of American sailors. The U.S. Navy, Thornberry asserted, "suffered a sneak attack from Typhoon Cobra that did more damage to Halsey's fleet than the Imperial Japanese Navy had managed to inflict in the preceding three years."

U.S. Navy and Coast Guard vessels were ravaged between December 17 and 20 in 150 mile per hour winds, and 70-foot seas. Courageous destroyer commanders and crews rescued ten percent of the 900 sailors trapped below destroyer decks, or washed into the sea. More than 100 aircraft were wrecked on or blown off aircraft carrier decks.[18]

William L. McGee dedicated his book about amphibious operations in the South Pacific "to the hundreds of thousands of home-front warriors who built the amphibious ships and craft ... the skippers and assault boat coxswains who were trained to run their craft at full throttle toward a fiercely defended beach ... and to the Marine Corps and Army troops who stormed ashore." Petty Officer McGee joined the U.S. Navy in 1942, after a stint as a shipyard welder building LSTs and Liberty (cargo and transport) ships. McGee took U.S. Navy gunnery training, served in the Naval Armed Guard on U.S. Merchant Marine ships, and experienced enemy air and torpedo attacks in the Pacific war.[19]

McGee describes the contributions of U.S. Navy officers and enlisted personnel in a myriad of ranks and rates, U.S. Coast Guard personnel directing beach traffic as attack transports unloaded supplies under fire, and U.S. Marines at Guadalcanal "storming ashore" on "D-Day," 7 August 1942.[20]

The skills and responsibilities of Navy and Coast Guard coxswains in variable surf conditions were perceptively described by the author: "The inexperience of most coxswains took a toll on the landing craft. One ship lost eighteen of twenty-five boats employed in the first wave. Except for two ships manned by the Coast Guard with a more solid core of experienced boat handlers, the other transports suffered disproportionately high losses of landing craft." McGee noted that in addition to "the normal difficulties of beaching a landing craft ... coxswains had been asked to beach on an ebbing tide, a problem of seamanship that was beyond most of their capabilities." Despite general landing successes, McGee explained, "other boats landed hundreds of yards from their assigned beaches ... [and] there were collisions, engine failures, faulty compasses, and boats holed by rocks."[21]

Ken Wiley joined the Coast Guard in 1943, attended landing craft school with the U.S. Marines at Camp Lejeune, North Carolina, and was assigned to the attack transport USS *Arthur Middleton* (APA-25) in the Pacific Theater. Petty Officer Third Class Wiley was the young coxswain of *LCVP-13* ("Lucky Thirteen"). PO3 Wiley transported supplies and troops to the beaches under enemy fire in variable weather, explored dangerous rivers and inlets in enemy territory, and evaded Japanese suicide boats and combat aircraft.[22]

USS *Middleton* carried Wiley's *LCVP-13* and other landing craft. The Navy flagship *Middleton* carried out missions at Kwajalein, Eniwetok, Guadalcanal, in the Philippines, and at Okinawa. Coxswain Wiley described missions onboard the *Middleton* and in landing craft in combat zones.[23] The bonding that existed between troops and sailors in harm's way was a significant fact of life. Wiley described his fellow service personnel with perception and admiration. Among them was combat artist Seaman First Class Kenneth P. Riley (USCG) whose illustrations of shipboard life and wartime action gained national attention and a permanent place in Navy and Coast Guard archives as official documentation of the Pacific war. Wiley also described the excitement and pride Coast Guard personnel felt when championship boxer and military physical trainer Cmdr. Jack Dempsey (USCGR) visited the USS *Middleton*. Then, in full combat gear and carrying a rifle, Cmdr. Dempsey climbed aboard Coxswain Wiley's *LCVP-13* for the invasion run to the beaches of Okinawa.[24]

Among the most difficult duties Petty Officer Wiley performed were the burials at sea while onboard the USS *Arthur Middleton*. Wiley described the ceremony: "The bodies, wrapped carefully in white linen and weighed down with iron, were laid out on the deck with a flag draped across each corpse. We evacuated these men as wounded, but they died before they could get to the hospital at Pearl Harbor." The ship's flag would be lowered to half-mast, and, Wiley recalled, "Taps would be played over the PA system." PO Wiley quoted the chaplain's final words: "Oh Lord, we commit their souls to you for all eternity. We now commit their bodies to the deep." Pallbearers would lift "each linen-wrapped body," which would then be "slid over the side and plunged into the dark waters below."[25]

Clarence Storla served as a petty officer on *LST-831* in the Pacific. In basic training, Petty Officer Storla learned semaphore and light signaling and small boat handling. Storla's eclectic interests led to his achieving the rates of water tender and fireman first class, and a brief stint as a Coast Guard correspondent. After the war, Storla used the GI bill to earn advanced degrees in sociology and anthropology, and then he commenced a teaching career. Petty Officer Storla explained in an oral history interview the unloading of supplies and taking Marines into Okinawa on D-Day, a chance meeting on Saipan with his brother who had come ashore in an LCI, and shooting at Kamikaze suicide planes. "There were also Kamikaze swimmers and kamikaze suicide boats," Storla recalled: "We captured one of those speed boats, took the ammo out of it, and the skipper used it for a gig."[26]

Dale Killian signed up with the Coast Guard before conscription (the draft) could determine his choice of military services. After basic training, Killian was assigned to an LST that carried supplies, vehicles, and Army and

Marine personnel to invasion sites on New Guinea. The LST also made trips to the Philippines and Dutch East Indies. When an LST in his convoy was torpedoed, Killian was ordered to coxswain a smaller LCVP, go into the night with a flashlight, and rescue the sailors who had been thrown into the ocean. Killian was honored and pleased to carry out the successful mission.

When Killian's LST came under Japanese kamikaze attacks, the ship's guns fired back at the suicide pilots. His LST was not hit. Killian recalled worrying about his two brothers overseas, one in the Army, the other in the Navy. The Army brother was killed in Europe. After the war, Killian was stationed in Seattle, Washington, attended several service reunions, and proudly concluded that he had "always been proud to have played a small part in the war. I think our generation can take some pride in what we did out there in the Pacific during WWII."[27]

Between 1941 and 1944, six Great Lakes seagoing buoy tenders were built and launched at the Lake Superior port of Duluth, Minnesota, by the Zenith Dredge Company and the Marine Iron and Shipbuilding Corporation. These 180-foot Coast Guard cutters were designed for icebreaking, aids to navigation, search and rescue, and other Coast Guard missions. The vessels were named after vegetation, and by the Coast Guard classification system were called Iris, Cactus, and Mesquite Class cutters.

The 180-foot cutters were the *Sassafras* (WAGL-401), *Papaw* (WAGL-308), *Balsam* (WAGL-62), *Tupelo* (WAGL-303), *Woodbine* (WAGL-289), and *Sweetbrier* (WAGL-405). A seventh tender, the CGC *Ironwood* (WAGL-297), was built at Coast Guard Yard in Curtis Bay, Maryland, and launched in 1943. The buoy tenders kept shipping lanes marked, maintained the navigation buoys, came under enemy fire, shot down Japanese aircraft, performed salvage and ship repair operations on damaged Allied ships, and carried out SAR missions. The buoy tenders fought shipboard fires, dodged and deactivated floating mines, and survived typhoons and kamikaze attacks. The CGC *Papaw* secured a Japanese aircraft on Iwo Jima (21 May 1945), and the CGC *Ironwood* salvaged a Japanese submarine off Guadalcanal (January 1945).[28]

During the war, these cutters were sent from Duluth on the western terminus of Lake Superior, east down the Great Lakes and St. Lawrence River, into the Atlantic, then to the Gulf of Mexico and Caribbean Sea, through the Panama Canal to California, west across the Pacific to Hawaii, and into the insular Pacific combat zones.[29]

In an autobiography, Radio Man First Class Tanney Edward Oberg (USCG) described his tour of duty on the CGC *Sweetbrier* (WAGL/WLB-405), on which he sailed from Duluth (7 August 1944) to Okinawa. RM1 Oberg arrived in the Ryukyu Islands (350 miles south of Japan) and Okinawa on 6 May 1945.[30]

"The USCGC *Sweetbrier* (WLB-405) was small as military ships go. Despite our small crew [of 7 officers and 74 enlisted men]," Oberg asserted, "we took part in the final major naval campaign of the war [Okinawa]." Ten thousand naval personnel casualties occurred in the three-month campaign, "mostly by Kamikazes, and 34 ships were sunk, and 368 damaged."[31]

RM1 Oberg described the *Sweetbrier* as "armed and equipped for battle," but "its primary mission was to maintain (navigation) marking buoys ... crucial in wartime for the success of amphibious operations. In addition to our 3"/50-caliber anti-aircraft gun, machine guns, and other weapons, we were equipped with a 20-ton boom for buoy work."[32] The "other weapons" were formidable and included 30-caliber machine guns, 2 K-gun depth charge ejectors, 2 depth-charge racks, and 2 mousetrap depth-charge throwers. The seagoing buoy tender was equipped with sonar and radar, two single screw diesel engines, and an electric motor and two generators. The CGC *Sweetbrier* had a 37-foot beam (width) and a 12-foot draft that allowed stability in deep water and inshore operations.[33]

RM1 Oberg experienced the shock of seeing deceased enemy soldiers when he and several exploring *Sweetbrier* crew members carelessly walked unarmed into a combat zone on Guam. Oberg described naval combat action in which *Sweetbrier* gun crews struck and splashed a diving kamikaze plane (6 May 1945) with the assistance of two U.S. Corsair fighter aircraft, carried a Navy CB (Construction Battalion) unit ashore in an LCVP loaded with dynamite used to eliminate coral obstructions in the amphibious landing routes, and witnessed the accidental shoot-down of an American combat aircraft by U.S. naval guns.[34]

RM1 Oberg reported that the *Sweetbrier* Deck Log (on 15 June 1945) recorded the reception of a letter that Lt. Paul Lybrand (USCG), the cutter commander, received dated 7 June 1945 "from Commander Amphibious Force, Pacific (Serial 678) stating that *Sweetbrier* was given credit for destroying one Japanese plane on 18 May and one on 20 May."[35] The CGC *Sweetbrier* also received wartime Commendations from the commander of the Pacific Fleet, U.S. Navy, Admiral Chester W. Nimitz (22 June 1945), British Prime Minister Winston Churchill (2 July 1945), and James Forrestal, secretary of the U.S. Navy (14 August 1945). Squadron Commander L.S. Fiske (USN) sent letters of commendation (dated 17 December 1945) for outstanding wartime service to the commanding officers of the six cutters built in Duluth, Minnesota: the "*Balsam* (CGC-62), *Papaw* (CGC-308), *Sassafras* (CGC-401), *Sweetbrier* (CGC-405), *Tupelo* (CGC-303), and *Woodbine* (CGC-289)" for "assignments performed in a superior manner" that "were a credit to you, the personnel under your command, and to the United States Coast Guard."[36]

The danger of typhoons was ever present in the Pacific. On 2 August 1945, RM1 Oberg experienced a particularly severe typhoon with "74 mph winds, heavy swells" and "an angry sea [which] tossed our 180-footer bow to stern and beam to beam and back again. Most of us were miserably sick. Some on-deck crewmen [gun crews at battle stations] suffered bruises and contusions when the raging sea smashed them against bulkheads." On that occasion the

USCGC *Sweetbrier* (WLB-405). The armed 180-foot buoy tender was constructed in Duluth, Minnesota, and served in combat zones in the Pacific, including Okinawa.

Navy had ordered smaller vessels (cutters, tugboats, destroyers) out to sea. On 8 October 1945, the Navy issued another typhoon warning, but this time larger ships were ordered out to sea to ride it out. Smaller vessels like the *Sweetbrier* were now ordered into supposedly protected harbors at anchor with running engines for control. After watching one small boat sink, and being narrowly missed by an out of control ocean tugboat, RM1 Oberg credited the enlisted helmsman and bridge officers who guided the cutter into open waters at the height of the storm for exhibiting "great seamanship, controlling our tossing 180-footer, and repeatedly avoiding misfortune."[37]

The atomic bombing of the Japanese cities of Hiroshima (6 August 1945) and Nagasaki (9 August 1945) convinced Japan to surrender. On 2 September 1945, in Tokyo Bay, Japanese diplomatic and military officials signed the formal surrender documents on the U.S.S. *Missouri* (BB-63) in proceedings presided over by General Douglas MacArthur (USA).[38]

RM1 Tanney Edward Oberg was transferred to the USCGC *Woodbine* (WLB-289) in November 1945 for return to the United States and honorable discharge from the United States Coast Guard. Oberg was disappointed that he could not sail under California's Golden Gate Bridge on the *Sweetbrier*, which was still in the Pacific.[39]

In civilian life, Oberg became a corporate executive and business consultant, but he stayed connected with the CGC *Sweetbrier* (WLB-405) and its crews at reunions. Oberg was present (27 August 2001) when the *Sweetbrier* was decommissioned in Cordova, Alaska, and at the ceremony (26 October 2001) at U.S. Coast Guard Yard in Baltimore, Maryland, when the intrepid cutter was transferred to the navy of the African Republic of Ghana.[40]

Signalman First Class Douglas Munro (USCG) is a testimonial to courage and sacrifice in combat. SM1 Munro was an LCVP coxswain at Guadalcanal. The 22-year-old sailor returned to the beach in charge of five other boats to rescue 500 U.S. Marines they had disembarked into overwhelming Japanese gunfire. SM1 Munro landed his boat on shore and opened fire to draw enemy fire away from the Marines. After the Marines had cleared the beach and were underway in other landing craft, Munro and two other Coastguardsmen were wounded, Munro mortally, as they put to sea. Before he died, SM1 Munro asked, "Did they get off?"

At Munro's posthumous awards ceremony, the citation described his award for "Extraordinary heroism and conspicuous gallantry in action above and beyond the call of duty." President Franklin Roosevelt ended the proceedings with these words: "[Munro] and his courageous comrades saved the lives of many who otherwise would have perished."[41]

Douglas Munro was born in Vancouver (British Columbia), Canada, in 1919, grew up in Cle Elum, Washington, and enlisted in the U.S. Coast Guard in 1939, two years before the United States entered World War II. For his bravery and sacrifice on Guadalcanal on 27 September 1942, SM1 Munro, the coxswain of Higgins boat landing craft P1021, received the U.S. Navy Medal of Honor.[42]

Historic Fort Snelling National Cemetery in Minnesota is the final resting place of more than 170,000 men and women of the U.S. Armed Forces who served in uniform from the Civil War to the present. Among their ranks is Seaman First Class Patrick E. Ward (USCG). The south Minneapolis native enlisted in the USCG in April 1943, and served in the Pacific Theater. In January 1944, SN1 Ward was a gunner in a fleet of 300 ships that invaded the Marshall Islands, Guam, the Philippines, and Peleliu in the central Pacific. Guam was recaptured in July and August. The Philippine, Leyte, landings occurred in late October 1944. Coast Guard crews served on USN and USCG ships. The 35 Coast Guard vessels in the fleet included armed attack transports, cargo vessels, destroyers, frigates, and LSTs. SN1 Ward was on an attack transport. The naval vessels faced gunfire, artillery bombardments, and Kamikaze attacks as ships and landing craft unloaded supplies, vehicles, and troops. SN1 Patrick Ward (USCG) was honorably discharged at the age of twenty. Ward was buried at Fort Snelling in 1994.[43]

Hal Buell, the author of *Uncommon Valor, Common Virtue,* paid tribute to the USN, USCG, and USMC personnel who fought and died on Iwo Jima.

SM1 Douglas Munro (USCG) was awarded a posthumous Medal of Honor for his performance in combat with Coast Guard colleagues and a U.S. Marine detachment at Guadalcanal on 27 September 1942. Petty Officer Munro was the coxswain of LCVP-P-1021. (Painting of SM1 Munro and his landing craft at Guadalcanal by Bernard D'Andrea courtesy Mary Ann Bader, director, Coast Guard Art Program, Washington, D.C.)

Buell, an experienced Associated Press photo editor, did not neglect the civilian and military combat photographers who covered the bloody 3-week invasion of February-March 1945. The author chronicled the two famous flag raising ceremonies performed by courageous Navy and Marine personnel on the top of Mt. Suribachi, and the Pulitzer Prize winning photograph of the second event by Associated Press photographer Joe Rosenthal.

Buell included historic photographs from the National Archives taken by "Marine, Coast Guard, and Navy photographers made as Americans literally inched their way across a 4.5 mile island in 36 days of fiery hell, and 36 nights of constant vigilance against infiltrators, surprise attacks, and hand grenades thrown from the shadows ... and the most vicious kind of hand to hand fighting."[44]

Coast Guard combat photographs from the National Archives illustrate Marines, Navy and Coast Guard personnel praying on a landing craft headed for Iwo Jima on D-Day.[45] The Battle of Iwo Jima caused 28,000 American casualties, with 21,000 wounded, and 7,000 military personnel killed. More than 20,000 Japanese died out of a total of 100,000 American and Japanese combatants.[46] Combat photographer Robert Warren (USCG) took a picture which showed the impact of heavy surf and enemy gunfire on scattered and damaged "amtracs, tanks, and boats" scattered along the Iwo Jima shoreline.[47] Photographer Paul Queenan (USCG) captured the brute strength involved as Navy, Marine, and Coast Guard personnel hand-carried supplies from LSTs through the raging surf and shifting sands that bogged down tractors and trucks.[48]

The editors of *Time* magazine and *Time Books* compiled a magnificent collection of World War II photographs from civilian, military, and archival sources. *V-J Day* (2005) is a visual chronicle of the Pacific War and victory over Japan. The special edition magazine includes photographs, maps, other graphics, and a concise, informative narrative. The contributions and photographs of U.S. Navy, Army, Marines and Coast Guard missions are featured. One photograph illustrates 2 Coast Guard LSTs unloading on Leyte beach in the Philippines, as troops construct sandbag piers to facilitate the unloading process in surf conditions.[49] Sailors are photographed playing chess in the storeroom of a Coast Guard ship. A hospitalized soldier is reading a book while on a cot in the sick bay of the hospital ship, USS *Solace* (AH-5), in 1945.[50]

Military chaplains risked their lives and some suffered combat wounds and death ministering to the spiritual and psychological needs of military personnel at sea and ashore. The U.S. Army had 8,000 clerics with officer rank. The Navy, which ministered to USN, USCG, and USMC personnel, had 3,000 ministers, priests, and rabbis. The *V-J Day* journal produced by *Time* featured a photograph of a memorial mass being held for Americans lost in battle on Ie Shima Island in the Ryukyus islands. An adjacent photo showed a Coastguardsman leading a prayer on the deck of an LST heading for Iwo Jima. Another photograph captured a Coast Guard chaplain baptizing 30 soldiers in the waters of a peaceful tropical lagoon.[51]

One striking combat photograph featured a USN-USCG ship armada off Iwo Jima waiting to disembark military personnel, equipment, and supplies onto the beach. Approximately 70 ships and landing craft are visible in the compelling aerial photograph.[52] The wounded warriors of Iwo Jima were escorted back to landing craft for transfer to medical units on LSTs and larger vessels. Another compelling photograph showed Coastguardsmen assisting "a wounded Marine into a landing craft for evacuation" out to a hospital ship.[53]

The *Time* editors narrated and photographed the generally unpublicized threats Japanese submarines, aircraft, and incendiary balloons posed to the Pacific Coast of the United States between 1941 and 1945. In the first few weeks after the Pearl Harbor attack, nine Japanese submarines (I-boats) patrolled West Coast sea-lanes, torpedoed eight and sank two American cargo vessels, and killed six merchant mariners. A *Time* photograph showed a Japanese torpedo that was discovered ashore near the Golden Gate Bridge. U.S. Navy ord-

SM1 Douglas Munro (USCG), a posthumous Medal of Honor winner, with his sidearm.

nance specialists detonated the high explosive device. In September 1942, a seaplane launched from an I-boat dropped incendiary bombs in an Oregon forest. Firefighters extinguished the conflagration. In 1945, an inflammable Japanese balloon ignited a blaze in which six Americans died.[54]

The editors of *V-J Day* described and photographed celebrations by U.S. Armed Forces personnel that occurred after President Harry Truman's 2 September 1945 announcement of the Japanese surrender. President Franklin Roosevelt passed away before V-J Day, but he had celebrated V-E (Victory in Europe) Day the previous May.[55]

A commemoration of the U.S. Coast Guard's contributions in the Pacific war was celebrated in January 2008. Dignitaries present at the National Monument Cemetery of the Pacific in Hawaii included Governor Linda Lingle, U.S. Coast Guard Commandant, Admiral Thad Allen (USCG), Lt. Cmdr. William Clark (USN and USCG, Ret.), and Rear Adm. Sally Brice O'Hara (USCG), commander of the 14th Coast Guard District, which includes the Hawaiian Sea Frontier.

Also present at the unveiling of the plaque and memorial were relatives of Signal Man First Class Douglas Munro (USCG), the landing craft coxswain who earned a posthumous Medal of Honor for his 1942 rescue of 500 U.S. Marines on Guadalcanal. Admiral Thad Allen (USCG) narrated the story of Petty Officer Munro at Guadalcanal. Patty Sheehan, Munro's sister, spoke of her brother's pride in the Coast Guard. Commander Douglas Sheehan (USCG, Ret.) was present with his mother to honor his famous uncle.

Petty Officer Todd Minnick, a crew member on the USCGC *Walnut* (WLB-205), contributed to the ceremony. The previous summer, PO Minnic and the *Walnut* crew sailed out of the cutter's homeport of Honolulu, Hawaii, to Guadalcanal for the 65th anniversary of the invasion. The crew acquired a 2,000-pound boulder from the beach where SM1 Munro was struck down by enemy bullets. The boulder will be placed at the base of the U.S. Coast Guard Memorial on Punchbowl Drive.[56]

17

Return to the Philippines and Victory

When the air, sea, and land forces of Imperial Japan attacked the United States colony of the Philippines (1941–1942), American and Filipino military and civilian personnel waged a courageous and valiant defense. But eventually, in the face of Japanese victory and atrocities, the Philippines Islands fell to the enemy.

General Douglas MacArthur (USA), the U.S. military commander of the Philippines and commander of U.S. Army Forces Far East, was unprepared to successfully defend the Philippines. Gen. MacArthur lost all the U.S. Army Air Force aircraft on the ground in Manila to Japanese air attacks despite a nine-hour period of warning after the Pearl Harbor attack. President Franklin Roosevelt ordered Gen. MacArthur to vacate the Philippines, escape to Australia, and plan Allied offensive operations in the Southwest Pacific.[1] After vowing his famous pledge, "I shall return," MacArthur, his wife and son, and military aides climbed aboard *PT-41*. Under the skillful command of Lt. John D. Bulkeley (USN), Gen. MacArthur commenced a rough and dangerous voyage through enemy waters to the island of Mindanao and a U.S. Air Force B-17 bomber flight to Australia.[2]

The American Philippine invasion commenced in September and October of 1944. By mid–1945, Allied forces generally controlled the Philippines, despite the resistance of Japanese air and naval forces, suicide aircraft and boats, and persistent enemy troops dispersed in the tropical forests and highlands.[3]

Dr. Robert Browning, chief U.S. Coast Guard historian, and his staff of associate historians have done extensive research and writing about U.S. Coast Guard operations in the Atlantic and Pacific theaters during World War II. In his Pacific theater research, Dr. Browning wrote, "Coast Guard cutters and Coast Guard manned ships participated in nearly all amphibious landings in the Philippine Islands, and suffered through the Kamikaze attacks with the rest of the fleet." Thirty Coast Guard amphibious ships landed U.S. Army and Marine troops on the ten major Philippine Islands, including the beaches of Leyte. The Philippine fleet included 35 U.S. Coast Guard vessels and seven U.S.

Navy ships with combined USN/USCG crews. The Coast Guard ships included ten frigates (small destroyers), 12 LSTs, and seven attack transport and cargo ships.[4]

The 622-foot USS *General William Mitchell* (AP-114) was manned by Coast Guard crew members from 20 January 1944 to 22 February 1946.[5] The 13 large (17,830-gross ton) Coast Guard manned AP transports carried 450 officers and 4,700 troops at an average 19-knot speed. The nine smaller (522-foot, 12,347 gross ton) Coast Guard–manned APs carried 5,700 troops at a sustained flank speed of 18 knots. The USS *General Mitchell*, named after the prophetic and controversial U.S. Army air power advocate, carried thousands of American troops across Atlantic and Pacific waters, took wounded troops to military hospitals, shipped 5,000 U.S. troops to Luzon in the Philippines, and served as a "Magic Carpet" ship carrying American military personnel home after the war.[6]

The invasion fleet entered Leyte Gulf in the evening of 19 October 1944. At 0700 the crew of the USS *Leonard Wood* (APA-12) was ordered to General Quarters. At 0816 landing craft were lowered into the water. An hour later, 2,500 troops were heading to shore. An LCVP from the USS *Aquarius* (AKA-16) carried a beach master team ashore, the first military unit to land on Leyte after the U.S. naval bombardment of enemy positions. Mortar fire landed close to Coast Guard vessels, but kamikaze suicide aircraft did not arrive until after the initial troop landings. Coast Guard LSTs unloaded vehicles, supplies, and troops, then sailed back out to sea and returned with more supplies. Coast Guard attack transport crews took wounded ground troops and paratroopers onboard their vessels.[7]

On 12 November 1944, *LST-66* was struck alongside the starboard gun mounts by a kamikaze aircraft. The casualty count was 14 U.S. Army and Coast Guard personnel wounded and eight killed. Coast Guard–manned frigates carried out fire support, antisubmarine and escort patrols, and supply missions, and landed Army Rangers on a strategic island 48 hours before the Leyte landings.

The next American naval amphibious target was the island of Luzon. Manila, the capital city of the Philippines, is located on Luzon. Seven of the invading U.S. Navy ships had mixed Navy and Coast Guard crews. The Coast Guard–operated vessels included 10 LSTs, and the *Leonard Wood, Aquarius, Cavalier, Callaway, Cambria,* and *Arthur Middleton*. On 8 January 1945, the gunners on the *Callaway* (APA-35) splashed two kamikaze planes, but a third one hit the superstructure of the vessel. Firefighters doused the flames, but the Coast Guard casualty count was 20 wounded and 29 killed. No troops were killed, and the limited and repaired damage allowed the *Callaway* to navigate the 30 miles toward shore, where landing craft completed the journey and brought supplies and soldiers to the beachfront.

On the morning of 9 January 1945, the USS *Leonard Wood* (APA-12)

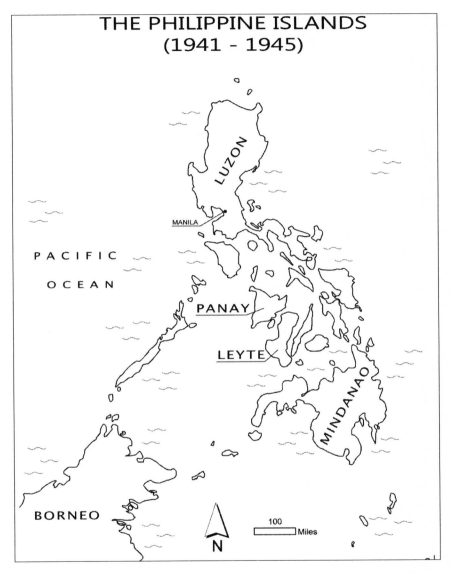

THE PHILIPPINE ISLANDS
(1941 - 1945)

LUZON

MANILA

PACIFIC

OCEAN

PANAY

LEYTE

MINDANAO

BORNEO

100
Miles

N

debarked 1,000 troops and 450 tons of supplies. Amphibious landing craft and barges got the supplies and troops ashore under sparse but dangerous enemy artillery and mortar fire. On 31 January, the 327-foot amphibious force flagship, USCGC *Spencer*, directed landings in Manila Bay. On 16 February, the 327-foot CGC *Ingham* directed landings on the enemy-held island fortress of Corregidor. Within three days, Coast Guard historian Browning described, "Troops had captured most of the important points on the island, returning the American flag to the scene of the 1942 United States capitulation."[8]

The 738 vessels of the Seventh Fleet that participated in the Leyte campaign consisted of 157 combat ships, 420 amphibious vessels, 73 service ships, and 84 hydrographic, minesweeping, and patrol vessels. Seven U.S. Navy ships had mixed Navy and Coast Guard crew complements: USS *William P. Biddle, Bellatrix, Crescent City, Fuller, George F. Elliott, President Hayes,* and *Heywood.*

Thirty-five Coast Guard–manned ships participated in the Leyte campaign. The 14 landing ship tanks were *LST-20, LST-22, LST-24, LST-26, LST-66, LST-67, LST-68, LST-168, LST-169, LST-170, LST-204, LST-205, LST-206,* and *LST-207.* The 21 ships were the USS *Allentown, Aquarius, Arthur Middleton, Bisbee, Burlington, Buttonwood, Callaway, Cambria, Carson City, Cavalier, Centaurus, Coronado, El Paso, Eugene, Gallup, Hutchinson, Leonard Wood, Muskogee, Ogden, San Pedro,* and *Spencer.*

Landing craft came to shore through mine fields, rough surf conditions, and enemy fire in crowded, chaotic circumstances. Disabled landing craft had to be secured, rescued, and towed off the beaches if possible. Coast Guard beach salvage units undertook the dangerous salvage missions. Beach conditions were made more uncertain when starved, grateful, liberated Filipino citizens flocked to the beaches to welcome U.S. Coast Guard, Army, and Navy forces. Military personnel provided the Filipinos with K-rations and medical care. Manila Harbor, one of the best ports in Asia, served as the entreport for the large LSTs, which opened their huge bow jaws, lowered the ramps, and discharged soldiers and supplies on to the beaches, at the same time tending to wounded troops.

Captain Frank D. Higbee (USCG) led the landing craft flotilla that brought the first naval contingent of four Coastguardsmen from the USS *Aquarius* to the Leyte beach. Capt. Higbee came ashore with the first wave of troops.

On 25 October 1944, *LST-207* was attacked by five kamikaze aircraft. It shot down three. While carrying out a resupply landing on 12 November, *LST-66* was struck by a kamikaze plane. Eight crewmembers were killed. Fourteen were wounded as the gun crew destroyed another enemy plane, was credited with hitting a second plane, and shot down two more Japanese planes in a subsequent attack.

On 5 December 1944, patrol frigate USS *Coronado* (PF-38) was escorting a ship convoy to Leyte when one of the merchant ships (SS *Antoine Saurian*) was struck by torpedoes from two Japanese aircraft. The merchant seamen abandoned the sinking vessel. The Coast Guard–manned *San Pedro, LST-454,* and *Coronado* put lifeboats in the water to rescue the mariners. The *Coronado* saved 31 merchant seamen, including the captain of the vessel, eight U.S. Navy Armed Guard gunners who had been stationed on the vessel, and 223 Army troops. A few hours later, the *Coronado* gunners hit an attacking Japanese aircraft at a distance of 1,000 yards. Unfortunately, in one of the gunnery exchanges, when a Japanese aircraft crossed the bow of the *Coronado*, a U.S. Coast Guard officer was killed when he stepped into the line of fire.

The last amphibious assault in the Philippines in 1944 occurred south of Luzon on the island of Mindora. The U.S. Navy Attack Force, under Rear Adm. Arthur D. Struble (USN), included destroyers, aircraft carriers, and PT (Patrol Torpedo) boats. The only Coast Guard–manned vessel in the operation was the U.S. Army supply ship, *FS-367* under the command of Lt. (jg) R.H. Greenless (USCGR). The landings were successful, despite incessant Japanese air attacks. It is estimated that, by the end of December, 373 enemy aircraft had attacked U.S. naval and merchant vessels and bombed American troop positions on Mindora. More than half of those Japanese planes were shot down. *FS-367* stood by to rescue crews and tow damaged vessels out of harm's way during the attacks that damaged and sank Navy and merchant vessels, blew up an ammunition ship, and forced naval crews into fuel-filled burning waters.[9]

By 28 January 1945, the U.S. Army had occupied the Philippine island of Leyte all the way to the former U.S. Army Air Force base at Clark Field, with the assistance of Filipino guerrillas. On 30 January American forces controlled Subic Bay. The Coast Guard–manned attack transport *Cavalier* (APA-37) was a casualty of the Subic Bay operation. Torpedoed by a Japanese submarine (I-boat), the *Cavalier* maintained seaworthiness due to the skill of a Coast Guard damage control team, and reached Leyte under tow.

On 31 January, an attack group of more than 80 U.S. Navy support, amphibious, landing craft, destroyer, and destroyer escort vessels landed U.S. Eighth Army and Eleventh Airborne Division troops south of Manila to attack defending Japanese troops. The naval force included the USCGC *Spencer* (WAGC/WHEC-36), and the Coast Guard–manned U.S. Army transport *FS-309*. The *Spencer* served at Leyte and Luzon. Onboard *Spencer* in the Luzon campaign was U.S. Army commanders Maj. Gen. Joseph M. Swing and Lt. Gen. Robert L. Eichelberger. The *Spencer* was the flagship of the Eighth Amphibious Group commander, Rear Adm. W.M. Fechteler (USN).

In his book, *Our Jungle Road to Tokyo* (1950), Gen. Eichelberger described the combat action of the naval campaign, including Japanese suicide vessels (Q-boats) that challenged Navy ships and gun crews and destroyed one patrol craft. Of the Coast Guard flagship, Gen. Eichelberger later wrote, "I found the *Spencer* to be extremely comfortable. Unlike my week enroute to Hollandia [New Guinea] on a destroyer, the *Spencer* I thought a grand ship ... outstanding. Discipline on this Coast Guard ship was very fine."[10]

The Coast Guard–manned U.S. Army freight ship *FS-309* was attacked at 0335 on 14 February 1945 by a Japanese Q-boat. *FS-309* was moored at a wharf inside a protective raft of wooden timbers. The Q-boat hit the timber raft, exploded, and disintegrated. The *FS-309* crew escaped casualties, but the ship had to be cleared of sand, water, and timber debris and pumped out.[11]

After the fall of Manila, Japanese troops still needed to be confronted at

Corregidor and on the Bataan Peninsula. On 15 February 1945, CGC *Ingham* (WAGC-35), the Task Force flagship of Adm. Arthur D. Struble (USN), led 62 landing craft into Mariveles Harbor on Bataan. Naval fire support ships, under Adm. R.S. Berkey (USN), suppressed enemy gunfire. The 4,300 troops of two U.S. Army Regimental Combat teams secured the Mariveles harbor and airstrip. On 16 February, military commanders stationed on the *Ingham* directed beach landing and paratroop operations on Corregidor. The 6,000 trapped Japanese troops fought ferociously, but the island was secured by the end of the month.

In late February, Task Force flagship USCGC *Spencer* (WAGC-36) carried Brigadier General Harold H. Haney (USA) and 8,000 Infantry Division troops into successful battle operations. *LST-66*, under Lt. Wendell J. Holbert (USCGR), guided a March amphibious assault that included 6,200 U.S. Army and Marine personnel and a company of tanks.

On 26 March (1945), Capt. Albert T. Sprague, Jr. (USN) led an Amphibious Group on to Cebu Island. The CGC *Spencer* joined the operation that put 14,000 Eighth Army American Division troops onshore following a heavy naval bombardment by Adm. Berkey's support ships. Japanese troops battled U.S. forces in caves, jungles, swamps and highlands until the end of June, when courageous and battle-hardened American forces secured most of the Philippine archipelago.[12]

On 1 July 1945, more than 100 ships of the U.S. Navy Third Fleet, under the command of Adm. William F. Halsey (USN), headed north through the Philippine Sea to begin the naval bombardment and air attack upon Japan. The Third Fleet consisted of destroyers, battleships, cruisers, and aircraft carriers. American aircraft took off from Okinawa and other captured airfields to bomb the Japanese islands of Kyushu and Honshu, and Tokyo and other major cities. Key industrial sites, fuel and mineral resource centers, and military bases were targeted. By 25 July, it was estimated that most of the Imperial Japanese Fleet that had sought refuge in Japan's Inland Sea had been destroyed.

On 6 August 1945, a U.S. B-29 bomber piloted by Col. Paul W. Tibbets (USAAF) dropped the atomic bomb on Hiroshima and destroyed the city. Absent a subsequent surrender declaration from Emperor Hirohito and other political and military leaders, a second nuclear bomb was dropped, which devastated Nagasaki on 9 August. On 14 August, in a prerecorded message, Emperor Hirohito announced the Japanese surrender on Radio Tokyo. On the previous evening, Japanese military and civilian officials thwarted a plot by military extremists to kidnap the Emperor, impound the Emperor's recorded surrender declaration, and assassinate compliant officials. The Truman administration subsequently received official notice of the Tokyo broadcast. At 1900 on 14 August 1945, President Harry Truman announced the Japanese surrender and the end of World War II.[13]

Defenders of the nuclear bombing of Japan believe it saved millions of lives that would have been lost in a homeland attack against determined, nationalistic, tenacious civilian and military fighters. The suicide planes and boats used in the Pacific war, and examples of Japanese soldiers fighting to the death and committing suicide, were testimonials to the battles that would have been waged on the islands of Kyushu, Hokkaido, Honshu, and Shikoku. Kamikaze troops and thousands of kamikaze aircraft were scattered throughout the islands. Millions of men and women were prepared to fight the Allied invaders. After the war, tons of ammunition were discovered. The alternative suggestion of using Allied bombers and submarines to bomb and starve the Japanese into submission would have required months of application, Soviet involvement and the probable Cold War division of Japan into Communist and Euro-American regions[14] would have appeared inhumane.

General Douglas MacArthur (USA) was appointed by President Truman to be supreme commander of the Allied Powers for the surrender and occupation of Japan, and governor general of the defeated nation, with the responsibility of demilitarizing, democratizing, and Westernizing it.

On 2 September 1945, a total of 258 Allied warships and hundreds of carrier planes in the vicinity of Tokyo Bay stood by as General MacArthur, on the battleship USS *Missouri,* conducted the surrender ceremonies with several leading Japanese military and civilian officials. Watching from the deck of the *Missouri* and other combat vessels were thousands of grateful Allied officers and enlisted personnel.[15]

U.S. Coast Guard and Navy vessels transported occupation troops and supplies into Japan. Navy and Coast Guard ships commenced the rewarding process of taking eligible military personnel back to the United States in Operation Magic Carpet. On 1 January 1946, the U.S. Coast Guard was transferred from U.S. Navy jurisdiction back to the U.S. Department of the Treasury.[16]

For most American veterans, discharge from active duty and return to civilian life were primary objectives. Returning regulars and reservists would take advantage of the innovative congressional "G.I. Bill," and use federal assistance programs to attend trade and technical colleges, schools, colleges, and universities, and return to civilian life, homes and families. Thousands of soldiers, sailors, and marines did not return to civilian life. Many had fallen in combat and noncombat incidents. Others chose to continue their military careers in the U.S. Armed Forces.

"Magic Carpet" and other postwar duties occupied the U.S. Navy and Coast Guard into the following year. The Coast Guard inevitably returned to its multi-mission peacetime and national security duties and responsibilities.[17]

Lt. Cmdr. Samuel Eliot Morison (USNR) received his officer's commission in 1942, and subsequently was asked to write a World War II naval history. Dr. Morison (Ph.D.), a Harvard historian, sailed on eleven U.S. Navy vessels, including the USCGC *Campbell* (WPG-32/WAGC-32). From his seafaring experience, and postwar research in military archives and oral interviews, Captain Morison (1945) crafted the classic 15-volume *History of the*

United States Naval Operations in World War II (Little, Brown & Company) between 1947 and 1962. The U.S. Navy promoted him to rear admiral in 1951. In 1963, Little, Brown & Company published Professor Morison's single volume naval history synthesis, *The Two Ocean War: A Short History of the United States Navy in the Second World War.*[18]

Admiral Morison attributed the Allied victory in the Pacific to several factors, including the fortuitous amphibious warfare technology and techniques developed by the U.S. Marine Corps in the prewar period. The U.S. Navy and Coast Guard adopted and adapted the amphibious warfare strategy and put insular Japanese forces on the defensive. Antisubmarine tactics, radar and sonar, mobile aircraft carrier fleets, and the support provided by Navy battleships, cruisers, destroyers, attack transports, landing craft and their well-trained, courageous crews, were essential to victory. The training, technology, strategy, tactics, logistics, leadership, and professionalism of U.S. Army and Army Air Force, Marine Corps, Navy, and Coast Guard leaders and the coordination between the U.S. Armed Forces led to victory on land and sea, over unimaginable geographic expanses and conditions.

Adm. Morison expressed admiration for the officers and crews "of the destroyers ("tin cans"), which operated in every theater of the war. They not only had to be first rate seamen and ship handlers ... but assimilate the new techniques of anti-submarine warfare and air defense." He also praised the submariners "of the silent service," who "destroyed the Japanese merchant fleet ... sank warships ... and scouted in advance of amphibious landings." The submarine crews cooperated with indigenous "patriots" in intelligence and support operations.[19] Submarines also performed, along with surface naval vessels, search and rescue operations and picked up downed aviators.

With his scholarship, eloquence, and perception, Dr. Morison instructed his readers to "remember ... the gunboats, mine [sweepers], destroyer escorts, PTs, beaching and other lettered craft ... and small cutters ... largely officered by reservists." Morison recalled that small craft "were forced to perform functions and make long voyages for which they had not been designed" and operated "under the most hazardous conditions." Adm. Morison the professional educator did not neglect "the training at special schools set up for that purpose." Professor Morison the historian extracted lessons and admonitions from his Pacific war studies, and recollected that at the beginning of the American participation in the war, "The Navy was woefully deficient in escorts and small craft, and should resolve never to be caught short again."[20] Dr. Morison was prescient. That naval debate over ship numbers, sizes, and functions extended into the Vietnam War and the contemporary war on terror as priority planners considered the balance between littoral ("brown water") vessels and "blue [deep] water" ships.

Equally prescient, and in modern times more problematic, was Morison's assessment of the peace and wartime contributions of the then "vastly expanded

American Merchant Marine," their intrepid civilian crews, and the "know-how of master mariners and seamen ... whose world-wide operations ... were indispensable to support the Navy, Army, and our Allies. Merchant mariners and the Naval Armed Guards on the ships showed exemplary courage in combat duty ... and in replenishing the Fleet under constant threat of Kamikaze attack."[21]

The world owes a debt of gratitude to the men and women who served at home and abroad, on land and sea, in each of the U.S. Armed Forces in every theater of war in World War II.

Epilogue

The contributions of the U.S. Coast Guard to World War II and the Allied victories over the Axis powers of Germany, Italy, and Japan have been explored in this book. The coordinated missions of the U.S. Armed Forces and our military allies, Canada, Great Britain, Australia, and New Zealand, and the freedom fighters in the enemy occupied territories of Europe and Asia, achieved hard fought victories between 1939 and 1945.

The joint missions of the U.S. Navy, U.S. Marine Corps, U.S. Army and Army Air Force were tactically and strategically challenging and brilliant, carried out as they were over vast and often inhospitable terrestrial and maritime environments in every geographic theater of war. The transoceanic challenges were compelling and enormous. Good military training, innovative technology, and a patriotic and nationalistic spirit galvanized the U.S. and Allied Armed Forces, and facilitated victory over dedicated and formidable foes.

American men and women stepped forward to serve the United States military at home and abroad, in the Reserves and National Guard, in the enlisted rates and commissioned officer ranks, and auxiliary units. American civilians played a critical role in fund-raising, rationing, volunteer work, and the contribution of their skills to the industrial and agricultural production needed for global victory. The U.S. Merchant Marine contributed competent civilian seafarers to crew the cargo vessels that carried supplies and personnel into combat zones in every corner of the globe and suffered significant casualties in the process. Merchant ships were armed. U.S. Navy Armed Guards manned the guns.

The U.S. Coast Guard had contributed to maritime law enforcement and national defense since its founding as the Revenue Marine in 1790. The U.S. Revenue Marine evolved into the Revenue Cutter Service. In 1915, the USRCS merged with the U.S. Life-Saving Service to form the U.S. Coast Guard. The USCG performed convoy escort and antisubmarine, patrols, port security, and search and rescue missions during America's participation in World War I (1917–1918). In 1939, the U.S. Lighthouse Service joined the Coast Guard. In the World War II era, the U.S. Coast Guard Women's Reserve was formed. Its personnel were called SPARS, an acronym based on the Coast Guard motto, "Semper Paratus." The well-trained and intrepid civilian members of the fledgling U.S. Coast Guard Auxiliary ably supplemented domestic Coast Guard regular and Reserve personnel in World War II, and ever since.

During World War II, the USCG merged with the U.S. Navy and performed coordinated and independent missions. Coast Guard personnel served on U.S. Navy and U.S. Army vessels independently or in joint-crews and manned Coast Guard cutters and landing craft independently. Coastguardsmen ran Navy destroyers, attack transport and cargo ships, and patrol boats. Coast Guard personnel joined their Navy compatriots in beach master units and as combat photographers and aviators. Large Coast Guard cutters served as flagships for U.S. Army, Marine, and Navy commanding officers.

Auxiliarists and SPARS administered Coast Guard office, hospital, search and rescue, radio communications, and port security units to free up regular and reserve Coast Guard personnel for maritime duty. Enlisted Coastguardsmen, civilian Auxiliary, and Temporary Reserve personnel performed home front duties that contributed to national defense. Early in the war, Beach Patrols carried out SAR missions and deterred and assisted in the capture of enemy saboteurs and espionage agents. Some members of the civilian Coast Guard Auxiliary served as Temporary Reservists. The "TRs" served many functions, including rear echelon support, local and regional waterfront patrols, and security at federal facilities and stations.

The U.S. Coast Guard Auxiliary was established in 1939 to promote boating safety. The civilian organization evolved into a "force multiplier" for the USCG, conducting SAR and port security missions. World War II Coast Guard commandant Adm. Russell R. Waesche assisted in the establishment of the USCGAUX. Civilian boat owners were organized into flotillas within Coast Guard Districts, and were led by elected civilians with nonmilitary "officer" ranks and guided by restricted statutory regulations. By the end of 1940, one year before the United States entered the war, the USCGAUX consisted of 150 flotillas, 3,000 members, and 2,700 boats operated by civilians. Civilian owned aircraft and their pilots were organized into aviation flotillas, conducted surveillance patrols, and scouted in SAR missions. One hundred and thirty-seven auxiliarists died during World War II from injuries and illness related to duty assignments.

During the war, 50,000 Auxiliarists wore civilian uniforms, guarded docks and ships, did port security and antisubmarine patrols, assisted firefighters, made arrests, performed beach patrol duty, manned radios, conducted SAR missions in response to civilian boating accidents, and reported or assisted victims of torpedoed ships struck by German U-boats off the East Coast. By 1943, the civilian Auxiliary boaters and aviators had 100 women in their ranks. Some Auxiliarists joined the Coast Guard Reserve or Temporary Reserve and performed joint duty assignments.[1]

The men and women of the U.S. Public Health Service served merchant mariners, and members of the U.S. Armed Forces at home and abroad. The

PHS traces its origins to the earliest years of the federal republic, and gradually acquired military status with its commissioned officer and nursing corps. The USPHS commanding officer held the rank of U.S. Surgeon General. The USPHS personnel complement consisted of civilians and commissioned officers. Specialists included members of social minority groups and included nurses, dentists, physicians, scientists, sanitation experts, and pharmacists. USPHS medical personnel were assigned to all of the Armed Forces. More than 700 PHS medical officers served with the U.S. Coast Guard in combat zones, where many suffered casualties.[2]

Traditions Military Videos produced excellent videotape featuring the Coast Guard in World War II. The video captures the war in the Atlantic, Normandy, the Mediterranean, and across the Pacific. The variety of Coast Guard actions and missions included landing craft operations; beach masters; kamikaze attacks; canine patrols on Pacific islands; 83-foot patrol boats which saved more than 1,000 lives; buoy tenders preparing navigation routes for combat vessels; USCG crews on cutters, destroyers, and transport and supply vessels; aviation and ocean weather patrols; medical units at sea and onshore; security patrols ashore; the Greenland Patrol; the capture of German troops and vessels; and commentary from Adm. Russell R. Waesche, the exemplary wartime commandant of the U.S. Coast Guard.[3]

Most of the World War II Coast Guard cutters have been decommissioned and scrapped for steel. A few of the venerable World War II cutters still exist, however, and serve as floating maritime history museums. The 327-foot USCGC *Ingham* (WPG-35) served in the Atlantic and the Pacific in World War II, and later in the Korean and Vietnam theaters. The *Ingham* is now stationed as an historic landmark at Patriots Point Naval and Maritime Museum in Mount Pleasant, South Carolina, in Charleston Harbor, east of Charleston.[4] The 327-foot USCGC *Taney* (WPG-37) was in combat at Pearl Harbor on 7 December 1941 and served as an escort cutter and flagship in the Pacific and in Vietnam. Today the CGC *Taney* is a museum ship in the Baltimore, Maryland, Inner Harbor.[5]

Seven Treasury Class "327" cutters were launched in the mid–1930s. The sleek, comfortable ships were equivalent to U.S. Navy destroyers and destroyer escorts (DDs, and DEs) and performed search and rescue and antisubmarine warfare patrols. Crew complements averaged about 230 men. Flank speed on the 327s was 20 knots. A variety of deck guns (5-inch), and smaller anti-anti-aircraft, machine guns and small arms were available aboard the 327s, as were a variety of depth charges. In 1944, the 327s served as amphibious force flagships for invasion commanders of the U.S. Navy, Army, and Marine Corps. The destroyer/frigate sized cutters were supplemented in combat by smaller Coast Guard–manned landing craft, large landing ship tanks (LSTs), and smaller sub-chaser patrol boats.[6]

The 165-foot USCGC *Mohawk* (WPG-78) served on escort duty and antisubmarine patrol in Atlantic, and on the Greenland Patrol in Arctic waters. The *Mohawk* is now a museum ship at Key West, Florida, a fitting testimonial to the U-boat presence and anti-submarine patrols that occurred in the Atlantic and Gulf regions during World War II.[7]

On 6–7 June 2003, seventy World War II veterans celebrated their 20th D-Day (7 June 1944) Anniversary in Duluth, Minnesota, and, 70 miles east, in Bayfield, Wisconsin. The site of the Bayfield celebration was a World War II LCT boat, the 150-foot *Outer Island*. The former Normandy landing craft survived German artillery and mortars fire, and is now a company construction boat used for dredging, hauling cargo, and carrying supplies in marine construction projects. Ken Dobson, one of the boat owners, said he has enjoyed preserving the World War II landing craft, one of the few LCTs, if not the last one, in the United States. Dobson said he "enjoys watching veterans relive their memories aboard the boat" and starting the engines to excite veterans who "figured they'd never hear that sound again."[8]

Writers of Coast Guard history who have served in the U.S. Armed Forces add special insight and appreciation in their analyses of the Sea Services. Rear Adm. Samuel Eliot Morison, the eminent Harvard historian, sailed the seas to better understand maritime history, technology, tactics, and logistics. President Franklin Roosevelt assigned Dr. Morison the responsibility of chronicling a history of the U.S. Navy in World War II. In his initial assignment, Lt. Cmdr. Morison sailed on U.S. Navy and Coast Guard vessels in combat zones. The result of his scholarship was the classic 15-volume *History of United States Naval Operations in World War II,* written and published between 1947 and 1962.

In volume seven of his naval history, Adm. Morison described the Aleutian Islands, Alaska, cruiser task force, commanded by Rear Adm. W.W. Smith (USN) in 1942, as consisting of "a destroyer strike group, six S-class submarines, and a flock of Coast Guard cutters and other small craft." Morison described the challenging Aleutian seafaring and aviation conditions of "fog and unsettled thick and rough weather. The hazards of surface and air navigation are greater there than in any other part of the world."[9] Coast Guard veterans of the Greenland Patrol would likely challenge Morison's assertion of unique climatic conditions in the Aleutians.

Professor Morison gave a vivid description of the technology and operations of LVT amphtrac and LCI landing craft and crews in the Gilbert and Marshall islands in 1943. The amphibious vessels were well armed for offensive and defensive combat support, supply, and troop transport missions to hostile beaches in varying sea and surf conditions. The LVTs carried a crew of six and 20 troops. LVTs were "armed and armored," Morison wrote, and "both driver and passengers were protected by ¼-inch armor plate, two machine guns of .50 caliber and one of .30." The LCIs were "shoal draft gunboats" which carried infantry troops to shore, gave "close-in fire support to a landing force," and were equipped with "machine guns ... and six rocket racks with 72 rockets which were effective at 1,100 yard range." In addition, Morison explained, "Alternate LVT-As were equipped with flame throwers, but these got so wet in the Kwajalein and Eniwetok landings that they did not work."[10]

The tactical problems and challenges of landing craft operations were perceptively described by Morison in the Kwajalein invasion of 1944: "Each LVT was to go on board its mother LST for the night to fuel, make repairs, and load Marines. But some could not find their way back to the LSTs in the dark. Others ran out of gas, and stranded on various islets ... their crews completely exhausted. There had been a heavy chop in the lagoon. When darkness fell, crews were soaked and chilled."[11]

Admiral Morison tracked Coast Guard–manned vessels in the Aleutians, Gilberts, and Marshalls from June 1942 to April 1944. Attack transport USS *Leonard Wood* (APA-12), under Capt. H.C. Perkins (USCG), served in the Gilbert Islands and the Makin Atoll in November 1943, lowering LCVP landing craft with soldiers aboard in early morning operations. At Eniwetok (February 1944), Capt. D.W. Loomis (USN), on the Coast Guard's manned flagship *Leonard Wood,* commanded 11 transport vessels carrying U.S. Army and Marine units, tanks, and scout detachments.[12]

The USS *Cambria* (APA-36), under Capt. C.W. Dean (USCG), was the flagship of Adm. H.W. Hill (USN), who commanded the Majuro Attack Group of one cruiser, two escort carriers, three transports, two minesweepers, and a U.S. Army infantry regiment. The Majuro mission (February 1944) was followed by Eniwetok, with Adm. Hill still on the *Cambria* utilizing the attack transport's sophisticated communications equipment.[13]

The Coast Guard–manned USS *Arthur Middleton* (APA-25), under Capt. S.A. Olsen (USCG), had performed distinguished service at Tarawa the previous year (November 1943) in support of the 2nd Battalion, 8th Regiment, commanded by Major H.P. Crowe (USMC).[14] In the invasion of Kwajalein Atoll (31 January–7 February 1944), field artillery bases had to be established to support assaults on Japanese positions by three landing teams of the 25th U.S. Marine Regiment, commanded by Brig. Gen. James L. Underhill (USMC). The Marines embarked on the Coast Guard–manned USS *Callaway* (APA-35), under the command of Capt. D.C. McNeil (USCG).[15]

Captain Stephen H. Evans (USCG) published his scholarly history, *The United States Coast Guard, 1790–1915: A Definitive History,* in 1949, four years after World War II ended. The war directly impacted on the author. Capt. Evans dedicated his Service history "To my brother, Arthur Bliss Evans, Jr., Lieutenant (junior grade), U.S. Coast Guard Reserve, lost in action against the enemy while serving on board USS *Leopold* (DE-319), North Atlantic Ocean, 9 March 1944."

At the end of his *Definitive History* (1790–1915), which ended two years before the entry of the United States into World War I, Capt. Evans included a "Postscript: 1915–1949," in which he wrote this summation of the Coast Guard role in World War II: "The Coast Guard, acting as part of the Navy, furnished trained forces for combat operations in all theaters of war," which included an extension of the peacetime missions of "aids to navigation, search and rescue, beach patrol, port security, and enforcement of marine safety laws and regulations." Then (with the consolidation of the Bureau of Marine Inspection and Navigation under Coast Guard control in 1942), Evans concluded, "To perform all these varied duties under conditions of total war, the Coast Guard expanded to nearly 200,000 officers and men."[16] The total Coast Guard complement also included the 8,000 officers and enlisted personnel of the U.S. Coast Guard Women's Reserve, under the command of Capt. Dorothy C. Stratton (USCG). Added to the supplemental ranks were 50,000 civilian members of the Coast Guard Auxiliary. Most of the Auxiliaries were gradually added to the U.S. Coast Guard Temporary Reserve list to give them military status. It was feared that with purely civilian status in wartime, Coast Guard Auxiliary members might be captured and executed as spies while out on antisubmarine patrol.[17]

Howard Van Lieu Bloomfield, a maritime author and sailor, wrote a history of the Coast Guard that included five chapters on World War II. Bloomberg expressed specific appreciation to his "former history teacher, Rear Adm. Samuel Eliot Morison (USN, Ret.), for permission to quote freely from his *History of United States Naval Operations in World War II*."[18]

Bloomfield studied USCG Patrol Bomber Squadron Six, which supported the maritime Greenland Patrol and aided in convoy protection and weather patrols. The Coast Guard–manned U.S. Navy Squadron was dispersed to bases in Greenland, Iceland, Arctic Canada, and Newfoundland, on the coast of eastern Canada. "Squadron Six flew," Bloomfield graphically explained, "[in] all weathers, mostly bad, in fogs, gales, sleet and snow ... over ice or rough seas where there was no landing [and performed] rescues, drops of emergency or medical supplies, transporting injured men, [and did] submarine spotting over convoys and ice patrols on instrument flying ... and at night."[19]

The Coast Guard wartime seaplane complement consisted of around seventy sea (float) planes, and eighty other aircraft the USCG operated for the U.S. Navy. The skilled Coast Guard aviators set the float planes down in rough ocean waters on rescue missions, took injured and lost mariners out of life rafts and lifeboats, rescued merchant mariners who survived enemy torpedo attacks, and even German crew members of sunken U-boats. Coast Guard aviators also pioneered in the use of the fledgling helicopters during the war. In 1943 and 1944, Commander F.A. Erickson (USCG), the commanding officer of Floyd Bennett Field in Brooklyn, New York, pioneered in helicopter training and piloted rotor-winged aircraft in rescue missions.[20]

Coast Guard cutters and Coast Guard–manned U.S. Navy and U.S. Army vessels carried out a plethora of wartime missions and suffered casualties in the process: 4 Army, 12 Navy, and 16 Coast Guard vessels were destroyed or sunk in the war. Of the nearly 200,000 Coast Guard personnel who served at home and abroad in World War II, 572 were killed in action, 1,035 were killed overseas in accidents, and a total of 1,878 Coast Guard personnel died in service. Bloomfield calculated that one Coastguardsman earned the Medal of Honor, six were awarded U.S. Navy Crosses, 67 received Legion of Merit honors, and one got a Distinguished Flying Cross.[21] However, World War II Coast Guard historian Lt. Malcolm F. Willoughby (USCGR-T) calculated that 12 Coast Guard personnel earned the Distinguished Flying Cross, and one Coastguardsman (Cmdr. Richard L. Burke) was awarded the "Gold Star in lieu of a second DFC award."[22]

A secret mission involving U.S. Coast Guard and U.S. Navy personnel in Japanese-occupied China was revealed after the war. Expert Coast Guard horsemen joined a U.S. Naval Group to train Chinese forces in their fight against the Japanese invaders. The USCG group consisted of members of the Coast Guard Horse Patrol, a wild animal trainer, and former mounted police officers and ranchers. Coast Guard and U.S. Navy demolition and munitions experts trained Chinese guerrillas in horse-mounted missions using guns and explosives. Military historian Howard Bloomfield calculated that "these pupils of Naval Group China killed 23,540 Japanese and destroyed 209 bridges, 84 locomotives, and 141 ships and river craft" in 1944 and 1945.[23]

U.S. Coast Guard historian Robert Browning wrote that Naval Group China trained Chinese military personnel to handle horses and dogs in the region of Chunking, China. Dogs were used for sentry duty and horses for long-range reconnaissance missions to observe and prevent the infiltration of Japanese forces behind Chinese lines. The twenty Coast Guard instructors who had been flown over the mountains into China to train Chinese troops in patrol and sentry duty were under the command of Lt. Cmdr. Clayton Snyder (USCG).[24] The U.S. Navy and Coast Guard members of Naval Group China might be considered predecessors of today's U.S. Navy SEAL (Sea, Air, Land) special operations forces.

After the surrender of Japan, U.S. Coast Guard cutters joined the Allied occupation forces in coastal and harbor mine sweeping missions. Coast Guard transport ships began the postwar transfer of thousands of U.S. troops back to the United States in operation "Magic Carpet."[25]

After the transfer of the Coast Guard from the U.S. Navy back to Treasury Department jurisdiction in 1946, Navy Secretary James Forrestal observed that the Coast Guard "earned the highest respect and deepest appreciation of the Navy and Marine Corps. Its performance of duty has been without exception in keeping with the highest traditions of the naval service."[26]

Colonel Gene Gurney (USAF), a B-24 pilot in the U.S. Army Air Force in World War II, served subsequently in the U.S. Air Force as an aviator, intelligence officer, public information officer, and combat officer in Vietnam. Col.

Gurney also authored numerous military books and articles. From that formidable professional background, Col. Gurney wrote a perceptive history of
the peacetime and wartime missions of the United States Coast Guard from
1790 through the Vietnam era. In his book, *The United States Coast Guard*
(1973), Col. Gurney devoted more than 60 pages of photographs and narrative to World War II. In his book acknowledgements, the author credited several civilian archivists, National Archives sources and researchers, and Coast
Guard photojournalists, officers, and enlisted personnel at Coast Guard headquarters in Washington, D.C.

Colonel Gurney explained specialized Coast Guard missions, activities,
and little known incidents, including the following: crewmen from the combat-
damaged USCGC *Campbell* (WPG-32/WAGC-32) boarded the Polish destroyer
and rescue ship *Burza* with survivors of German U-boat *U-606*, which the
Campbell had sunk; USCG crews manned eight Canadian corvette warships[27];
photographs of damaged Coast Guard LCIs struck by mines and German
gunfire, still afloat and running, with some landing craft later sinking[28]; Coast
Guard LSTs taking wounded soldiers to hospital ships and shore stations, U.S.
Navy medical officers, corpsmen, and Coast Guard pharmacists mates treating wounded American combat personnel on ships and ashore, and administering medical aid to German prisoners of war, and a Coast Guard transport
ship loading more than 300 German POWs for detention in America.[29]

Colonel Gurney's photographic research illustrated the salvaging of an
abandoned midget Japanese submarine (I-boat) at Guadalcanal, which was
turned over to U.S. Navy intelligence officers,[30] Coast Guard and Navy signal-
men waving semaphore flags on a Pacific combat beach,[31] the unloading of war
dogs from a landing barge at Guam to be used on canine patrol to "ferret out
Japanese hidden on the island,"[32] and the former champion heavyweight boxer,
Cmdr. Jack Dempsey (USCGR), at Okinawa conversing with famed war correspondent Ernie Pyle.[33]

Ernie Pyle chronicled the war, and military journalists chronicled him.
Coast Guard combat correspondent Chief Specialist Evan Wylie (USCGR)
wrote about Pyle's death on the island of Ie Shima, just north of Okinawa. On
18 April 1945, an enemy bullet struck Pyle in the midst of Army and Marine
troops with whom he shared a bond born in combat. Chief Wylie's story (dated
18 May 1945 the following month) appeared in *Yank*, the weekly U.S. Army
periodical. The Japanese sniper fired on Pyle as Pyle leaped from a jeep to take
cover in a ditch. "The small, gray, weary little guy," wrote Wylie, "had died
instantly from a bullet that penetrated the left side of his helmet and entered
the left temple. The litter bearers placed the body on the stretcher and worked
their way along the ditch under sniper fire." Chief Specialist Wylie concluded,
"Ie Shima will be remembered as the place where America's most famous war
correspondent met the death he had been expecting for so long."[34]

The June 2008 issue of *Naval History* paid tribute to the role of the U.S.

Coast Guard in defeating the U-boat menace in the Atlantic in World War II. Without the successful Navy and Coast Guard strategies and tactics and the assistance of Canadian and British warships, Britain might have been defeated. Jeff Barlow underscored the significance of the executive order that placed the U.S. Coast Guard under U.S. Navy jurisdiction in 1941 and the role the 327-foot Coast Guard cutters would play in convoy duty and antisubmarine warfare. Barlow credited the U.S. Navy Armed Guards for their skillful manning of the guns on merchant vessels.[35]

Michael G. Walling, a former Coast Guard petty officer and commissioned officer and author of an acclaimed book on the Atlantic U-boat war, wrote, "The [six] reliable Coast Guard Secretary-class cutters were the backbone of the U.S. North Atlantic escort fleet during World War II."[36] Walling described the sinking of the torpedoed USCGC *Alexander Hamilton* (WPG-34) on 29 January 1942 and the successful attacks and sinking of *U-626* by the USCGC *Ingham* (WPG-35); *U-606* by the USCGC *Campbell* (WPG-32); *and U-175* by the CGC *Spencer* (WPG-36) in the winter of 1942–1943. The respective commanding officers of the *Ingham, Campbell,* and *Spencer* were Cmdr. George McCabe, Cmdr. James A. Hirschfield, and Cmdr. Harold S. Berdine. The USCGC *Duane* (WPG-33) assisted the *Spencer* in destroying *U-175* by firing its deck guns at the submarine and aiding in the rescue of the 41 survivors of the U-boat crew. The U.S. Navy Armed Guards on adjacent merchant vessels also fired on *U-175* and influenced the German submariners to surrender.[37]

As the population of World War II veterans sadly diminishes, contemporary events to celebrate them are increasingly important. Veterans are being honored in books and in the media, and at ceremonies and wartime memorials in Washington D.C., and communities across the nation. In the September 2007 issue, associate editor Matt Grills of *American Legion* magazine interviewed World War II Petty Officer Marvin Perrett (USCG). Perrett was a coxswain on landing craft at Normandy, Iwo Jima, and Okinawa. The former Coastguardsman proudly recalled his boat, *PA 33–21,* a replica of which he visited at the National World War II Museum in New Orleans. PO Perrett recalled the invasions, near misses and close calls, troops wounded and killed, and the loss of one landing craft "sunk out from under me." He described the 10–12 mile trips back and forth, transporting troops and supplies in and wounded soldiers out to the USS *Bayfield* (APA-33). Recalling his combat experience, Perrett said, "I had to fend for myself and my crew. It scares heck out of me today. How'd I manage to make it?"[38]

Captain Dorothy Stratton (USCG) founded and directed the U.S. Coast Guard Women's Reserve and named the members SPARS, after the Service motto, "Semper Paratus." Prior to entering the Coast Guard, Stratton was dean of women and a psychology professor at Purdue University. Lt. Dorothy Stratton (USN) initially served in the Women's Appointed Volunteer Service (WAVES). Six months later, she transferred to the USCG to direct the SPARS, which grew to a force of 11,000 enlisted women and officers. Captain Stratton retired from the Coast Guard in 1946 and received the Legion of Merit. She later served as executive director of the Girl Scouts of America. Capt. Stratton passed away on 17 September 2006, at the age of 107.[39]

Lois Bouton served under Captain Dorothy Stratton in the SPARS. In 1943, Bouton resigned her position as an elementary school teacher in Illinois and went to basic training in Palm Beach, Florida. Petty Officer Bouton (USCGWR) served as an instructor and then a radio operator from 1943 to 1945. RM Bouton was stationed in Bethany Beach, Delaware, where she sent weather reports and ship location coordinates to Coast Guard units ashore and afloat. After the war, PO Bouton returned to her teaching career, volunteered at veterans hospitals, and, in 2007, at the age of 87, was still sending letters and making contact with Coast Guard stations and personnel throughout the nation.[40]

Chief Journalist Alex Haley (USCG) joined the Coast Guard in 1939. Due to the restrictions African Americans faced in the service then, Haley's enlisted rate options were limited to mess attendant and steward. Haley honed his writing skills on long patrols on several cutters and in the Pacific combat theater, and his literary talent led to his breaking the ratings barriers. Haley got assignments as reporter and editor for Coast Guard publications, and earned promotions to Journalist First Class and Chief Journalist. Chief Petty Officer Haley retired from the Coast Guard in 1959. He won the Pulitzer Prize for his novel *Roots* in 1976. In 1991, the Coast Guard commissioned the 210-foot USCGC *Haley* (WMEC-39), home-ported in Kodiak, Alaska. CPO Haley died in 1992.[41]

Sixty-two years after D-Day, Wilfred Eberhart was on a Seattle, Washington, dock, being reunited with CG-11 (later redesignated CG-83366), the Coast Guard cutter he served on at Normandy on D-Day (6 June 1944). The 83-foot rescue boat, now a restored yacht, had been in Seattle since it was decommissioned in 1962. Signalman Third Class Eberhart (USCG) explained how the 12-person crew of CG-11, and the crews of each of the 60 cutters in Coast Guard Flotilla 1, rescued 1,400 injured troops in the waters off Omaha Beach during the invasion. SM3 Eberhart recalled pulling dead and injured troops out of the water and tracking German submarines.[42] Lt. (jg) Art Lehne (USCG, Ret.) was also reunited with SM3 Eberhart and the landing craft in the Armed Forces Day ceremonies at Seattle on 19 May 2007. SM3 Eberhart, 85 years of age on the day of the celebration, was the radio operator and flag signalman on the boat. Lt. Lehne, 86 years old in 2007, was the commanding officer of CG-11 (83366).[43]

Honorary Chief Petty Officer Raymond F. O'Malley (USCG, Ret.) was laid to rest on 13 March 2007 in Chicago, Illinois, at age 86. Seaman First Class O'Malley and Boatswain's Mate Second Class Melvin A. Baldwin, who died in 1964, were the only two survivors of the torpedoed USCGC *Escanaba* (WPG-77). The Great Lakes cutter was sunk in the North Atlantic on 13 June 1943, with the loss of 103 Coastguardsmen. At the conclusion of the military funeral, Rear Adm. John E. Crowley (USCG) presented the American flag to O'Malley's spouse, Dolly. Raymond O'Malley had attended 64 memorial services for his fallen Coast Guard comrades on the annual Coast Guard Day memorial celebration in Grand Haven, Michigan, the home port of the 165-foot CGC *Escanaba*.[44]

Coast Guard personnel were responsible for Port Security, firefighting, and explosives loading and unloading in harbor and port areas in the United States and in combat zones overseas. Coast Guard Captains of the Port (COTPs) were responsible for the training and administration of port security units. Coast Guard port security teams deterred espionage and sabotage and contributed to military and civilian safety with preventive action and intervention. Ports and merchant ships and military cargo and tanker ships were hazardous zones, given the vase quantities of fuel and ordnance that were on warships and transported and stored. Fires and explosions were prevented or controlled through Coast Guard preemptive action that contained the repercussions of incidents in often dangerous and life-threatening circumstances.

Just one major fire incident that occurred in the New York City maritime region illustrates the significance of the port security and firefighting teams and the dangers they faced. Seaman Second Class Seymour L. Wittek (USCG) was on Port Security duty in New York Harbor on 24 April 1943, when a fire erupted on the Panamanian ammunition ship *El Estero* at 1720. The fire started when an oil feed line ruptured. SN2 Wittek wrote the author of this book, stating, "Sir: I am sending you new material I have gathered [on the *El Estero* catastrophe]: "I was a volunteer to board the SS *El Estero*." [45]

Coastguardsmen of the "Munitions Detail" in Jersey City, New Jersey and 60 Coast Guard volunteers from the barracks, including SN2 Seymour Wittek (USCG), reported to the dock in Bayonne, New Jersey, and responded under the command of Lt. Cmdr. John T. Stanley (USCG). New York and New Jersey firefighters joined in the battle. Coastguardsmen fought the shipboard fire from the U.S. Army dock, from fireboats, and from onboard the *El Estero*. Lt. Cmdr. Arthur F. Pfister coordinated the response to the fire with Lt. Cmdr. Stanley, and they concluded the *El Estero* should be scuttled. Rear Adm. Stanley V. Parker, the COTP of New York, agreed. But the seacocks were in the midst of the inferno and could not be reached or removed to commence the scuttling (sinking) process. Coastguardsmen volunteered to remain aboard the vessel to man the fire hoses and fill the *El Estero* with enough water to quench the flames before the ammunition cargo exploded. Coast Guard and civilian fireboats poured water on the flames. At 1820, tugboats commenced to tow the ammunition ship further out to sea. Public safety officials and medical personnel stood by in case the conflagration led to massive explosions; they also warned the urban community to seek safety. At 2045, the water-logged ship began to keel over. The tugs cut the towing lines, and Lt. Cmdr. Stanley ordered the 20 remaining Coastguardsmen off the ship and into the fireboats. The *El Estero* sank minutes later in 35 feet of water. Coast Guard munitions experts calculated the tonnage of ammunition cargo on the *El Estero,* the two other ammunition ships at the dock, and the ordnance on adjacent railroad cars and concluded that, had the *El Estero* exploded at the dock and ignited the adjacent ammunition cargoes, half of New York City would have been damaged or destroyed, and one million area residents would have been killed or seriously injured.[46]

Had the *El Estero* exploded at its berthing dock, Staten Island storage tanks containing millions of gallons of fuel could have ignited, adding to the urban inferno. The four tugboat captains and their crews attached hawsers to the 11,500-ton, 325-foot ammunition transport. Coast Guard firefighters on the dock stood their ground even as their shoes began to burn. Hundreds of civilian mariners, law enforcement officers, firefighters, and Coastguardsmen on boats and ashore bravely carried out their hazardous duties, knowing at any second a cataclysmic blast could take their lives. Several small explosions occurred as the ship was towed further out into the harbor and as the vessel sank beneath the sea. Security measures prevented the public from hearing the full story of the disaster. The brave civilian and Coast Guard personnel who risked their lives to save lives would be publicly honored in awards ceremonies the following year, when media coverage informed the nation of the incident.[47]

The Bayonne New Jersey Times (25 and 26 September 1944) covered the ceremonies that were sponsored by the city of Bayonne and the *Times* to honor and present medals to the 168 Coast Guard officers and enlisted personnel who risked their lives to control the *El Estero* conflagration. Admiral Charles A. Parks (USCG) represented U.S. Coast Guard commandant Adm. Russell R. Waesche. Admiral W.R. Munroe (USN), commander of the Third Naval District, was present, as was Adm. Stanley V. Parker, the New York City Captain of the Port. An estimated 3,000 people were present to honor the Coast Guard heroes who were credited with saving thousands of lives and two cities. Bayonne Mayor Bert Daly and New York City Mayor Fiorello La Guardia were on hand to honor the Coastguardsmen, who marched to the ceremonies behind the Manhattan Beach Station Coast Guard Band.[48]

In his description of the *El Estero* disaster, Coast Guard historian Lt. Malcolm F. Willoughby (USCGR-T) wrote, "Lt. Cmdr. John T. Stanley (USCG), was on his first day of duty as Munitions Officer. For his part, he was awarded the Legion of Merit. The citation read: 'Lt. Cmdr. Stanley boarded the vessel and for three hours directed a large detail of men in controlling and extinguishing the fire; by his calm and courageous leadership [an explosion was prevented] which might have done incalculable damage to other vessels and vital installations in the harbor.'"[49]

The 14 December 1942 edition of *Life* magazine paid tribute to the missions and contributions of the U.S. Coast Guard in World War II. The popular periodical featured narrative and magnificent photographs and drawings of the Coast Guard missions ashore and on the high seas. The topics and illustrations included 165-foot and 83-foot antisubmarine patrol cutters; combat ship ordnance and armament; port security operations; Coast Guard air stations and reconnaissance aircraft; and patrols off American shores by civilian Coast Guard auxiliary and U.S. Coast Guard Temporary Reserve (USCGR-T) personnel.[50]

The *Life* cover featured a photograph of Lt. Maurice Jester (USCG), the commander of the 165-foot patrol craft *Icarus* (WPC-110). A former enlisted chief boatswain's mate, Lt. Jester earned the Navy Cross for "extraordinary achievement" in ASW operations against German U-boats in the Atlantic theater.[51]

The multi-mission role of the Coast Guard in World War II was significant, as were its missions prior to the war. While carrying out overseas combat responsibilities, the Coast Guard continued its inspection of merchant vessels; safety training for merchant mariners; surveying and mapping missions; cold-weather operations in the high latitudes; and oceanic weather station duties. The Coast Guard assisted in the defense of Iceland and Greenland; located German weather stations that relayed meteorological information to U-boats; and conducted sea and air convoy protection and ASW patrols.[52]

Within its multi-mission responsibilities, the Coast Guard provided minorities with enhanced military opportunities in an era of racial segregation. Progress in all of the Armed Forces was slow, and integration was expedited by political pressure. Nonetheless, the Coast Guard had offered enlisted and commissioned officer opportunities to Blacks ashore and afloat since the late nineteenth century. Strict segregation was nearly impossible in the small Sea Service. African Americans served in mess and steward capacities and in World War II battle stations. A Black gun crew on the USCGC *Campbell* (WPG-32) earned citations for assisting in the sinking of a U-boat. The USCGC *Sea Cloud* (WPG-284), a North Atlantic weather ship, was integrated in 1943 and boasted a complement of African-American commissioned officers and rated petty officers.[53]

The competence with which the U.S. Coast Guard carried out its naval missions earned the Service the gratitude and respect of U.S. Navy officials. In the Official Report of the Fleet Admiral of the U.S. Navy, Adm. Ernest J. King (USN) summarized his perspective on the Coast Guard contribution to the war effort: "Under the general direction of Admiral R.R. Waesche (USCG), Commandant, the Coast Guard has done an excellent job in all respects, and as a component of the Navy in time of war has demonstrated an efficiency and flexibility which has been invaluable in the solution of the multiplicity of problems assigned. The organization and handling of local defense in the early days of the war were particularly noteworthy."[54]

World War II Era
Coast Guard Chronology

1915 (28 Jan.) The U.S. Coast Guard (USCG) was officially created with the consolidation of the U.S. Life-Saving Service (USLSS) and the U.S. Revenue Cutter Service (USRCS) under the Treasury Department. The USRCS (Revenue Marine) was established in 1790 by Congress under the direction of Treasury Secretary Alexander Hamilton.

1916 (1 April) Coast Guard aviation began with the acceptance of USCG officers and enlisted personnel into U.S. Navy flight training at Pensacola, Florida.

1917 (6 April) During World War I the USCG was placed under the jurisdiction of the USN and returned to Treasury Department control in 1919.

1917 (15 June) The Espionage Act tasked the USCG with safeguarding vessels, ports, harbors, anchorages, and waterfront infrastructure.

1918 (26 Sept.) The U.S. Coast Guard cutter (USCGC), USS *Tampa* was sunk by a German U-boat torpedo while escorting an Allied convoy in the North Atlantic. All 115 crewmembers were lost.

1918 (11 Nov.) The Armistice ended World War I.

1919 (16–27 May) Lt. Elmer F. Stone (USCG) was the pilot of USN seaplane NC-4 in the first aircraft transatlantic crossing.

1919 (Dec.) Coast Guard boats, oceangoing cutters, and aircraft began patrols against the rumrunners of the Prohibition era (1919–1933).

1920 (24 March) The first USCG Air Station (USCGAS) was operational in Morehead City, North Carolina.

1939 (23 June) The Coast Guard Reserve was formed as a civilian organization to assist recreational boaters. In 1941 the "Reserve" became the USCG Auxiliary. The new USCG Reserve (USCGR) provided trained military personnel to supplement Coast Guard Regular forces. Most of the 240,000 World War II Coast Guard complement were Reservists.

1939 (1 July) The U.S. Lighthouse Service (USLHS) was incorporated into the USCG.

1939 (1 Sept.) World War II began with the German invasion of Poland.

1939 (5 Dec.) President Franklin Roosevelt declared the U.S. neutral in the war in Europe and established a protective air and naval Neutrality Patrol.

1940 (10 February) The USCGC *Duane* initiated the USCG Weather Patrol. Weather Patrol cutters were replaced in 1976 by electronic buoys and space satellites.

1941 (6 June) USS *Hunter Liggett* (APA-14) became the first USN attack transport to be crewed completely by USCG personnel.

1940 (27 June) The Espionage Act of 1917 invoked by President Roosevelt activated the USCG Port Security mission.

1941 (12 Sept.) USCGC *Northland* (WPG-49) made the first U.S. naval capture of an enemy trawler and crew off the coast of Greenland during the U.S. neutrality period.

1941 (14 Sept.) USCGC *Northland* destroyed a German weather station in Greenland and captured enemy personnel.

1941 (1 November) The USCG was transferred to USN control just prior to U.S. entry into World War II and for the duration. The Coast Guard returned to Treasury Department jurisdiction on 1 January 1946.

1941 (7 Dec.) Japanese naval units attacked the U.S. military base at Pearl Harbor, Hawaii.

1941 (8 Dec.) The United States declared war on Japan.

1942 (30 January) USCGC *Alexander Hamilton* (WPG-34) was torpedoed and sunk by a German U-boat off the coast of Iceland with the loss of the 20 crewmembers.

1942 (21 Feb.) USCGC *Spencer* sank a German submarine.

1942 (28 Feb.) The Bureau of Marine Inspection was transferred to the Coast Guard.

1942 (9 May) USCGC *Icarus* (WPC-110) sank U-352 and saved and captured 33 prisoners.

1942 (15 May) USCGC *Acacia* (WAGL-200) was sunk in the Caribbean Sea by a U-boat.

1942 (9 July) USCGC *McClane* (WSC-146) and USS *YP-251* sank a Japanese submarine off the Alaskan coast.

1942 (1 Aug.) A Coast Guard aircraft (Grumman J4F-1*Widgeon* V-212) sank a German U-boat in the Gulf of Mexico.

1942 (9 Sept.) USCGC *Muskegat* (WAG-48) was sunk by a U-boat with the loss of the 121 crewmembers.

1942 (27 Sept.) Petty Officer First Class Douglas Munro (USCG) used his landing craft and a machine gun to protect U.S. Marines at Guadalcanal. PO1 Munro posthumously received the Medal of Honor.

1942 (17 Dec.) USCGC *Natsek* (WYP-170) was lost off Newfoundland (Canada) with all 22 crewmembers.

1942 (17 Dec.) USCGC *Ingham* (WPG-35) sank U-626.

1942 (Dec.) The Coast Guard Women's Reserve (SPARS) was organized under the command of Lt. Cmdr. (later Captain) Dorothy Stratton (USCG).

1943 The LORAN (long-range navigation system) was initiated and maintained by the Coast Guard.

1943 (Jan.) USS LCI(L)-83 (Landing Craft Infantry, Large) and USS LCI(L)-84 were the first U.S. Navy landing craft of that type to be Coast Guard manned.

1943 (21 Feb.) USCGC *Spencer* (WPG-36) sank U-225.

1943 (22 Feb.) USCGC *Campbell* (WPG-32) rammed and sank U-606.

1943 (17 March) USS LST-16 was the first Landing Ship Tank to be CG manned.

1943 (17 April) USCGC *Spencer* sank U-175. Coast Guard crew members boarded the submarine before it sank in an attempt to salvage intelligence information and capture the vessel.

1943 (13 June) USCGC *Escanaba* (WPG-77) sank off the Greenland coast with the loss of 101 members of the crew. There were two survivors.

1943 (30 August) USS *Hurst* (DE-250) was the first World War II Destroyer Escort with a CG crew. The Coast Guard had previously manned Navy destroyers during Prohibition.

1943 (8 Sept.) USS *Long Beach* (PF-34) was the first USN Patrol Frigate to be CG manned.

1944 (3 Jan.) The first mercy mission performed by a helicopter occurred when Cmdr. Frank A. Erickson (USCG) flew a supply of blood plasma in a snowstorm to a New Jersey hospital where U.S. Navy survivors of a destroyer explosion were patients. Floyd Bennett Field in Brooklyn (New York) became a Coast Guard helicopter-training base that trained American and British aviators and mechanics.

1944 (20 Jan.) The USS *General Billy Mitchell* (AP-114) was the first Navy Transport to be CG crewed.

1944 (10 Feb.) The 705-foot USS *Wakefield* (AP-21), a former passenger liner, was the largest ship manned by the USCG.

1944 (22 Feb.) The National Air-Sea Rescue Agency was established and administered by the USCG in cooperation with the other U.S. Armed Forces.

1944 (10 March) The CG-manned destroyer USS *Leopold* (DE-319) on convoy duty 400 miles south of Iceland attacked a U-boat, but was sunk by a second U-boat in heavy seas with the loss of 171 crew and 28 survivors.

1944 (14 March) USCGC began to run U.S. Army Transportation Corps vessels. In April CG crews began to furnish crews for USA LTs (Large Tugs).

1944 (1 April) The first helicopter rescue of a civilian occurred when Lt. (jg) W.C. Bolton (USCG) rescued a boy marooned on a sandbar in high tide off Jamaica Bay, New York.

1944 (21 June) Coast Guard 83-foot patrol and rescue boats USCG-83415 and USCG-83471 sank off the coast of Normandy in the D-Day invasion.

1944 (29 June) The shipboard landing of a helicopter occurred on the deck of the USCGC *Cobb* (WPG-181) off Long Island, New York. Cmdr. Frank Erickson (USCG) was the helicopter pilot. The Navy assigned the Coast Guard to develop helicopter operations for Search and Rescue (SAR) and Anti-Submarine Warfare (ASW).

1945 (29 Jan.) The USS *Serpens* (AK-97), a Navy warship manned by the Coast Guard, blew up at Guadalcanal with the loss of the entire crew. During World War II, USCG crews manned 650 vessels for the Navy and Army and sank 11 submarines.

1945 (7 May) Germany capitulated.

1945 (8 May) Officially designated as V-E (Victory in Europe) Day.

1945 (11 May) The U.S. Army freight ship FS-255 was sunk off the Philippines by a Japanese submarine with the loss of four Coast Guard crew members.

1945 (15 June-21 July) USS *Admiral C.F. Hughes* (AP-114) and its Coast Guard crew sailed the longest troop transport voyage in naval history. Five thousand U.S. Army troops were transferred 15,500 nautical miles from Europe to the Pacific theater.

1945 (6 August) Atomic bomb dropped on Hiroshima (Japan) by a U.S. bomber.

1945 (9 August) Atomic bomb dropped on Nagasaki (Japan) by a U.S. bomber.

1945 (14 August) President Truman announced Japan's surrender and the end of World War II.

1946 (1 Jan.) The USCG was returned from U.S. Navy and Defense Department authority to the jurisdiction of the Treasury Department after World War II.[1]

Documents

A Letter Home from LCI-91 (29 December 1943), by Robert Morris [EDITED]

Robert Morris
Dec. 29, 1943
Falmouth, England.

This letter was taken home by a man returning to the states. Thus it will not have to be censored. I can say a few of the things that I have been restricted from saying heretofore.

LCI-91 ACTION SUMMARY PRIOR TO THE D-DAY INVASION OF NORMANDY

Dear Folks.

I don't know exactly when you will receive this letter, but I am in on particular rush. Since it is coming to you in rather an unorthodox manner, and hence will miss the censorship that blots out most of the interest from other letters, I shall be able to include a few dates and facts. I am keeping in mind that I must nevertheless be reserved with information that may be of use to the enemy, but things that have happened, and some of the places that we have been can now be mentioned without endangering future operations.

To begin, we started with our whole flotilla and many other ships from Norfolk, Virginia on April Fool's day of last April. So by now we have much the better part of a year overseas. First we stopped at Bermuda. Made a few liberties there. This island is one of the beauty spots of the earth of that I am sure. I have never seen more really beautiful spots even in pictures. Of course, it is still British although we have bases there and much of the stuff there is U.S. The Negro situation there is peculiar. They do not consider themselves as a class by themselves. They call themselves "subjects of the King." The cost of living there is very high, but I should like very much to go back there again, for it is really a beautiful and scenic spot.

So we took off across the Atlantic with many ships and a heavy escort of navy warships. We weren't bothered much going over, as a matter of fact, we had a good time. It took us around 18 days to get from Bermuda to our African port. In the meantime we soaked up lots of sunshine, and also cut our hair in various fantastic manners. I had the noon to 4, and the midnight to 4 a.m. watch every day, and during the day I would be up on the conning tower with almost no clothes. I really had a nice tan when we got to Africa. I wore a sun helmet most of the time, so I did not get my mug as well tanned as I hoped I would.

April 28, we steamed (after leaving most of the rest of the convoy to go to another port) into the Wadi Sebu (Wadi Sebu means river), and up to the town of Port Lyautey (was known as Kyentra), French Morocco. This is about 60 miles north of Casablanca, and about 8 miles up the river inland. Interesting place. There was everything from educational sights to the most sordid of things. The champagne costs about $2.00—the bottle costs $1.50 and the liquid the remaining four bits. There are a number of ships scuttled by the Germans around here and the process of reclaiming them is going on.

May 9—my birthday, I had liberty and decided to visit Rabat a city about 40 miles away. We had orders not to go, so we slipped through some vineyards, and through a native village and hitched a ride with an army truck. Spend an enjoyable time there. It is a rather metropolitan city, and in many ways reminds one of home. But the native sections are prevalent enough to help one keep in mind that he is in Africa. We had to hitch a ride back in an Arab truck. Had a rather miserable, but memorable time.

May 27—Left Lyautey, and proceeded to Gibraltar. On the afternoon of the 28th, we passed through the straights of Gib. We had an easy time until we got into the Mediterranean, but after we got in we had a few airplane scares. They were our first real scares, and they scared us plenty. Next day we acted as escorts for the convoy, and we did all sorts of interesting investigations. If we had been attacked, we would have been in a mess no doubt.

May 30—Pulled into Nemours, French Algeria. Practiced beaching operations at a place called Sidna Yucha nearby. Lots of things operations at a place called Sidna Yucha nearby. Lots of things happened here that I will have to save until I can tell you.

June 6—We loaded with American Rangers and headed out. That night we put into Arzew, Algberia. Early on the 8th we departed again. We were rid of the rangers but head taken on other cargo. We passed Oran and Algiers.

June 11—Pulled into Bizerte, which was to be our base for the coming operations. The place was in a horrible mess. The street fighting had been going on in the town and had really knocked hell out of everything. Only the rats and the booby traps were left. It was once quite a town, and a large French naval base, but now it is a shamble. There are sunken ships and damaged planes everywhere. Bizerte shall be a place that I shall never forget. It was here that we had our first real air raid. As a matter of face, we had no more than reached the place when we saw our first JU-88s.

There is a large lake near the city called the Lake of Bizerte. It was here that we anchored for so many days awaiting the days of the invasions. We did lot of maneuvers in and about the city of Bizerte. We had night maneuvers, and air rid after air raid. We even used to bet as to the time when Jerry would be over that night. There were periods of lots of work when we would load up with all sort of things, and then again there were periods of unloading. We took a jeep ride thru the wreck that was Bizerte, and the sight was appalling.

The period just prior to the invasion of Sicily was one of the thoughts that I want to think about. For weeks before the invasion we were forced to lay at anchor out in the Lake of Bizerte. We had no radio, no form of pastime. We about went batty. We knew what was coming, but we didn't know where or when. Besides, this was our first action, and we were afraid whether we admit it or not and we all do. So there we were for weeks, day in and day out, setting on this cast iron tub in the hot African sun—just waiting—and waiting. Some of the nerves were getting a little jangled, and we were all eager to get going and it over with.

July 5—Finally things started to roll—and we were happy. We loaded with troops, maneuvered some, and later anchored out in the lake. That night Hitler sent over enough Junker 88's to make a circus. But they got Hitler sent over enough Junker 88's to make a circus. But they got the worst of it by far. I have never seen such a display of fireworks. We had some heavy stuff because we were starting out on the bid adventure, and so there was a lot of stuff to greet the Axis boys with. The alarm came in the wee-hours of the morning, and so it was plenty dark. I recall one JU [Junkers JU-88] in particular, he came right over to us, and since there were so many ships and guns about he was just literally blasted in pieces. He came down like a wounded duck. It was dark as pitch, and by this time the boys had itchy trigger fingers. Well, one of the Jerry boys had managed to jump from the 88, I will never know how he managed to live thru that hail of steel that came up at him. Well, as he came down, the boys caught sight of the chute in the darkness. As I said, they had nervous fingers. So about a hundred heavy caliber antiaircraft guns cut loose at the object. I am afraid that there was not much left of the chute or the man when they got down. So next morning we got underway and proceeded out thru the smoke screen that had been thrown around things to hinder the bombs. The aim of the Jerries was not so good. They got a lot worse beating than we did. By July 7 we landed with a huge convoy in Sousse, Tunisia. It was here that Patton gave the soldiers a talking to.

Sousse, by the way was as bad a wreck as Bizerte. This war makes a hell of a mess of everything and everyone—you should see some of the people around here—those that are left. July 9 found us by Malta, and so we went on to Sicily. As luck would have, a storm came up. And we were having a miserable time. I pent most of the time either praying or cussing. It made me so confounded mad to think that we would have to have a storm on this night that so much depended upon. The soldiers that we had along were a miserable sight. They were not used to this rolling thu, and some of them were so sick that they wanted to die where they were rather than going on to the beach to die—if they were going to.

Thus came the morning of July 10—the Invasion of Sicily. This is a story in itself. I saw enough to last a lifetime. The navy shelling the beach, the planes bombing, the flares, the antiaircraft fire, the bombing, the machine guns going off right ahead of us, the pill box that just about got us, but punctured the ship next to us instead. The big ammunition ship that was bombed and exploded to high heaven. The LST that was hit and burned. The wounded that was carried back aboard for us to take and burned. The wounded that was carried back aboard for us to take back to Africa, the mines, and the thousands and thousands we started back to Africa, I don't think that I have ever been quite so tired—nervous exhaustion. In passing I must say that every man and officer on our ship did a swell job, and non-faltered in any way.

We made numerous runs back to Sicily (we had hit the beach just east of Licata). Took back reinforcements of our soldiers, and one trip even took about 200 of the wild North African Gouimers (Gooms). These natives have been trained as modern soldiers, but they are wild yet. Man when you give a wild-man a mortar and modern grenades and rifle, what a spectacle he makes. These fellows fight for the love of it—and for the booty that they can capture. It is told they are pain extra for Italian or German ears that they get—I am glad that they are on our side. Then as a contrast, we took about 200 American nurses to Licata. This was a pleasant time—the best that we had since leaving the states. They are swell people those nurses—bless em all.

One time returning from Sicily, we got lost. We were supposed to sight Pantelleria (the island) about 2 a.m., but we did not see it. That meant one thing—that we were lost, and that we were wandering around in the German minefield. Every second we expected to go sky high, boy, that was a long night. But we got back to Bizerte O.K. Made a liberty in Ferryville, which is across the lake from Bizerte. It too is a miserable town, racked by the war, and stinking in filth and dirt. We made some "private" expeditions and collected a lot of enemy helmets, guns, bullets, bayonets, machine guns, etc. also got some things from some crashed planes.

So began another session of training (more training) in and around Bizerte, Tunisia. But August 4, we were on the go again—and this time in a westward direction. And so we came to Oran, Algeria. But we anchored in Mers El Kebir, an small town about 8 miles removed from Oran. Had a good time in Oran. It is removed from the front, there is a large Red Cross there, and lots to see. It is not blasted by the war, and there are churches and lots of things of beauty. But it was not all vacation. We were sent to a place called Andalouses, Algeria to help train more troops—for the next invasion.

Aug 30—We left Oran to return to Bizerte.

Sept 6—We left Bizerte loaded with troops again, and headed for Sicily once more, and on Sept 7 we docked in Palermo, the capital of Sicily, we made an unauthorized liberty, found an old wine cellar and had some real Marsala and Vermouth. Could buy it for next to nothing, and it was really good. But it packed a whallop. Palermo had felt the war. Our planes had blasted it steadily. The area around the waterfront is a big pile of shambles. The force of the some of the bombs was so great that one ship longer than our house was lifted clean out of the water and up on dry land. Boy, what a sock those eggs carry! But uptown the city was in good shape. There was a lot of interesting things to see here. It was quite different than Africa, and wouldn't trust of those [locals] as far as I could throw the 91. Those monkeys are for the guy that is winning. I didn't forget that a month ago, these same punks were throwing hot lead in our direction. And I would just as soon see them in a pile as walking around with the silly smile of friendship that they showed.

Sept 8—and again we knew we were going into battle again. We steamed out of Palerma, and joined a huge convoy. By now this is old business. Passed by the Isle of Ustica. That night the Jerrys found us and we received a nice bombing. Some of the eggs that they dropped looked as large as a house. They didn't hit anything with them, but when they exploded in the water even though they hit far away, it shattered the ship. All that night we slept out on deck near the guns. We could see and hear firing all around us at times.

Sept 9—Invasion of Italy, the same story. The hugeness of the thing is almost breathless. There are thousands of ships and men. The beaches are black almost with army and navy gear. Men and machines are everywhere. And further up on the beach are the ones—the men—who were not so lucky. In the shell holes were piled the dead. Some of them had been burned in tanks and looked like badly burned hams. Others had been blasted and only parts of them remained. There were Italian, German, and American together. They were enemies no longer. A liberty ship had been hit and her stern was sticking up in the air. Their were lots of other smaller ships hit too. We had control of the air, and the air was full of all sorts of places. Our bombers would go over in droves and our fighters were always overhead. Once in a while the Jerry would and our fighters were always overhead. Once in a while the Jerry would pull a fast sneak-in and bomb and strafe us. Boy how we would duck—and shoot back at them when they came over. There ware a half dozen or so of us that went up on the beach to help the soldiers to unload. Got to see a lot more that way. Even took a walk about and looked things over in general. Not far away was an old Roman temple, that was now full of war and the things of war. I picked up a big knife from the body of a headless soldier. The burial parties would be around soon as they were starting to decompose, and had to be buried. Got some souvenirs from one of the planes that had been shot down, even did some diving and brought up some heavy machine gun ammunition that had been lost to the bottom. It was in quite shallow water, so got it out easily. We spent two days running in reinforcements. Then that night we made up convoy to

go back to Sicily. (During the battle of the beach of Salerno, we got our reinforcements off the big transports that lay miles off the beach.) Anyhow, we had
not even succeeded in making up convoy, when we had a beaut of a raid. The
place was lit up like Times Square. Flares from the bombers, and flashes from
the bombs and all sorts of gun fire. When a large ship cut loose at the bombers
it looked like a huge volcano erupting. Such a blaze and what a noise. The fragments of shells started falling all around us. And I gave my time bonnet a love
tap.

We made a couple of trips back to Salerno. The soldiers were having a
tough time of it, and the second time we came back we almost thought that
we were going to have to evacuate them. That would have been bad. As an
example, on our second trip back we were unloading on the beach, and I had
occasion to signal to a British ship. I had to set up on the edge of a conning
tower to do so. All I had above my waist was my helmet, and I guess that I
made a good target. All of a sudden I heard first one then another slug whis-
tle past. I assure you I lost no time in getting down behind the protection of
the conning tower. But after all that time, Jerry had not been pushed back out
of rifle range. But the job was done as you know—and give that army of ours
the credit. Those guys in army togs do the dirty work and no kidding. Saw the
Isle of Capri in the distance, sure would have liked to gone up. Some of our
ships did—to help kick the hell out of the Germans thereupon. Jon was successful.

Oct 16—We left Bizerte for good, and we were not sorry to go. We have
too many unpleasant memories of the place. (We had lots of other little too
many unpleasant memories of the place. (We had lots of other little adven-
tures such as our trip to Tunis, LaGouletta, and the ancient ruins of Carthage.
In Tunis, we had the party with the French girls, and also there we did the job
of drydocking this tub and painting her bottom.)

Back we went to Oran. Then to Gibraltar. The fellows really made a liberty there. They liked to have torn the great rock out by the roots. You recall
that this was the first liberty in months that was anything like making one in
a civilized country. For the first time in a long time we were among English
speaking people again. Some of the sorry cases that came back to the ships!
The whole Flotilla was together again. We had established a record. Came thru
two major invasions, and tho some of the ships had been shot up a bit, and
some had been battered a bit, we had not lost one ship—a tribute to the Coast
Guard. Then off again, thru Gibraltar, around Spain, and thru the Bay of Bis-
cay and to England.

Landed in Plymouth, England. Boy, was it nice to be around civilization
again. The town has been almost blasted to the ground in many placed—rather
in most places. I t was a large city, but now only four shows are in operation.
Everything is completely black. Then came my London leave. I went by train,
and saw quite a bit of the country. Been to Falmouth, and other places. I like

it here, but I want to get this next invasion over with, and get back to those good old states. We are in for more training pretty soon. And so, there is a summary of it. Of course, not even a fraction of all has been told. I will have to save that until I see you, but here we are, and hoping that it will not be soon until we are there.

You understand that this letter is confidential, and not to be shown around. It is just for your information. I am sorry for the typing errors, but I have to do this in a hurry, and want just to get the information to you, I am sure that you can read it.

[Historians' Office]
[USCG Home Page]
Added: October 2001

A Letter to His Minister (13 January 1944),
by Robert Morris [EDITED]

Jan. 13, 1944

Dear Dr. Stewart:—
I have your letter dated Oct. 12; I want you to know that I really did appreciate it very much. We have a great assortment of persons and articles in our flotilla, but one of the things that we do not have is a Chaplain. However, since we have been in England we have had quite a bit of opportunity to attend services on Sundays. The story was definitely the opposite in Africa and even in Sicily. I suppose that there were provisions set up on the bases, but these floating units are constantly getting the meager end of everything. Not from selfish reasons do I say that the situation should be the converse, but it is and probably always will be as is. The boys on the shore bases have the first opportunity at anything desirable and by the time we get in we had pretty shallow pickings sometimes. The same was true of recreation and entertainment while in Africa. Even in the advanced bases there were movies and various sorts of shows. But the fellows on the ships just stayed on the ships. Of course, there is a reason I suppose. It would be difficult for the floating units to come in to dock, there would be no room for them anyhow, but we did envy somewhat the others. But we have our innings too.

We have got to travel and see and do a lot of things that the base personnel have not. Most of the base boys did not even get to Sicily or Italy, and I had some very interesting times in those places. One of them, of course, was getting shot at and shelled and bombed. I don't suppose those occurrences could be classified as good times, but since we came out of it all O.K., I guess we are still ahead in certain respects. Looks as I drifted a bit from my topic of Chaplains, but I guess that we do rather well even in their absence. Perhaps you would be interested if I elaborated just a little more. To me it has been an interesting form of observation to just a little more. To me it has been an interesting form of observation to watch the attitudes toward Religion as displayed by the American Youth. I suppose that you as a minister know better than anyone the attitude the so called "younger generation" has pertaining to Church and Christ. My observation has been that the most of us understand and appreciate—and duly respect all the fundamental concepts of that which is blanketed by the term "Religion." But there is something in the composition of the young people that restrains them from openly declaring themselves dependent upon the Lord. I haven't the comprehension nor wisdom to explain why this is so, though my supposition is that youth has an almost unconquerable desire to be "big" and self-sustaining. The admittance of any weakness or the need for support just doesn't fit into the figure, which it is desired to present to others. In short, youth takes its religion in a passive sort of way for the h most part. Certainly, there are exceptions; but even the regular attendants at services are inclined to be just a bit reserved in their attitude.

But here is the point that I am attempting to make. I have been fortunate during my life, and so have never had the opportunity to see the effect that a real crisis and impending doom has upon young people; that is, I never had the opportunity before the morning of July 10, 1943—the day of the invasion of Sicily. To me that will be a memorable day for the remainder of my life. Lots was happening on that dark and stormy morning between midnight and the wee hour at which we hit the beach and walked in the surf and upon the sands of that enemy land. Our craft is not large, and riding in and upon it was a sizeable group of America's Youth. Besides our own Coast Guard crew we had a full "cargo" of U.S. soldiers. Everywhere on board one might have observed the aspects of war. Our own crew was never out of its clothes—nor far removed from the battle stations. Everyone carried his gas mask, helmet, and life jacket. But the troop compartments filled with mines, torpedoes, etc.

I went off watch at midnight, but for obvious reasons, did not feel very sleepy. So I went below to talk with the soldiers for awhile. I recall that the compartment full of trained young men had an atmosphere of potence and strength. I imagine all the battle gear and the battle dress aided in creating that effect. Here before me was a group which appeared outwardly to be strong and indomitable—here was youth self-sustaining and self-sufficient, strong and courageous. But closer self-sustaining and self-sufficient, strong and courageous. But closer observation taught me other things. A silence prevailed in the compartment, and as I wandered about I saw interesting things. Some of them just lay in their bunks staring at the overhead or at the bunk above them—

staring in apparent silence. Others sat on their bunks and stared across into nothingness. Another group scattered about in reposing or sitting position were reading—not comic books this time—but little blue or brown editions of the Bible. Others were scanning again little pictures in their wallets. All of us knew that in a few hours a shell or bullet would end some of these lives. Here was the unique situation of American Youth in a crisis—facing a doom. And here Youth came out of its shell. There was an open frank admittance of the need for strength and courage.

There was unabashed recourse to God both thru prayer and reading of the Bible. I recall one soldier telling me that he had, "prayed and prayed plenty since we left North Africa." I could not observe our own crew as closely as we are a small number comparatively, and were scattered about the ship on our various watches. Later, when we were back in North Africa, I made a casual survey, and found that we too, had "prayed and prayed plenty." None of us denied it, nor did we deny it when we went into Italy. At present we are in England, presently there will be need for much more prayer—they will not go unsaid, for I am convinced, as are the others, that they are not unheeded. Well, I guess I had better bring this to a close. I wish that I had a more capable command of words to better explain some of the things that I would like to, but since I have not, we will have to let it go as is.

Please convey my greeting to all those back there whom I haven't seen for almost these two years. Good luck and success to you and all the seen for almost these two years. Good luck and success to you and all the improvements you are making.

Sincerely,

Robert Morris
[Historians' Office]
[USCG Home Page]
Added: October 2001

Operation Neptune, LCI(L)-91 (10 June 1944)

10 June, 1944
From: Commanding Officer, USS LCI (L) 91
To: Commander, Task Group 124.4
Via: Deputy Commander, Task 124.4
Information: Commander, Group 29, LCI (L) Flotilla 10
Commander LCI (L) Flotilla 10

Subject: Operation Neptune, Participation in by USS LCI (L) 91

1. This vessel departed from Weymouth, England, in company with Convoy Group One (0–1) at 1715 on 5 June, 1944. In addition to the regular crew, a total of two hundred and one (201) men from Headquarters 116th Infantry, 147th Engineers Battalion, 121st Engineers Battalion, and 7th Beach Battalion were aboard.

2. Approach to the Omaha Assault Area was made according to plan without eventful action. Departure was made from the Trans- port Area as scheduled and contact made with the Primary Control Vessel.

3. Upon approach to Dog White Beach it became evident that proposed markers for a cleared channel through the underwater obstructions had not been placed. A small break in the Element "C" was blocked by what appeared to be a sunken DUWK.

4. A beaching was made between units of Element "C" at the scheduled time, H-70, 0740 on 6 June, 1944, approximately 225 yards from the back of he beach and 75 yards from the water line. A man rope was led to the beach through a maze of stakes each topped by a teller mine. Troops disembarked reluctantly over both ramps in the face of heavy enemy machine gun and rifle fire.

5. The rapidly rising tide and slow departure of troops made it necessary to move the ship forward to keep grounded. About twenty minutes after grounding it was impossible to move farther in because of the mined stakes. The ship was swinging with the tide toward the stakes on the port bow so the ship was retracted. While doing so a taller mine was exploded at the port bow injuring a few soldiers but not causing fatal damage to the ship.

6. About sixty troops were still on board so a signal was hoisted requesting assistance from small boats. No such aid was forthcoming so a second beaching was made about 100 yards West of the original one in an effort to get in beyond the obstructions.

7. A portion of the remaining troops had disembarked over the port ramp when what appeared to be an "88" struck the center of the well deck and exploded in the fuel tanks below. A blast of flame immediately followed and within seconds the entire well deck was a mass of flames. Water pressure was inadequate to fight the flames. Small caliber enemy fire continued near the beach and fight the flames. Small caliber enemy fire continued near the beach and intermittent "88" fire near the ship.

8. Because the fire could not be gotten under control to enable the ship to retract the order was given to abandon ship. Personnel disembarked over the side and proceeded in to the beach. Right to ten men, mainly ship's crew, were disembarked seaward in an LCS. Two wounded soldiers were removed to the beach by raft. No living personnel were left aboard the ship.

9. No accurate account of survivors is yet available. As far as can be determined, Numbers 1 and 2 Troop Compartments had been evacuated and most of the personnel had left the exact location of the hit.

10. Orders for the operation were thrown in the fire. Secret and confidential communication publications were removed sea-ward by the Chief Radio Man. All other ship's records were consumed by the fire.

11. One of the soldiers whose name unfortunately is not available was exceedingly helpful in disembarking personnel and checking the ship for survivors. All compartments, except Numbers 1 and 2 which were ablaze were checked to be sure everyone had been evacuated.

12. The hydrographic data regarding this beach, furnished before the operation, was remarkably accurate. The gradients were as reported and the ship grounded at the position predicted by the graphs. The underwater obstructions were a hindrance but the mines and enemy fire were their most effective defense.

Arend Vyn, Jr.
Lt. (jg), USCGR
Commanding

Letter to the Secretary of the Navy: Loss of Ship (19 June 1944)

19 June, 1944
From: Commanding Officer, USS LCI (L) 91
To: The Secretary of the Navy
Via: (1) Commander Task Group 124.4
    (2) Commander Task Group 124
    (3) Commander Task Group 123
    (4) Commander Task Group 122
    (5) Commander Twelfth Fleet
    (6) Commander in Chief, United States Fleet

Subject: Loss of ship—Report of
Reference: (a) Article 841 (3) U.S. Navy Regulations

1. The following report is submitted in accordance with reference (a).

2. The USS LCI (L) 91 departed from Weymouth, England, in company with Convoy Group One (0–1), Operation Neptune, late in the afternoon of 5 June, 1944. Approach to the Omaha Assault Area was made according to plan without eventful action. Departure was made from the Trans-port Area as scheduled and contact made with the Primary Control Vessel.

3. Upon approach to Dog White Beach it became evident that proposed markers for a cleared channel through the underwater obstructions had not been placed nor a channel cleared. A small break in the Element "C" was blocked by what appeared to be a sunken tank.

3. A beaching was made between units of Element "C" at the scheduled time, H-70, 0740 on 6 June, 1944, at the left center of Dog White Beach. Troops disembarked reluctantly over both ramps in the face of heavy enemy machine gun and rifle fire. A man rope had been led by a member of the ship's crew, from the ship through a maze of stakes each topped by a teller mine, to the beach.

5. The rapidly rising tide and slow departure of troops made it necessary to move the ship forward to keep grounded. About twenty minutes after grounding it was impossible to move farther forward without detonating mines on the stakes, so the ship was retracted. While doing so a teller mine on a stake at the port bow was exploded injuring a few soldiers and blowing a hole about two (2) feet in diameter in the bow just above the water line, but apparently causing no more serious damage to the ship.

6. After retracting, about sixty (60) of the original two hundred and one (201) troops were still on board so a signal was hoisted requesting assistance in unloading from LCVP's standing off shore. No such aid was forthcoming so a unloading from LCVP's standing off shore. No such aid was forthcoming so a second beaching was made about one hundred (100) yards west of the first one, in an effort to get in beyond the obstructions.

7. A portion of the remaining troops had disembarked after the second beaching when a violent explosion occurred forward, immediately followed by a blast of flames. Within second the entire "well deck" was a mass of flames. Water pressure was inadequate to fight the flames. Small caliber enemy fire continued near the beach and intermittent "88" fire near the ship.

8. Because the fire could not be gotten under control to enable the ship to retract and because of the obvious damage to the hull and bulkheads, the order was given to abandon ship. Personnel disembarked over the side and proceeded in to the beach. A portion of the ship's crew were evacuated seaward in an LCS. All compartments except Troop Compartments Numbers One (1) and Two (2) which were ablaze, were checked to be sure everyone had been evacuated.

9. The original theory was that an "88" shell had penetrated the main deck above Number Two Troop Compartment, exploding in the fuel tanks below. Later investigation, however, supported the theory that mines had done the major damage. The hull was damaged beyond repair, the deck of Number Two (2) Troop Compartment completely blown up. With an incoming tide all compartments below the main deck and forward of the engine room flooded. All combustible equipment and gear in these compartments, in the house, and in the pilot house were destroyed by fire.

10. The salvage crew was making a survey of the material which might be taken from the engine room, Number Four (4) Troop Compartment, magazine, and steering engine room. The 20mm gun barrels, and commissary stores from the commissary locker had already been removed by unknown parties from the beach.

11. Orders for the Operation and classified communication publications were through in the fire. All other ship's records were consumed in the fire.

Arend Vyn, Jr., Lt.(jg) USCGR
Copies to: Commanding
Cominch (Via Air Mail)
Commander Group 29, LCI (L) Flotilla 10
Commandant, U.S. Coast Guard via: Commander LCI (L) Flotilla 10

[Historians' Office]
[USCG Home Page]
Added: October 2001

Coast Guard Unit Commendation for D-Day (6 June 1944)

THE COMMANDANT OF THE UNITED STATES COAST GUARD
WASHINGTON 20593
13 October 2000
The Commandant of the Coast Guard takes great pleasure in presenting the
COAST GUARD UNIT COMMENDATION to:
FLOTILLA 10—GROUP 29—DIVISION 57
for service as set forth in the following
CITATION:
    "For exceptionally meritorious service during Flotilla 10—Group 29—Division 57's participation in the allied force's invasion of Normandy, France on 6 June 1944. Consisting of 24 Coast Guard–manned Landing Crafts (LCI), Flotilla 10 distinguished itself in the face of heavy enemy fire in delivering hundreds of allied troops and tons of equipment to Omaha Beach at the outset of the invasion. The gallant efforts of the crews of these LCIs were key to clearing channels through minefields and hedgehogs to enable the rest of the allied force to reach the beaches. Although continually exposed to heavy gunfire, the LCIs dodged sunken obstacles and sailed through heavy seas, shuttling between the landing areas and the transport ships delivering badly needed supplies and reinforcements to the beaches. After delivering their human cargo and equipment, the LCIs served as rescue platforms, recovering and transporting injured soldiers and sailors to hospital ships off shore.
    Through out the invasion, 4 of the LCIs, Numbers 85, 91, 92 and 93, were lost while distinguishing themselves in the heat of battle. LCI-85 was one of the first to ram its way through sunken obstacles and successfully clear a path to

the beach before being hit by an 88mm shell that penetrated the hull and exploded in the forwarded troop compartment. After unloading troops to smaller landing craft, LCI-85 stuck a mine and was simultaneously struck by 25 artillery shells. Listing badly, LCI-85 returned to [USS *SAMUEL*] *CHASE* and unloaded its wounded before it sank. LCI-91 and LCI-92 were both struck by German shells shortly after reaching the beach and both burst into flames. The crews fought the fires while unloading troops. These LCIs burned throughout the day, giving off thick smoke that served as a key landmark for other allied forces approaching the coast. Further down the beach, LCI-93 successfully delivered its first load of troops, but grounded on a sandbar during their second delivery and took 10 direct artillery hits. As the invasion progressed, the remaining LCIs of Flotilla 10 successfully rescued over 400 injured allied personnel.

These were instrumental in the successful invasion of Normandy and in turning the tide of World War II. The dedication and devotion to duty exhibited by the crew of Flotilla 10—Group 29—Division 57 during this period are in keeping with the highest traditions of the United States Coast Guard.

JAMES M. LOY
Admiral, U.S. Coast Guard
Commandant

[Historians' Office]
[USCG Home Page]
Added: October 2001

A Letter to Parents on the Death of Their Son Douglas Munro

Lieutenant Commander D. H. Dexter, USCG
The following is a copy of LCDR Dexter's letter to the parents of Douglas Munro written soon after their son was killed in action with the enemy at Guadalcanal on 27 September 1942. LCDR Dexter was Munro's commanding officer at the time of Munro's death.

"Guadalcanal, BSI
Dear Mr. and Mrs. Munro:
    Believe me when I say sincerely that this is a very sad letter for me to write advising you of the death of your son Douglas, but as Commanding Officer of the unit to which he was attached at the time of his death, I have pride in telling you that he covered himself with honor and I hope Glory, and fulfilled the mission so satisfactorily that almost all of the men he had under his charge returned

to their unit and, without exception, all had praise for your son's execution of his duties.

It was a year ago last June that Douglas and Raymond Evans came to me and asked if they could be transferred to Captain Ashe's staff. I succeeded in getting them and since that day have felt that Douglas was one of my boys, for both Douglas and Ray Evans have been with me and his loss has left a very decided space which I feel will never be filled so far as I am concerned.

On Sunday the 27th of September and expedition was sent into an area where trouble was to be expected. Douglas was in charge of the ten boats which took the men down. In the latter part of the afternoon, the situation had not developed as had been anticipated and in order to save the expedition it became necessary to send the boats back to evacuate the expedition. Volunteers were called for and, true to the highest traditions of the Coast Guard and also to traditions with which you imbued your son, he was among the first to volunteer and was put in charge of the detail.

The evacuation was as successful as could be hoped for under fire. But as always happens, the last men to leave the beach are the hardest pressed because they have been acting as the covering agents for the withdrawal of the other men, and your son, knowing this, so placed himself and his boats so that he could act as the covering agent for the last men, and by his action and successful maneuvers brought back a far greater number of men than had been even hoped for. He received his wound just as the last men were getting in the boats and clearing the beach. Upon regaining consciousness his only question was 'Did they get off?' and so died with a smile on his face and the full knowledge that he had successfully accomplished a dangerous mission.

I am sending this to you direct for I feel that you should have the privilege of knowing the facts, but request that you keep it confidential until such time as the official notification is received. I regret having to make this request but feel that it is for the good of all concerned. I consider this is a personal letter and not an official report.

In the year and a half that I have known Douglas, I have grown to admire him and through him, you. He was the true type of American manhood that is going to win this war and I hereby promise that I will make all efforts to personally call on you whenever it is my privilege to be near Cle Elum and to pay homage to you both as parents of Douglas.

Sincerely and respectfully,
(Sgd) D. H. Dexter
Lt. Comdr., U.S. Coast Guard

[Historians' Office] [Douglas Munro Index]
[USCG Home Page]
Added: January 2003

Chapter Notes

Chapter 1

1. Thomas P. Ostrom, *The United States Coast Guard, 1790 to the Present* (Oakland, OR: Red Anvil/Elderberry Press, 2006), 205–212, and selected material from chapters 1 to 15.
2. Tom Beard, ed., *The Coast Guard* (Seattle: Foundation for Coast Guard History, and Westport, Connecticut: Hugh Lauter Levin, 2004), 54–55.
3. Beard, *Coast Guard,* 76, 182–185.
4. *Ibid.,* 41–52.
5. *Ibid.,* 53–54.
6. *Ibid.,* 71.
7. George Brown Tindall and David E. Shi, *America: A Narrative History* (New York: W.W. Norton), 1996, 1228.
8. Beard, *Coast Guard,* 78, 79.
9. David J. Bercuson and Holger H. Herwig, *The Destruction of the Bismarck* (Woodstock, NY: Overlook Press), 2003, 342.
10. *Ibid.,* 343.
11. *Ibid.,* 338.
12. *Ibid.,* 341, 344, 345.
13. Tindall and Shi, *America,* 1218–1219.

Chapter 2

1. William J. Bennett, *America: The Last Best Hope,* vol. 2 (Nashville, TN: Thomas Nelson, 2007), 189.
2. *Ibid.,* 192.
3. *Ibid.,* 194.
4. James F. Dunnigan and Albert A. Nofi, *The Pacific War Encyclopedia* (New York: Checkmark Books), 1998, 350, 562.
5. *Ibid.,* 303, 518.
6. *Ibid.,* 385.
7. Robert E. Johnson, *Guardians of the Sea: A History of the Coast Guard, 1915 to the Present* (Annapolis, MD: Naval Institute Press, 1987), 89.
8. Mike McLaughlin, "Profiles: Intelligence Officer Edwin Layton Had Nimitz's Ear and Guided the Way Across the Pacific," in *World War II History* (January 2002): 27–28.

9. *Ibid.,* 20.
10. *Ibid.,* 22.
11. C.A. "Sandy" Schwaab, CWO (USCG, Ret.), ed., "Project News 2: Guardian Spies: The Secret Story of the U.S. Coast Guard and the OSS During World War II," *The Cutter* 22 (Spring 2007), 13–14. *The Cutter* is the newsletter for the Foundation for Coast Guard History (FCGH), published in Seattle, Washington. The primary source material for this article is from the National Archives and the FCGH Oral History Project.
12. *Ibid.,* 14.
13. Rear Adm. Edwin T. Layton (USN, Ret.), Capt. Roger Pineau (USNR, Ret.), and John Costello, *And I Was There: Pearl Harbor and Midway-Breaking the Secrets* (New York: William Morrow, 1985), 111.
14. Dunnigan and Nofi, *Pacific War,* 478–479.
15. *Ibid.,* 480–483.
16. Richard P. Klobuchar, *Pearl Harbor: Awakening a Sleeping Giant* (Bloomington, IN: lstBooks Library, 2003), 46–47.
17. *Ibid.,* 105.
18. *Ibid., 249–250.*
19. Barrett Thomas Beard (Lt. Cmdr., USCG, Ret.), *Wonderful Flying Machines: A History of U.S. Coast Guard Helicopters* (Annapolis, MD: Naval Institute Press, 1996), 1–3.
20. RM1 George C. Larsen (USCG), "Pearl Harbor: A Memoir of Service," *The Cutter* (Spring 2007), 4–7; U.S. Coast Guard Historian's Office, USCG, http://www.uscg.mil/history/weboralhistory/georgeclarsen_ww2_memoir.asp (added November 2005) and www.military.com (December 2006).
21. Gwenfread Allen, *Hawaii's War Years (1941–1945)* (Honolulu: University of Hawaii Press, 1950), 40–41.
22. *Ibid.,* 89–90.
23. *Ibid.,* 222.
24. John W. Chambers II, ed., *The Oxford Companion to American Military History* (New York: Oxford University Press), 1999, 669.
25. Allen, *Hawaii's War Years,* 365.

26. Sally Van Wagenen Keil, *Those Wonderful Women in Their Flying Machines: The Unknown Heroines of World War II* (New York: Rawson Wade, 1979), 270.

27. Chambers, *Oxford Companion*, 669.

28. Allen, *Hawaii's War Years*, 231.

29. Richard P. Klobuchar, *The USS "Ward": An Operational History of the Ship That Fired the First American Shot of World War II* (Jefferson, NC: McFarland, 2006), 56–57.

30. Thomas P. Ostrom, *The United States Coast Guard, 1790 to the Present* (Oakland, OR: Red Anvil/Elderberry Press, 2006), 69.

31. H.R. Kaplan and Lt. Cmdr. James F. Hunt (USCG), *This Is the Coast Guard* (Cambridge, MD: Cornell Maritime Press, 1972), 163.

32. *The Coast Guard at War: Coast Guard Units in Hawaii, December 7, 1941,* U.S. Coast Guard Historian's Office, USCG, http://www.uscg.mil/history/articles/PearlHarbor.asp (added November 1999; updated April 2001), 1–2.

33. U.S. Coast Guard Historian's Office, *The Coast Guard at War* (April 2001), 3–6.

34. *Cutters and Craft List,* U.S. Coast Guard Historian's Office, USCG, http://www.uscg.mil/history/cutterindex.asp (added December 2001; updated July 2003), 6–11. The USCGC *Taney* was decommissioned in 1986 and assigned to a berth at the Maritime Museum in Baltimore, Maryland.

Chapter 3

1. Thomas Parrish, ed., and S.L.A. Marshall, *Encyclopedia of World War II* (New York: Simon and Schuster, 1978), 644.

2. Parrish, *Encyclopedia*, 593.

3. John W. Chambers, ed., *The Oxford Companion to American Military History* (New York: Oxford University Press, 1999), 145.

4. Thomas P. Ostrom, *The United States Coast Guard, 1790 to the Present* (Oakland, OR: Red Anvil/Elderberry Press, 2006), 57–58.

5. Parrish, *Encyclopedia*, 400.

6. *Ibid.*, 367.

7. *Ibid.*, 25, 659.

8. Frederick Chapin Lane, *Ships for Victory* (Baltimore: Johns Hopkins University Press, 1951), 408, 566.

9. Parrish, *Encyclopedia*, 429.

Chapter 4

1. Tom Beard, ed., *The Coast Guard* (Seattle: Foundation for Coast Guard History, and Westport, CT: Hugh Lauter Levin, 2004), 238–239.

2. Beard, *Coast Guard*, 240–245.

3. *Ibid.*, 244.

4. *Ibid.*, 86, 87, 89.

5. Thomas P. Ostrom, *The USCG on the Great Lakes: A History* (Oakland, OR: Red Anvil/Elderberry Press, 2007), 41–42, 48–49, 102–103.

6. H.R. Kaplan and James E. Hunt, *This Is the Coast Guard* (Cambridge, MD: Cornell Maritime Press, 1972), 70–72.

7. Malcolm F. Willoughby (USCGR-T), *The U.S. Coast Guard in World War II* (Annapolis, MD: U.S. Naval Institute, 1957/1989), 45–47. Willoughby's 1957 book was reprinted in 1989. The revised 1989 printing was completed by the Naval Institute Press, under the 1957 copyright of the United States Naval Institute, Annapolis, Maryland. The 1989 edition is essentially the same as the 1957 edition in format, chapters, photographs, maps, diagrams, and page numbers. Vice Adm. Alfred C. Richmond, Commandant, U.S. Coast Guard, wrote the foreword to the 1957 edition. The 1989 edition foreword was written by Adm. Paul A. Yost, Commandant, U.S. Coast Guard. The 1989 edition features a dedication "To all members of the United States Coast Guard Regular, Reserve, and Temporary Reserve who served their country during World War II. The 1989 edition also features a book jacket cover print of the painting by Bernard D'Andrea. The print is an illustration of the combat action of Coast Guard Signalman First Class Douglas Munro (USCG) and his role in the evacuation of U.S. Marines at Guadalcanal on 27 September 1942. Petty Officer Munro was posthumously awarded the congressional Medal of Honor. References to Willoughby's history and the 1957/1989 editions will be used intermittently throughout this book because this author acquired both Willoughby editions, and the page numbers are the same in each edition.

8. *Ibid.*, 50–53.

9. *Ibid.*, 54–63.

10. *Ibid.*, 64–65, 67, 69–71.

11. *Ibid.*, 71–73.

12. Robert E. Johnson, *Guardians of the Sea: A History of the U.S. Coast Guard, 1915 to the Present* (Annapolis, MD: U.S. Naval Institute Press, 1987), 220–221.

13. John Whiteclay Chambers II, ed., *The Oxford Companion to American Military History* (New York: Oxford University Press, 1999), 145–146.

14. Willoughby, *Coast Guard in World War II*, 150–168.

15. Thomas P. Ostrom, *The United States Coast Guard, 1790 to the Present* (Oakland, OR: Red Anvil/Elderberry, 2006), 61.

16. Bill D. Ross, *Iwo Jima: Legacy of Valor* (New York: Vanguard, 1985), 353–354.

17. Ostrom, *Coast Guard on the Great Lakes,* 2006, 43–44.

18. Beard, *Coast Guard,* 306.

19. *Ibid.,* 283.

20. *Ibid.*

21. Thomas Parrish, ed., and S.L.A. Marshall, *Encyclopedia of World War II* (New York: Simon and Schuster, 1978), 485–86.

22. Beard, *Coast Guard,* 284–85, 288, 291.

23. *Ibid.,* 284.

24. Willoughby, *Coast Guard in World War II,* 37–38.

25. *Ibid.,* 38.

26. *Ibid.,* 38–39.

27. *Ibid.,* 40.

28. *Ibid.,* 42–44.

29. Beard, *Coast Guard,* 287.

30. "Patrol Squadron Six (VP-6)," Pensacola, Florida: National Museum of Naval Aviation, http://naval.aviation.museum.html (accessed January 2, 2007), 1–8.

Chapter 5

1. Malcolm F. Willoughby, *The U.S. Coast Guard in World War II,* Annapolis: United States Naval Institute, 1957/1989, 169–170.

2. *Ibid.,* 172–175.

3. *Ibid.,* 176–177.

4. David M. Hamilton, "The Amphibious Revolution," *Naval History* (October 2006), 62–63.

5. Robert L. Scheina, *U.S. Coast Guard Cutters and Craft of World War II* (Annapolis, MD: Naval Institute Press, 1982), 13–14.

6. William J. Veigele, *PC Patrol Craft of World War II* (Santa Barbara, CA: Astral, 2003), 10–11.

7. *Ibid.,* 25–27, 30–32.

8. *Ibid.,* 55–59.

9. *Ibid.,* 223–224.

10. Scheina, *Coast Guard Cutters,* 37–38.

11. Willoughby, *Coast Guard in World War II,* 184.

12. Veigele, *PC Patrol Craft,* 236–238.

13. Leon Frederick, *Hooligan Sailor: The Saga of One Coastguardsman in World War II* (Ozark, MO: Hazelwood, 2005), 12–14.

14. *Ibid.,* 21–25, 45.

15. *Ibid.,* 25.

16. Willoughby, *Coast Guard in World War II,* 173.

17. *Ibid.*

18. Frederick, *Hooligan,* 50–51.

19. *Ibid.,* 56.

20. *Ibid.,* 59.

21. *Ibid.,* 66–67.

22. Scheina, *Coast Guard Cutters,* 260.

23. *Ibid.,* 298.

24. *Ibid.,* 299.

25. *Ibid.,* 306.

26. Willoughby, *Coast Guard in World War II,* 123.

27. *Ibid.,* 334.

28. *Ibid.,* 204.

29. Edgar M. Nash (Gunnery Officer, USCG), *World War Two USCG Warriors of USS Menges (DE-320)* (Modesto, CA: Author, 2003). Most of the pages were either unnumbered or renumbered in sequence in different sections. The manuscript features the naval experiences of Gunnery Officer E.M. Nash, a history of the *Menges,* combat action in the Atlantic and Mediterranean, photographs of the ship and crew, a commemoration listing and honoring *Menges* sailors who died while serving the United States, and autobiographies of the author and crew written in various postwar years up to 2002.

30. Oliver L. North, (Lt. Col., USMC, Ret.) and Joe Musser, *War Stories III: The Heroes Who Defeated Hitler* (Washington, DC: Regnery, 2005), 181–186.

31. Scheina, *Coast Guard Cutters,* 55.

32. Willoughby, *Coast Guard in World War II,* 334.

33. *Ibid.,* 110.

34. MOMM3c Warren D. Bonner (USCG), *The Mighty "E": A Ship and Her Crew* (Orange, CA: Author, 2004)8. Mr. Bonner sent the author an autographed copy of his book.

35. *Ibid.,* 13.

36. Thomas, Capt. Charles W. Thomas (USCG), *Ice Is Where You Find It* (Indianapolis: Bobbs-Merrill, 1951), dedication, xi-xiii.

37. Bonner, *Mighty "E,"* 14–15.

38. *Ibid.,* 72.

39. *Ibid.,* 74, 75, 88–89.

40. *Ibid.,* 114.

41. *Ibid.,* 324.

42. David Westwood, *The U-Boat War* (Drexil Hill, PA: Casemate, 2005), 190–192.

43. Gordon L. Rottman, Tony Bryan (Illustrator), *Landing Ship, Tank (LST) 1942–2002,* illust. Tony Bryan (New York: Osprey), 2005, 3–7.

44. *Ibid.,* 18–21.

45. *Ibid.,* 16–17.

46. *Ibid.,* 38.

47. Lt. (jg) George P. Alton (USCGR), *FS's: The Little Ships That Could* (San Leandro, CA: Author, 2000), 125–126, 135, 150–151. Mr. Alton sent the author an autographed copy of his manuscript from which the summary of themes and specific information were cited.

48. *Ibid.,* Appendix B, 139.

49. Alistair Cooke, *The American Home*

Front (1941–1942) (New York: Atlantic Monthly Press, 2006), 278.

50. *Ibid.*, 278–79.

51. *Ibid.*, 279.

52. Samuel Eliot Morison, *The Two-Ocean War: A Short History of the United States Navy in the Second World War* (Boston: Little, Brown, 1963).

53. *Ibid.*, 105.

54. *Ibid.*, 134–135.

55. *Ibid.*, 241.

56. *Ibid.*, 382.

57. *Ibid.*, 585.

58. *Ibid.*, 586.

59. Robert Erwin Johnson, *Guardians of the Sea* (Naval Institute Press: 1987), 238–239.

60. Thomas P. Ostrom, *The United States Coast Guard, 1790 to the Present* (Oakland, OR: Red Anvil/Elderberry: 2006), 63.

61. Admiral Ernest J. King (USN), *U.S. Navy at War: 1941–1945* (Official Reports to the Secretary of the Navy, Washington, DC: United States Navy Department, 1946), 3.

62. Willoughby, *Coast Guard in World War II*, ix.

Chapter 6

1. *Survival On Land and Sea* (Washington, DC: Publications Branch Office of Naval Intelligence, United States Navy, 1944), 1–187. Prepared for the United States Navy by the Ethnographic Board and the Staff of the Smithsonian Institution with contributions by the Bureau of Aeronautics and the Bureau of Medicine and Surgery, United States Navy.

2. *Ibid.*, 16–17.

3. Thomas P. Ostrom, *The USCG on the Great Lakes* (Oakland, OR: Red Anvil/Elderberry, 2007), 38.

4. *Ibid.*, 41–42.

5. Thomas P. Ostrom, *The United States Coast Guard, 1790 to the Present* (Oakland, OR: Red Anvil/Elderberry, 2006), 253–257. The information on World War II Coast Guard port security and national defense missions out of Charleston Harbor (South Carolina) came from the files of the COTP Office, Charleston. Captain K.F. Bennett, COTP and Commanding Officer, USCG Maritime Safety Office, Charleston, donated a copy of volumes 1 and 2 of *History of U.S. Coast Guard in the Sixth Naval District During World War II* to The South Carolina Historical Society library in Charleston. The author of this book reviewed the file of Coast Guard documents at the SCHS library. In his cover letter describing the gift donation to the SCHS, Capt. Bennett said, "This account was prepared shortly after World War II concluded. A copy was discovered in our files and was duplicated at Coast Guard Headquarters" (presumably in Washington, D.C.). The date on Capt. Bennett's letter and the date on the introductory pages of the file were unclear.

6. Lt. Malcolm F. Willoughby (USCGR-T), *The U.S. Coast Guard in World War II* (Annapolis, MD: United States Naval Institute, 1957), 65.

7. *Ibid.*, 70.

8. *Ibid.*

9. *Ibid.*, 86.

10. *Ibid.*, 70–71.

11. *Ibid.*, 71.

12. *Ibid.*

13. *Ibid.*, 86–87.

14. *Ibid.*, 87.

15. Ostrom, *The USCG on the Great Lakes*, 42.

16. Photojournalist First Class T. Michael O'Brien (USCG), *Guardians of the Eighth Sea: A History of the U.S. Coast Guard on the Great Lakes* (Honolulu: University Press of the Pacific, 1976, 2001, reprinted from the 1976 edition, published by the USCG, Ninth District), 69–71.

17. *Ibid.*, 73.

18. Ostrom, *The USCG on the Great Lakes*, 43.

19. *Ibid.*, 43–44.

20. *Ibid.*, 44.

21. Robert Ridder, "He Saw Four Cruisers Sunk in the South Pacific," *Duluth News Tribune*, May 21, 1944 (Duluth Public Library, USCG File).

22. Ostrom, *The USCG on the Great Lakes*, 45–46, 106, 141–142; and BMC Vermont Johnson's "Letter to the Zenith Dredge Co., Duluth, Mn.," May 8, 1985, Lake Superior Maritime Collection, Coast Guard File, Jim Dan Hill Library, University of Wisconsin-Superior.

23. Robert L. Scheina, *U.S. Coast Guard Cutters and Craft of World War II* (Annapolis: Naval Institute Press, 1982), 99.

24. Willoughby, *Coast Guard in World War II*, 162–163.

25. L.F. Chambers (PA3, USCG), "True Blue," *Coast Guard* (March 2005), 36.

26. Scheina, *Coast Guard Cutters*, 61, 96.

27. Bill Beck and C. Patrick Labadie, *Pride of the Inland Seas: An Illustrated History of the Port of Duluth-Superior* (Afton, MN: Afton Historical Society Press, 2004), 162.

28. *Ibid.*, 163.

29. *Ibid.*, 160–170.

30. *Ibid.*, 167.

31. *Ibid.*, 186–187.

32. Dennis L. Noble, *Lighthouses and Keep-*

ers: *The U.S. Lighthouse Service and Its Legacy* (Annapolis, MD: Naval Institute Press, 2004), 149–164.

33. "In Days Gone By," *Duluth News Tribune,* March 11, 1982, University of Wisconsin-Superior Maritime Collections, Jim Dan Hill Library, Coast Guard History File.

34. Cmdr. Jimmie H. Hobaugh (USCG), "Combined Group Station COTP Duluth Unit History Report, USCG," 5 March 1975, UW-S, JDHL Maritime Collections, Coast Guard History File.

35. Paul D. Mehney, "Continuing the Tradition," in *Guardian of the Great Lakes* (Ninth Coast Guard District, September-October 1999, UW-S, JDHL Maritime Collections, Coast Guard File).

36. "The Spirit Lives On," USCGC *Escanaba (WMEC 907),* USCGC *Escanaba* Home Page, Department of Homeland Security, http://www.uscg.mil/lantarea/cutter/escanaba,/History.htm (accessed 27 Oct. 2007; last update 17 August 2007).

37. Richard P. Klobuchar, *The USS "Ward": An Operational History of the Ship That Fired the First American Shot of World War II* (Jefferson, NC: McFarland, 2006), 40–43.

38. Lt. Cmdr. Tom Beard (USCG, Ret.), ed., *The Coast Guard* (Seattle: Foundation for Coast Guard History; and Westport CT: Hugh Lauter Levin, 2004), 123–125.

Chapter 7

1. Norman Polmar, *The Naval Institute Guide to the Ships and Aircraft of the U.S. Fleet* (Annapolis, MD: Naval Institute Press, 2005), 570.

2. "Russell R. Waesche (1936–1945)," in *Commandants of the Coast Guard,* FAQS from the Historian's Office, U.S. Coast Guard Historian's Office, USCG, http://www.uscg.mil/history/faqs/comm.asp (updated May 2002), 1.

3. Polmar, *Guide to Ships,* 570.

4. "Coast Guard Personnel: Commandants," USCG, http://www.uscg.mil/history/people/RRWaescheSRBio.asp (compiled March 2000), 1–2.

5. Robert Erwin Johnson, *Guardians of the Sea: History of the United States Coast Guard, 1915 to the Present* (Annapolis, MD: Naval Institute Press, 1987), 149–150.

6. *Ibid.,* 154.

7. *Ibid.,* 162–166, 179, 183–185.

8. "Training Merchant Marines for War: The Role of the United States Coast Guard," in *Coast Guard at War,* U.S. Coast Guard Historian's Office, USCG, www.uscg.mil/history (created October 2000; updated January 2001), 1–6.

9. Johnson, *Guardians,* 202.

10. "Coast Guard Personnel: Commandants," 1–2.

11. Johnson, *Guardians,* 260.

12. Adm. Ernest J. King (USN), *U.S. Navy at War (1941–1945),* Official Reports to the Secretary of the Navy (Washington, D.C.: United States Navy Department, 1946), 3.

13. Lt. Malcolm F. Willoughby (USCGR-T), *The U.S. Coast Guard in World War II* (Annapolis, MD: United States Naval Institute, 1957/1989), xi.

14. Johnson, *Guardians,* 254.

15. *Ibid.,* 254–255.

16. *Coast Guard Personnel: Facts, Images, History: Russell R. Waesche, 1936–1945,* USCG, http://www.uscg.mil/ (compiled March 2000), 2.

17. "Russell R. Waesche, Jr., 84, Rear Admiral," *New York Times,* June 15, 1998, http://query.nytimes.com/gst/fullpage.html?res=9804E0DB143DF936A25755C0A96E958260&sec=&spon= (accessed Friday, November 2, 2007).

18. Patricia Kime, "Former Coast Guard Commandant Dies," *Coast Guard* 5 (2007), 38.

19. *Ibid.,* 38.

20. Willoughby, *Coast Guard in World War II,* 1957/1989, 294.

21. Kime, "Former Coast Guard," 38.

22. "Out of the History Books: A Salute to the Many Heroes of World War II," *Coast Guard* 5 (2007), inside front cover, courtesy of CG Historian.

23. Willoughby, *Coast Guard in World War II,* 311–332.

Chapter 8

1. Lt. Cmdr. Tom Beard (USCG, Ret.), "Guarding Our Shores," in *U.S. Naval Aviation,* eds. M.H. Goodspeed and Rich Burgess (Pensacola, FL: Hugh Lauter Levin, 2001), 242, 243, 248.

2. *Ibid.,* 244.

3. *Ibid.,* 245.

4. *Ibid.,* 246.

5. Lt. Cmdr. Tom Beard (USCG, Ret.), ed., *The Coast Guard* (Seattle: Foundation for Coast Guard History, and Westport, CT: Hugh Lauter Levin, 2004), 283.

7. Ron Simon, "Coast Guard Veteran Followed the Navy During World War II," *Mansfield News Journal,* November 19, 2007.

8. Robert L. Scheina, *U.S. Coast Guard Cutters and Craft of World War II* (Annapolis, MD: Naval Institute Press, 1982), 21.

9. Lt. Malcolm F. Willoughby (USCGR-T), *The U.S. Coast Guard in World War II* (An-

napolis, MD: United States Naval Institute, 1957/1989), 334.

10. Scheina, *Coast Guard Cutters*, 13, 14, 16, 18.

11. *Ibid.*, 334.

12. *Ibid.*, 13, 14, 17.

13. Willoughby, *Coast Guard in World War II*, 334.

14. Scheina, *Coast Guard Cutters*, 13, 14, 16, 20.

15. *Ibid.*, 55.

16. Willoughby, *Coast Guard in World War II*, 334.

17. Scheina, *Coast Guard Cutters*, 1.

18. *Ibid.*, 14.

19. *Ibid.*, 21.

20. *Ibid.*, 37.

21. Willoughby, *Coast Guard in World War II*, 334.

22. *Ibid.*

23. *Ibid.*, 101, 198, 335.

24. *Ibid.*, 335.

25. Scheina, *Coast Guard Cutters*, 11.

26. *Ibid.*, 31.

27. Willoughby, *Coast Guard in World War II*, 335.

28. Daniel J. Hopkins, ed., *Merriam-Webster's Geographical Dictionary* (Springfield, MA: Merriam-Webster, 2001), 547. The *Merriam-Webster's Geographical Dictionary* has been the source used by this author for geographical information and accuracy regarding place names throughout this book.

29. Willoughby, *Coast Guard in World War II*, 335.

30. *Ibid.*

31. *Ibid.*

32. Scheina, *Coast Guard Cutters*, 15.

33. *Ibid.*, 40.

34. Willoughby, *Coast Guard in World War II*, 335.

35. *Ibid.*

36. Robert L. Scheina, *U.S. Coast Guard Cutters and Craft, 1946–1990* (Annapolis: Naval Institute Press, 1990), 7, 9.

37. Thomas P. Ostrom, Interview with Martin L. Jeter, FN1 (USCG), World War II, February 7, 2007. The interview occurred at a Rochester (Minnesota) restaurant, and at the home of Martin and Florence Jeter in Rochester.

38. Scheina, *Coast Guard Cutters 1946*, 11, 13. The author of this book took basic training at U.S. Coast Guard Station Alameda in 1961 and an exciting advanced training cruise on the USCGC *Dexter*. U.S. Coast Guard Station Alameda was then located on Government Island. USCG Station Alameda is still active. Government Island was later named Coast Guard Island. The author served in the USCGR unit at Duluth (Minnesota) from 1961 to 1969.

39. Jurgen Rohwer and Gerhard Hummelchen, *Chronology of the War at Sea (1941–1945)*, vol. 1 *(1939–1942)*, 1972–1973, and vol. 2 *(1943–1945)*, 1974 (New York: Arco, English translation copyright 1972, 1973, 1974, by Ian Allen). Distributed by United States Naval Institute Publications, Annapolis, MD. *Chronology of the War at Sea* contains a complete index of ship names and persons, operational code names, convoys, and surface and submarine forces. The volumes include 64 pages of photographs of Axis and Allied vessels and combat action. Sources consulted by the authors include German and Allied military and civilian documents. Military sources include the United States Army Air Force, United States Army, United States Marine Corps, and the United States Coast Guard. Among the historical sources listed are the writings and contributions of Capt. J.M. Waters (USCG), and the 15-volume *History of United States Naval Operations in World War II*, written by Rear Adm. Samuel Eliot Morison (USNR), the eminent Harvard historian. Professor Morison's volumes covered the war years from 1941 to 1945. The books were published in sequence by Little, Brown between 1947 and 1963.

40. J. Rohwer and G. Hummelchen, *Chronology of the War at Sea (1939–1945)*, vol. 1 (Arco, 1972), 104.

41. *Ibid.*, 185.

42. *Ibid.*, 213.

43. *Ibid.*, 223.

44. *Ibid.*, 226–227.

45. *Ibid.*, 234.

46. *Ibid.*, 247.

47. *Ibid.*, 253.

48. Robert L. Scheina, *U.S. Coast Guard Cutters and Craft of World War II* (Annapolis, MD: Navy Institute Press, 1982), 59–60.

49. Rohwer and Hummelchen, *Chronology*, vol. 1, 265–266.

50. *Ibid.*, 285–286.

51. Rohwer and Hummelchen, *Chronology of the War at Sea*, vol. 2, 376.

52. *Ibid.*, 495.

53. *Ibid.*, 500.

54. *Ibid.*, vol. 2, 503.

55. Rohwer and Hummelchen, *Chronology*, vol. 2, 503.

56. Rohwer and Hummelchen, *Chronology*, vol. 1, 253.

57. Willoughby, *Coast Guard in World War II*, 27.

58. *Ibid.*, 89.

59. *Ibid.*, 128, 199.

Chapter 9

1. Thaddeus D. Novak (Seaman First Class, and then advanced to Petty Officer/ Coxswain, USCG) and P.J. Capelotti (Senior Petty Officer, USCGR), *Life and Death on the Greenland Patrol, 1942* (Gainesville: University Press of Florida, 2005), editor's note, xi-xxii; editor's epilogue, 187–189; notes, 193–200. P.J. Capelotti is senior lecturer in anthropology and American Studies at Pennsylvania State University and Abington College and the author of several histories. Capelotti served on active duty as at the U.S. Coast Guard Historian's Office in Washington, D.C.

2. Danel J. Hopkins, *Merriam-Webster's Geographical Dictionary* (Springfield, MA: Merriam-Webster, 2001), 447.

3. Novak and Capelotti, *Life and Death on the Greenland Patrol*, 155–156.

4. *Ibid.*, 193.

5. *Ibid.*, 193–195.

6. Robert L. Scheina, *U.S. Coast Guard Cutters and Craft of World War II* (Annapolis, MD: Naval Institute Press, 1982), 187.

7. Lt. Malcolm F. Willoughby (USCGR-T), *The U.S. Coast Guard in World War II* (Annapolis, MD: United States Naval Institute, 1957/1989), 102–103.

8. Scheina, *Coast Guard Cutters,* 32–34.

9. Maurice Steinberg (RM3, USCG), *A Sailor at War* (Philadelphia: Xlibris, 2002). Steinberg listed his sources as official Coast Guard photographs; personal memories; excerpts from the official log of the CGC *Modoc* from 1 September 1944 to 15 August 1945; various U.S. Coast Guard publications; and *The Coast Guard at War* (Washington, D.C.: Greenland Patrol Historical Section-Public Information Division-U.S. Coast Guard Headquarters, 15 July, 1945).

10. *Ibid.*, 15–16.

11. *Ibid.*, 18.

12. *Ibid.*, 64–66.

13. *Ibid.*, 78–79.

14. *Ibid.*, 77,78, 79.

15. *Ibid.*, 107, 134, 135.

16. *Ibid.*, 14.

17. Capt. Charles W. Thomas (USCG), *Ice Is Where You Find It* (Indianapolis: Bobbs Merrill, 1951), xii.

18. *Ibid.*, xxi.

19. *Ibid.*, xxi-xxiv.

20. *Ibid.*, 27–36.

21. *Ibid.*, 38.

22. *Ibid.*, 43–51.

23. *Ibid.*, 52–56.

24. *Ibid.*, 76–80.

25. Willoughby, *Coast Guard in World War II*, 102.

26. *Ibid.*, 105–106.

27. *Ibid.*, 106–107.

28. *Ibid.*, 107.

29. *Ibid.*, 107–108.

30. *Ibid.*, 108.

31. *Ibid.*

32. Scheina, *Coast Guard Cutters,* 55.

33. Willoughby, *Coast Guard in World War II,* 110.

34. Scheina, *Coast Guard Cutters,* 199.

35. Willoughby, *Coast Guard in World War II,* 110.

Chapter 10

1. Capt. Alex R. Larzelere (USCG, Ret.), *The Coast Guard in World War I: An Untold Story* (Annapolis, MD: Naval Institute Press, 2003), xi-xiv.

2. *Ibid.*, 45–49.

3. Doris Kearns Goodwin, *No Ordinary Time: Franklin and Eleanor Roosevelt* (New York: Simon and Schuster, 1995), 277–288.

4. *Ibid.*, 282–283.

5. *Ibid.*, 262–267.

6. *Ibid.*, 233–234.

7. *Ibid.*, 210–211, 448–449.

8. Stuart Murray, *Atlas of American Military History* (New York: Checkmark Books, 2005), 163.

9. *Ibid.*, 170.

10. *Ibid.*, 164–165.

11. Reg Ingraham, *First Fleet: The Story of the U.S. Coast Guard At War* (Indianapolis: Bobbs-Merrill Company, 1944), 7–8.

12. *Ibid.*, 8.

13. *Ibid.*, 310.

14. *Ibid.*, 90.

15. *Ibid.*, 92–99.

16. *Ibid.*, 103–106.

17. *Ibid.*, 108–114.

18. *Ibid.*, 116–118.

19. Robert L. Scheina, *U.S. Coast Guard Cutters & Craft of World War II* (Annapolis, MD: Naval Institute Press, 1982), 14.

20. *Ibid.*, 21.

21. *Ibid.*, 59–60.

22. *Ibid.*, 187.

23. *Ibid.*, 132.

24. Robert Erwin Johnson, *Guardians of the Sea: History of the United States Coast Guard, 1915 to the Present* (Annapolis, MD: Naval Institute Press, 1987), 239.

25. *Ibid.*, 239.

26. Ingraham, *First Fleet,* 301–306.

27. *Ibid.*, 308.

28. "Around the Globe with the U.S. Coast Guard," *Coast Guard* (June 1943), 62; a reproduction taken from the inside front cover of

Coast Guard 6 (2007), U.S. Government Printing Office.

Chapter 11

1. John T. Mason, Jr., ed., an oral interview with Rear Adm. Odale Dabney, Jr. (USN), "Not for Heroes: Mine Disposal School in Washington, D.C.," in *The Atlantic War Remembered: An Oral History Collection* (Annapolis, MD: Naval Institute Press, 1990), 40.

2. *Ibid.*, 44.

3. *Ibid.*, 47.

4. John T. Mason, Jr., "Operation Torch: Landing in French Morocco," Interview with Adm. H. Kent Hewitt (USN), in *The Atlantic War Remembered*, 157–159.

5. John T. Mason, Jr., "New Help for the Admiral," Interview with Capt. Phil H. Bucklew (USN), in *The Atlantic War Remembered*, 265.

6. "Jack Dempsey," *Coast Guard Celebrities*, U.S. Coast Guard Historian's Office, USCG, http://www.uscg.mil/history/faqs/jackdempsey.asp (accessed March 2001), 1–2.

7. Mason, Bucklew interview, 265.

8. John T. Mason, Jr., *The Atlantic War Remembered*, 261–262. This reference was written by John T. Mason as a summary introduction to the interview with Capt. Phil H. Bucklew (USN). Mason is a trained historian whose interest and expertise in naval history came from his service with the Office of Naval Intelligence in Washington, D.C., from 1940 to 1945. In 1969, Mason organized the office of oral history at the U.S. Naval Institute. The biographical information on Professor Mason was acquired from *The Atlantic War Remembered: An Oral History Collection* (Annapolis, MD: Naval Institute Press, 1990), 481.

9. James M. Morris, *History of the U.S. Navy* (Greenwich, CT: Brompton, 1984), 146.

10. PA2 Christopher Evanson (USCG), "Looking Back: A Veteran Remembers the First Steps to Racial Equality," *Coast Guard* 4 (2007, Washington D.C.: Government Printing Office), 44–47.

11. PA2 Judy Silverstein (USCGR), "Adrift," *Coast Guard* 2 (2006, Washington, D.C.: U.S. Government Printing Office), 28–31.

12. Robert L. Scheina, *U.S. Coast Guard Cutters and Craft of World War II* (Annapolis, MD: Naval Institute Press, 1982), 44–49.

13. Silverstein, "Adrift," 28–31.

14. *Ibid.*, 29, 31.

15. Cmdr. Arch A. Mercey (USCGR) and Lee Grove, Chief Specialist (USCGR), eds., *Sea, Surf and Hell: The U.S. Coast Guard in World War II* (New York: Prentice Hall, 1945), 72–78.

16. Scheina, *Coast Guard Cutters*, 164–165.

17. Mercey and Grove, *Sea*, 72–78.

18. *Ibid.*, 113.

19. *Ibid.*, 114.

20. *Ibid.*, 112–119.

21. John Philo (Petty Officer/Gunners Mate 2nd Class (USN) World War II), "U.S. Navy Armed Guards in World War II," based on interviews and written communications with the author and Mr. Philo's presentation to the Scott Hosier World War II Roundtable in Rochester, Minnesota, in 2007. The written and oral interviews with the author of this book occurred in September 2005 and January 2008 and by his letter of correspondence to the author dated 23 January 2008. Philo retired as wrestling coach and mathematics instructor at Rochester Community and Technical College.

22. *Ibid.*

23. John Keegan, *Intelligence in War* (New York: Random House, 2003), 221–257.

24. *Ibid.*, 245.

25. *Ibid.*, 247.

26. *Ibid.*, 252–257.

27. Homer H. Hickam, Jr., *Torpedo Junction: U-boat War Off America's East Coast, 1942* (New York: Dell Publishing, 1989), xi-xvii, four photographs and descriptions between pages 198 and 199, and the description on the back cover page of the paperback edition.

28. Scheina, *Coast Guard Cutters*, 37–38.

29. Lt. Malcolm F. Willoughby (USCGR-T), *The U.S. Coast Guard in World War II* (Annapolis, MD: Naval Institute Press, 1957/1989), 145.

30. Hickam, *Torpedo Junction*, 98–103, 108, 134–135, 177–178, 296–298.

31. *Ibid.*, 38.

32. *Ibid.*, 285–292.

33. Thomas Parrish and S.L.A. Marshall, eds., *Simon and Schuster Encyclopedia of World War II* (New York: Simon and Schuster, 1978), 337.

34. *Ibid.*, 18–19.

35. *Ibid.*, 558.

36. Hickam, *Torpedo Junction*, 166–167.

37. *Ibid.*, 18–19.

38. *Ibid.*, 134.

39. "Cutters & Craft List," *Dione WPC-107*, U.S. Coast Guard Historian's Office, USCG, http://www.uscg.mil/history/webcutters/Dione1934.asp (added February 2003).

40. Capt. John M. Waters, Jr. (USCG), *Bloody Winter* (Princeton, NJ: D. Van Nostrand, 1967), viii.

41. *Ibid.*, ix.

42. Scheina, *Coast Guard Cutters*, 13–14.

43. Waters, *Bloody Winter*, 81.

44. *Ibid.*, 124–126.

45. *Ibid.*, 126–128.

46. *Ibid.*, 165–169.

47. Michael G. Walling, *Blood Stained Sea: The U.S. Coast Guard in the Battle of the Atlantic, 1941–1944* (Camden, ME: International Marine/McGraw Hill, 2004), 232–234.

48. Willoughby, *Coast Guard in World War II*, 199.

49. David Fairbank White, *Bitter Ocean: The Battle of the Atlantic, 1939–1945* (New York: Simon and Schuster, 2006), 213.

50. Scheina, *Coast Guard Cutters,* 32–34.

51. White, *Bitter Ocean,* 213–214.

52. Scheina, *Coast Guard Cutters,* 13, 14, 21.

53. White, *Bitter Ocean,* 216.

54. *Ibid.*, 1–2, 3, 6.

55. Martin Middlebrook, *Convoy: The Greatest U-Boat Battle of the War* (London: Cassell Military Publishers), 1976, 35.

56. *Ibid.*, photograph and caption opposite page 183.

Chapter 12

1. Robert L. Scheina, *U.S. Coast Guard Cutters and Craft of World War II*, Annapolis, MD: Naval Institute Press, 1982, 299.

2. Stuart Murray, *Atlas of American Military History* (New York: Checkmark Books, 2005), 164–165.

3. *Ibid.*, 168–169.

4. Lt. Malcolm F. Willoughby, (USCGR-T), *The U.S. Coast Guard in World War II* (Annapolis, MD: Naval Institute Press, 1957/1989), 169–172.

5. Craig L., Symonds (author) and William J. Clipson (cartographer), *The Naval Institute Historical Atlas of the U.S. Navy* (Annapolis, MD: Naval Institute Press, 1995), 158–159.

6. *Ibid.*, 160–161.

7. Willoughby, *Coast Guard in World War II*, 205–206.

8. *Ibid.*, 207–208.

9. *Ibid.*, 209, and the photograph adjacent to the page.

10. *Ibid.*, 210.

11. *Ibid.*, 210–211.

12. *Ibid.*, 211–214.

13. *Ibid.*, 214.

14. *Ibid.*, 215–218.

15. *Ibid.*, 219–220.

16. *Ibid.*, 220–221.

17. *Ibid.*, 223–227.

18. *Ibid.*, 228.

19. *Ibid.*, 229–237.

20. Cmdr. Arch A. Mercey (USCGR) and Chief Specialist Lee Grove (USCGR), eds., "To The Shores of Sicily," in *Sea, Surf, and Hell* (New York: Prentice Hall, 1945), 134–143.

21. Mercey and Grove, "Whistling Death," in *Sea, Surf, and Hell,* 144–145.

Chapter 13

1. Stuart Murray, *Atlas of American Military History* (New York: Checkmark Books), 170.

2. *Ibid.*, 170–171.

3. *Ibid.*, 179.

4. Craig L. Symonds, *Historical Atlas of the U.S. Navy* (Annapolis, MD: Naval Institute Press, 1995), 172–173. Craig L. Symonds served as professor of history at the U.S. Naval Academy. William J. Clipson, former chair of the graphic arts department at the U.S. Naval Academy, produced the exemplary maps that accompanied the *Atlas* narrative.

5. Stephen E. Ambrose, *D-Day* (New York: Simon & Schuster, 1995), 585–586.

6. David G. Chandler and James Lawton Collins, eds., *The D-Day Encyclopedia* (New York: Simon & Schuster, 1994), 610–611. Among the many distinguished editors and contributors associated with the *D-Day Encyclopedia* is Truman R. Strobridge. Strobridge served in the U.S. Merchant Marine and the U.S. Army. He has been the chief historian of the United States Coast Guard and has worked as a historian and archivist for several federal government agencies, including the Joint Chiefs of Staff (*D-Day Encyclopedia*, xxvii). *D-Day* editor David G. Chandler is the author of several military history books and served as the head of the war studies department at the Royal Military Academy, Sandhurst, UK. The second *D-Day* editor is Brig. Gen. James Lawton Collins, Jr. (USA, ret.). Gen. Collins landed at Utah Beach at Normandy and has served as the Army chief of military history (*D-Day*, xxi).

7. Ambrose, *D-Day*, 45.

8. James F. Dunnigan and Albert A. Nofi, *The Pacific War Encyclopedia* (New York: Check Mark Books/Facts on File, 1998), 268.

9. Ambrose, *D-Day*, 260, 372.

10. John A. Tilley, "A History of Women in the Coast Guard," U.S. Coast Guard Historian's Office, USCG, http://www.uscg.mil/history/articles/h_womn.asp (accessed January 1999).

11. Chandler and Collins, *D-Day Encyclopedia,* 160–161.

12. *Ibid.*, 98, 99.

13. *Ibid.*, 99, 373.

14. *Ibid.*, 373, 385, 478, 537. Dr. Howard A. Andersen was interviewed by the author of this

book in September 2005 and in subsequent conversations.

15. Lt. Malcolm F. Willoughby (USCGR-T), *The U.S. Coast Guard in World War II* (Annapolis, MD: Naval Institute Press, 1957/1989), 250–252. The quotes from Cmdr. Kenneth Edwards (RN) came from the book by this author, *The United States Coast Guard, 1790 to the Present,* (Oakland, OR: Elderberry, 2006), 65, and Cmdr. Kenneth Edward's own book, *Operation Neptune* (New York: Collins, 1946), 158.

16. Chandler and Collins, *D-Day Encyclopedia*, 147–149.

17. Cornelius Ryan, *The Longest Day: June 6, 1944* (New York: Simon and Schuster, 1959), 92.

18. *Ibid.*, 51.

19. *Ibid.*, 90.

20. *Ibid.*, 204–207.

21. *Ibid.*, 206–207.

22. Michael Korda, *Ike: An American Hero* (New York: HarperCollins, 2007), 39.

23. *Ibid.*, 44–45.

24. *Ibid.*, 52.

25. *Ibid.*, 290–291.

26. *Ibid.*, 412–413.

27. Cmdr. Arch A. Mercey (USCGR) and Chief Specialist Lee Grove (USCGR), eds., "Front Lines," in *Sea, Surf and Hell* (New York: Prentice-Hall, Inc., 1945), 146.

28. *Ibid.*, "Front Lines," 149–154.

29. *Ibid.*, "A Lucky Cox'n," 155–157.

30. *Ibid.*, "Cross Channel Trip," 158–171.

31. *Ibid.*, "Breaching the West Wall," 177–187.

32. *Ibid.*, "Picturing the War," 307–309.

33. Geoffrey C. Ward and Ken Burns, *The War: An Intimate History (1941–1945)* (New York: Alfred A. Knopf, 2007), 196–197. *The War* is based on the World War II film directed by Ken Burns and Lynn Novick. David McMahon researched the magnificent photographs.

34. *Ibid.*, 207.

35. Steven J. Zaloga, *D-Day 1944: Omaha Beach* (Oxford, UK: Osprey, 2003), 6, 33. Steven J. Zaloga is a military historian and prolific author. Zaloga's grandfather landed at Omaha beach in an engineering battalion with the First U.S. Army Infantry Division. Zaloga's father was in an engineering battalion that landed in the same sector a few days later. British designer and artist Howard Gerrard illustrated the book with illuminating maps, photographs, and drawings.

36. *Ibid.*, 56–58.

37. *Ibid.*, 40.

38. *Ibid.*, 46–47.

39. *Ibid.*, 51–52, 66–68.

40. Willoughby, *Coast Guard in World War II*, 246–248.

41. Stephen E. Ambrose, *D-Day June 6, 1944: The Climactic Battle of World War II* (Simon & Schuster, 1994), 258, 290.

42. *Ibid.*, 372.

43. *Ibid.*, 392.

44. Willoughby, *Coast Guard in World War II*, 245.

45. Flint Whitlock, *The Fighting First: The Untold Story of the Big Red One on D-Day* (Boulder, CO: Westview, 2004), 106. Colonel Walter T. Halloran is mentioned in the acknowledgments of the author of this book (*The U.S. Coast Guard in World War II*). At Omaha Beach, then-Corporal Halloran was a U.S. Army Signal Corps cinematographer. Halloran is mentioned by Flint Whitlock in *The Fighting First* on pages 70, 132, 136, and 145.

46. *Ibid.*, 134.

47. *Ibid.*, 143, 144.

48. Joseph Balkoski, *Omaha Beach: D-Day June 6, 1944* (Mechanicsburg, PA: Stackpole Books, 2004), 61.

49. Barrett Tillman, ed., *The Normandy Invasion: Brassey's D-Day Encyclopedia* (Washington, DC: Brasseys, Inc., 2004), 251–252.

50. Balkoski, *Omaha Beach,* 351.

Chapter 14

1. James F. Dunnigan and Albert A. Nofi, *The Pacific War Encyclopedia* (New York: Checkmark Books, 1998), x–xii, 418–421, 645–646.

2. Adm. Samuel Eliot Morison (USNR), *History of United States Naval Operations in World War II: Aleutians, Gilberts and Marshalls, June 1942-April 1944*, vol. 7 (Boston: Little, Brown, 1951).

3. *Ibid.*, 49–51.

4. Adm. Samuel Eliot Morison (USNR), *The Two-Ocean War: A Short History of the United States Navy in the Second World War* (Boston: Little, Brown, 1963), 265–266.

5. Lt. Malcolm F. Willoughby (USCGR-T), *The U.S. Coast Guard in World War II* (Annapolis, MD: United States Naval Institute (1957/1989), 191.

6. Morison, *The Two-Ocean War*, 266.

7. *Ibid.*, 266–271.

8. Willoughby, *Coast Guard in World War II*, 181–184.

9. *Ibid.*, 184–185.

10. *Ibid.*, 186.

11. *Ibid.*, 186–187.

12. *Ibid.*, 189–190.

13. Dunnigan and Nofi, *Pacific War*, 128, 218.

14. *Ibid.*, 40.

15. Willoughby, *Coast Guard in World War II*, 191.

16. Morison, *The Two-Ocean War*, 271.

17. Robert Erwin Johnson, *Bering Sea Escort: Life Aboard a Coast Guard Cutter in World War II* (Annapolis: Naval Institute Press, 1992). Since his appointment to the University of Alabama history department in 1956, Professor Johnson has written numerous articles and books on maritime history, the U.S. Coast Guard, and the U.S. Navy. Dr. Johnson is noted for his classic maritime book, *Guardians of the Sea: A History of the United States Coast Guard, 1915 to the Present* (Annapolis, MD: Naval Institute Press, 1987).

18. *Ibid.*, 44.

19. Robert L. Scheina, *U.S. Coast Guard Cutters and Craft of World War II* (Annapolis, MD: Naval Institute Press, 1982), 21, 22, 37, 38.

20. Johnson, *Bering Sea Escort*, 54.

21. *Ibid.*, 79–80, 86, 89, 90, 95.

22. *Ibid.*, 85.

23. *Ibid.*, 97–98, 100, 102.

24. *Ibid.*, 115–116.

25. Thomas P. Ostrom, *The United States Coast Guard, 1790 to the Present* (Oakland, OR: Red Anvil/Elderberry Press, 2006), 71.

26. Richard A. Russell, *Project Hula: Secret Soviet-American Cooperation in the War Against Japan* (Washington, DC: Naval Historical Center, Department of the Navy, 1997), 44. Richard A. Russell acquired most of his research material from the U.S. National Archives and Russian sources. Among the several people Russell acknowledged in his publication was Capt. John J. Hutson, USCG (Ret.), who participated in "Project Hula" and shared personal perspectives and photographs. Russell also acquired sources and personal information from Russian naval officers, archivists, and historians.

27. *Ibid.*, 3–8.

28. *Ibid.*, 8–13.

29. *Ibid.*, 12–28.

30. *Ibid.*, 29–35.

31. *Ibid.*, 35.

32. *Ibid.*, 36.

Chapter 15

1. Lt. Malcolm F. Willoughby (USCGR), *The U.S. Coast Guard in World War II* (Annapolis, MD: United States Naval Institute Press, 1957/1989), 8.

2. James F. Dunnigan and Albert A. Nofi, *The Pacific War Encyclopedia* (New York: Checkmark Books, 1998), x–xii, 418–421, 645–646.

3. Stuart Murray, *Atlas of American Military History* (New York: Checkmark Books, 2005), 158–159.

4. Adm. Mike Mullen (CNO, USN), "Why Midway Matters," *Naval History* (June 2007), 14–15. Adm. Mullin was sworn in as chairman of the Joint Chiefs of Staff on 1 October 2007. The CJCS is the top military advisor to the U.S. president, the secretary of defense, and the director of the Department of Homeland Security. The U.S. Coast Guard was transferred from the Treasury Department to the Transportation Department in 1967, and then to the Department of Homeland Security in 2003. The CJCS advises the Commandant of the Coast Guard on military and national security matters. The USCG and the USN and Pentagon maintain regular communications, and liaison contacts.

5. H.R. Kaplan and Lt. Cmdr. James F. Hunt (USCG), *This Is the Coast Guard* (Cambridge, MD: Cornell Maritime Press, 1972), 163.

6. Robert L. Scheina, *U.S. Coast Guard Cutters and Craft of World War II* (Annapolis, MD: Naval Institute Press, 1982), 15.

7. Willoughby, *Coast Guard in World War II*, 305.

8. Robert Erwin Johnson, *Guardians of the Sea: A History of the U.S. Coast Guard, 1915 to the Present* (Annapolis, MD: Naval Institute Press, 1987), 240–242.

9. *Ibid.*, 242–243.

10. Kim Kovarik, "A Failed Flanking Maneuver," ed. Fred Allison, *Naval History* (August 2007), 25–27.

11. Kaplan and Hunt, *This Is the Coast Guard*, 283–286.

12. Cmdr. Arch A. Mercey (USCGR) and Chief Specialist Lee Grove (USCGR), "Did They Get Off?" in *Sea, Surf and Hell: The U.S. Coast Guard in World War II* (New York: Prentice-Hall, 1945), 192–195.

13. Scheina, *Coast Guard Cutters*, 98–99.

14. Thomas P. Ostrom, *The USCG on the Great Lakes* (Oakland, OR: Red Anvil/Elderberry, 2007), 45–46.

15. *Ibid.*, 141.

16. Johnson, *Guardians*, 246, 252–254.

17. Robert M. Browning, Jr., *The Coast Guard and the Pacific War*, U.S. Coast Guard Historian's Office, USCG (January 1999), 5–7, http://www.uscg.mil/history/h_pacwar.html (accessed on Feb. 18, 2008).

18. Scheina, *Coast Guard Cutters*, 96–97.

19. Browning, *CG and Pacific War*, 4.

20. *Ibid.*, 8–11.

21. Willoughby, *Coast Guard in World War II*, 285.

22. Browning, *CG and Pacific War*, 11–12.

23. Scheina, *Coast Guard Cutters*, 98–100.

24. Browning, *CG and Pacific War,* 11–16.

25. Thomas P. Ostrom, Interviews with Navy Corpsman Leonard Jansen between 2005 and 2008. The author spoke with Jansen about World War II for a newspaper article interview in Jansen's oral presentations at the Scott Hosier World War II Round Table in Rochester, Minnesota.

26. Browning, *CG and Pacific War,* 19–21.

27. John Costello, *The Pacific War* (New York: Perennial/HarperCollins, 2000), v. *The Pacific War* was originally published in New York by Rawson, Wade in 1981; also New York: Quill, 1981, 1982.

Chapter 16

1. PA2 Judy L. Silverstein (USCG), "USCG Veteran Provided Stars and Stripes for U.S. Marines," *Reservist* (USCG) 51, no. 6 (U.S. Coast Guard Historian's Office, USCG, http:// www.uscg.mil/history/weboralhistory/Resnick _Iwo_Jima.asp (added July 2004), 1–4.

2. Cmdr. Arch A. Mercey (USCGR) and Chief Spec. Lee Grove (USCGR), *Sea, Surf and Hell* (New York: Prentice-Hall, 1945), 208–209.

3. *Ibid.,* 210–213.

4. *Ibid.,* 242–244.

5. *Ibid.,* 245–249.

6. *Ibid.,* 257–265.

7. *Ibid.,* 276–279.

8. *Ibid.,* 280–282.

9. *Ibid.,* 283–285.

10. *Ibid.,* 324–325.

11. Col. Joseph H. Alexander (USMC, Ret.), *Storm Landings: Epic Amphibious Battles in the Central Pacific* (Annapolis, MD: Naval Institute Press, 1997), 199.

12. *Ibid.,* 198.

13. Juliana Fern Patten, ed., *Another Side of World War II: A Coast Guard Lieutenant in the South Pacific* (Shippensburg, PA: Burd Street, 2005), ix, x, 155.

14. *Ibid.,* 15.

15. *Ibid.,* 15–27.

16. *Ibid.,* 59.

17. *Ibid.,* 60–62.

18. Larry Thornberry, "Fighting Nature: William Halsey's Battle Against a Typhoon," *Washington Times,* national weekly edition, June 11, 2007, 26. Thornberry reviewed the book, *Halsey's Typhoon: The True Story of a Fighting Admiral, an Epic Storm and an Untold Rescue* (New York: Grove/Atlantic Press, 2007), by Bob Drury and Ted Clavin.

19. William L. McGee, *The Amphibians Are Coming,* vol. I (Santa Barbara, CA: BMC, 2000), iii, v.

20. *Ibid.,* 18, 19.

21. *Ibid.,* 30.

22. Ken Wiley, *Lucky Thirteen: D-Days in the Pacific with the U.S. Coast Guard in World War II* (Philadelphia, PA: Casemate, 2007), xi–xiii, 1–6.

23. *Ibid.,* 83–84, 87–89, 142–145, 199–208, 212–217, 303–304.

24. *Ibid.,* 118, 283–284.

25. *Ibid.,* 110–111.

26. Rex Alan Smith and Gerald A. Meehl, *Pacific War Stories: In the Words of Those Who Survived* (New York: Abbeville Press), 2004, 324–330.

27. *Ibid.,* 479–481.

28. Robert L. Scheina, *U.S. Coast Guard Cutters and Craft of World War II* (Annapolis, MD: Naval Institute Press), 1982, 92, 96–97, 98–100.

29. RM1 Tanney Edward Oberg (USCG), *Lucky "Sweetbrier"* (Bloomington, IN: iUniverse, 2005), 10, 17, 21, 25, 28, 38, 42, 45.

30. *Ibid.,* 10, 45–46. In his 2005 book, Oberg refers to the CGC *Sweetbrier* hull number as WLB-405. Scheina's classic book, *U.S. Coast Guard Cutters and Craft of World War II* (Annapolis, MD: Naval Institute Press, 1982), 92, identifies the CGC *Sweetbrier* as WAGL-450. In his subsequent book, *U.S. Coast Guard Cutters and Craft, 1946–1990* (Annapolis, MD: Naval Institute Press, 1990), 142, Scheina lists the *Sweetbrier* as both WAGL-405 and WLB-405. Hull letter designations on some Coast Guard vessels were changed in 1965 and subsequently.

31. Oberg, *Lucky "Sweetbrier,"* 1.

32. *Ibid.,* 2.

33. *Ibid.,* 133–134.

34. *Ibid.,* 40–41, 46–47, 52–54.

35. *Ibid.,* 55, 139–141.

36. *Ibid.,* 163–166.

37. *Ibid.,* 77–79.

38. *Ibid.,* 105.

39. *Ibid.,* 107.

40. *Ibid.,* 110, 124.

41. Eugene Rachlis, *The Story of the U.S. Coast Guard* (New York: Random House, 1961), 155–157.

42. Fred Gaffen, *Cross Border Warriors: Canadians in American Force; Americans in Canadian Forces from the Civil War to the Gulf* (Toronto: Dundurn Press, 1995), 84–85.

43. Stephen Chicoine, *Our Hallowed Ground: World War II Veterans of Fort Snelling National Cemetery* (Minneapolis: University of Minnesota Press, 2005), 160–162.

44. Hal Buell, *Uncommon Valor, Common Virtue* (New York: Berkley/Penguin, 2006), 5–7.

45. *Ibid.,* 45.

46. *Ibid.,* 8.

47. *Ibid.*, 57.
48. *Ibid.*, 79.
49. Kelly Knauer et al., eds., *V-J Day: America's World War II Triumph in the Pacific* (New York: Time Books, 2005), 14.
50. *Ibid.*, 40, 41.
51. *Ibid.*, 76–77.
52. *Ibid.*, 81.
53. *Ibid.*, 85.
54. *Ibid.*, 88–89.
55. *Ibid.*, 116–118.
56. Gregg K. Kakesako, "Overdue Honor: New Memorial for the Coast Guard," *Honolulu Star Tribune*, vol. 13, issue 20, Sunday, January 20, 2008, 1.

Chapter 17

1. James F. Dunnigan and Albert A. Nofi, *The Pacific War Encyclopedia* (New York: Checkmark Books, 1998), 383.
2. Adm. Samuel Eliot Morison (USNR), *The Two-Ocean War: A Short History of the United States Navy in the Second World War* (Boston: Little, Brown, 1963), 85.
3. Dunnigan and Nofi, *Pacific War Encyclopedia*, 153–154.
4. Dr. Robert M. Browning, Jr. (U.S. Coast Guard historian), *The Coast Guard and the Pacific War*, U.S. Coast Guard Historian's Office, USCG, http://www.uscg.mil/history/articles/h_pacwar.asp (accessed February 18, 2008), 16.
5. Robert L. Scheina, *U.S. Coast Guard Cutters and Craft of World War II* (Annapolis: Naval Institute Press, 1982), 300.
6. Lt. Malcolm F. Willoughby (USCGR-T), *The United States Coast Guard in World War II* (Annapolis: United States Naval Institute Press, 1957/1989), 170–172.
7. Browning, *Coast Guard and Pacific War*, 17.
8. *Ibid.*, 17–18.
9. Willoughby, *Coast Guard in World War II*, 288–291.
10. *Ibid.*, 296–297.
11. *Ibid.*, 297.
12. *Ibid.*, 298–299.
13. Morison, *Two-Ocean War*, 570–571.
14. *Ibid.*, 572–573.
15. *Ibid.*, 573–575.
16. Willoughby, *Coast Guard in World War II*, 308.
17. *Ibid.*, 308–309.
18. Morison, *Two-Ocean War*, vii, ix-xii, and back cover biography.
19. *Ibid.*, 584–585.
20. *Ibid.*, 585.
21. *Ibid.*, 586.

Epilogue

1. C. Kay Larson (Coast Guard Auxiliary national historian) and Steven M. Budar, National Commodore (USCGAUX), *The United States Coast Guard Auxiliary, 1939–2007* (Nashville, TN: Turner, 2007, and St. Louis: MO: U.S. Coast Guard Auxiliary Association, 2007), 10–13.
2. Alejandro de Quesada, *The U.S. Home Front, 1941–1945,* illus. Stephen Walsh (Oxford: Osprey, 2008), 27–29.
3. Meredith R. Vezina, prod., *The Coast Guard in World War II* (Escondido, CA: Traditions Military Videos, USCG, ca. 1945–1949). The videotape cover states the production date as the "1940s." Assuming a postwar date, the author cited the date range as ca. 1945–1949.
4. "USCGC *Ingham*," in *Historic Naval Ships Visitors Guide* (Smithfield, VA: Historic Naval Ships Association, 2007), 1–3.
5. "USCGC *Taney*: From World War II to Baltimore Inner Harbor Museum," *Coast Guard News*, 2008, 1–2.
6. Mark Henry, *The U.S. Navy in World War II,* illus. Ramiro Bujeiro (Oxford: Osprey, 2002), 19.
7. Ed Schnepf, "SOS: Maligned Cutter Mohawk Welcomed to New Home at Key West, Florida," *Sea Classics* (May 2007), 34–35.
8. Derek Neas, "World War II Vets Get to Relive Memories: Highlight of Reunion Will Be Trip Aboard LCT Used at Normandy," *Duluth News Tribune,* Associated Press, and *Minneapolis Star Tribune*, Friday, June 6, 2003, B4.
9. Adm. Samuel Eliot Morison (USN), *Aleutians, Gilberts, and Marshalls, June 1942-April 1944*, vol. 7 (Boston: Little, Brown, 1951), 4–5.
10. *Ibid.*, 208–209.
11. *Ibid.*, 244.
12. *Ibid.*, 123–124, 288.
13. *Ibid.*, 226, 288.
14. *Ibid.*, 159.
15. *Ibid.*, 236.
16. Capt. Stephen H. Evans (USCG), *The United States Coast Guard, 1790–1915: A Definitive History* (Annapolis, MD: United States Naval Institute, 1949), 218, and the dedication page.
17. Lt. Malcolm F. Willoughby (USCGR-T), *The U.S. Coast Guard in World War II* (Annapolis, MD: United States Naval Institute/Naval Institute Press: 1957/1989), 17–22.
18. Howard V.L. Bloomfield, *The Compact History of the United States Coast Guard* (Hawthorn Books, 1966), ix.
19. *Ibid.*, 179.
20. *Ibid.*

21. *Ibid.*, 254.

22. Willoughby, *Coast Guard in World War II,* 313.

23. Bloomfield, *Compact History,* 255.

24. Robert Browning, "The Coast Guard and the Pacific War," U.S. Coast Guard Historian's Office, USCG, http://www.uscg.mil/history/articles/h_pacwar.asp (January 1999), 22.

25. *Ibid.*, 22.

26. *Ibid.*, 22–23.

27. Col. Gene Gurney (USAF), *The United States Coast Guard: A Pictorial History* (New York: Crown, 1973), 119.

28. *Ibid.*, 133.

29. *Ibid.*, 138–139.

30. *Ibid.*, 142.

31. *Ibid.*, 151.

32. *Ibid.*, 155.

33. *Ibid.*, 166.

34. Steve Kluger, *Yank: The Army Weekly: World War II from the Guys Who Brought You Victory* (New York: St. Martin's Press, 1991), 311–312. *Yank* in book form is a compilation of the *Yank* magazine articles written by military and civilian war correspondents and other contributors between 1941 and 1945. The particular article cited in *Yank,* "The Death of Ernie Pyle," was written by Chief Specialist Evan Wylie (USCGR) and dated 18 May 1945.

35. Jeffrey G. Barlow, "The Navy's Atlantic War Learning Curve," *Naval History* (June 2008), 24, 26.

36. Michael G. Walling, "Dangerous Duty in the North Atlantic," *Naval History* (June 2008), 31. Walling is the author of *Bloodstained Sea: The U.S. Coast Guard in the Battle of the Atlantic, 1941–1945* (Camden, ME: McGraw-Hill, 2004).

37. *Ibid.*, 32–35.

38. Matt Grills, "Just Another Day at the Races," *American Legion* (September 2007), 34–35. Former Coast Guard Petty Officer Marvin Perrett passed away in New Orleans on 7 May 2007.

39. John J. Galluzzo, "Captain Dorothy Stratton Dies at 107,"*Life Lines,* U.S. Life-Saving Service Heritage Association (Spring 2007), 13.

40. PA1 NyxoLyno Cangemi (USCG), "Coast Guard Lady," *Coast Guard* 2 (2007), 32–35.

41. PA2 Jennifer Johnson (USCG), "Alex Haley," *Coast Guard* 2 (2007), 1.

42. Donna Gordon Blankinship, "D-Day Veteran Reunited with His Coast Guard Cutter 62 Years after Invasion," *Associated Press,* June 6, 2006, 1–2.

43. Chuck Fowler, "Two World War II Coast Guard Vets Reunite with Their Wartime Patrol Craft," Office of Public Affairs: United States Coast Guard Thirteenth District, 18 May 2007, 1–2.

44. PAC Rob Lanier (USCG), "Requiem for a Sailor: World War II Veteran, CGC *Escanaba* Survivor O'Malley Laid to Rest," *Coast Guard* 2 (2007), 41.

45. SN2 Seymour L. Wittek (USCG), Personal Correspondence, which included Wittek's letter; also enclosed were source materials on the MV *El Estero* Fire. Information and correspondence mailed to the author from Seymour Wittek is dated 31 May 2006. The information files included Wittek's personal letter to the author, newspaper articles published about the incident, National Archives records of copies of the "U.S. Coast Guard Muster Roll for Captain of the Port, Coast Guard Barracks, Jersey City, New Jersey, from April 1943." Susan Abbott, Old Military and Civilian Records, Textual Archives Services Division, dated August 9, 2005, signed the National Archives letter accompanying the records. The Roster List is titled "Of the Officers and Crew of the U.S. Coast Guard Captain of the Port, New York, New York, for the Month of April 1943." SN2 Seymour L. Wittek is listed as "Number 1167, Serial Number 547–733, Sea.2c. (R), Date of Current Enlistment 10-22-42." The primary source articles submitted to the author by Mr. Wittek include *Harbor Watch,* "Coast Guard News," April 25, 2003, written by John Stamford (USCG World War II); articles and two photographs of the *El Estero* in (1) June 1942, and (2) on 25 April 1943 after the fire and explosions, with only the masts and superstructure of the ship above water, by Capt. Edward Oliver (USCG, Ret.) and Lt. North Clarey (USCGR, Ret.), with the source cited as the Coast Guard Historian; an article from *Readers Digest* (April 1955) by Stewart Sterling titled "Unsung Heroes of New York's Worst Hour of Peril" (147–150), condensed from *Cavalier.* Other information comes from the *Bayonne Times,* September 25, 1944, and September 26, 1944; and an article in the firefighter's professional paper, *Firehouse,* April 1988, by Bill Riepe, a retired deputy chief, who served for 32 years with the Jersey City (NJ) Fire Department, titled "Inferno in the Harbor: Munitions Ship Goes Ablaze on New Jersey Waterfront During World War II." Seymour Wittek put the following note on page 68, where the article appeared: "This was written by a NYC fireman. Very little credit given to the USCG." In his correspondence to the author, Wittek correctly asserted, "I know that you will appreciate having this information."

46. *Ibid.*, 31 May 2006.

47. *Ibid.*

48. *Ibid.*

49. Lt. Malcolm F. Willoughby (USCGR-T), *The U.S. Coast Guard in World War II* (Annapolis, MD: United States Naval Institute, 1957/1989), 67–68.

50. "U.S. Coast Guard," *Life* (December 14, 1942), 51–59. This particular edition of *Life* magazine was acquired and given to the author by Robert A. Knutson. Sgt. Knutson (USA) served in Vietnam combat zones on long-range reconnaissance patrols.

51. "U.S. Coast Guard," *Life* (December 14, 1942), 24.

52. Margaret E. Wagner, Linda Barrett Osborne, Susan Reyburn, and the Library of Congress staff, *The Library of Congress World War II Companion,* ed. David M. Kennedy (New York: Simon & Schuster, 2007), 319.

53. *Ibid.,* 295.

54. Adm. Ernest J. King (USN), *U.S. Navy at War, 1941–1945: Official Reports to the Secretary of the Navy* (Washington, DC: United States Navy Department, 1946), 28.

U.S. Coast Guard Chronology

1. *The World War II Era U.S. Coast Guard Chronology* was adapted and modified by the author from the following sources:

Ostrom, Thomas P. *The United States Coast Guard, 1790 to the Present: A History.* Oakland, OR: Elderberry/Red Anvil Press, 2006. 205–208.

Stent, Richard (President), and editorial staff members Baker Herbert, James C. Bunch, Pamela Wood, and Herbert Banks. *Coast Guard Combat Veterans.* Paducah, KY: Turner Publishing Company, 1994. 19–22.

Beard, Thomas Barrett. *Wonderful Flying Machines: A History of U.S. Coast Guard Helicopters.* Annapolis, MD: Naval Institute Press, 1996. 63–64.

Pearcy, Arthur. *A History of U.S. Coast Guard Aviation.* Annapolis, MD: Naval Institute Press, 1989. 3, 59–60.

Bibliography

Books

Alexander, Joseph H. *Storm Landings: Epic Amphibious Battles in the Central Pacific.* Annapolis, MD: Naval Institute Press, 1997.

Allen, Gwenfread E. *Hawaii's War Years, 1941–1945.* Honolulu: University of Hawaii Press, 1950.

Alton, George P. *FS's: The Little Ships That Could: A History of the Campaigns in the Pacific, and the Personal Experiences of the Author on the U.S. Army FS-268.* San Leandro, CA: Author, 2000.

Ambrose, Stephen E. *D-Day, June 6, 1944: The Climactic Battle of World War II.* New York: Simon & Schuster, 1995.

Balkowski, Joseph. *Omaha Beach: D-Day, June 6, 1944.* Mechanicsburg, PA: Stackpole Books, 2004.

Beard, Thomas Barrett. *The Coast Guard.* Seattle: Foundation for Coast Guard History; Westport, CT: Hugh Lauter Leven Associates, 2004.

_____. *Wonderful Flying Machines: A History of U.S. Coast Guard Helicopters.* Annapolis, MD: Naval Institute Press, 1996.

Beck, Bill, and C. Patrick Labadie. *Pride of the Inland Seas: An Illustrated History of the Port of Superior-Duluth.* Afton, MN: Afton Historical Society Press, 2004.

Bennett, William J. *America, The Last Best Hope: From a World at War to the Triumph of Freedom, 1914–1989.* Vol. 7. Nashville, TN: Thomas Nelson, 2007.

Bloomfield, Howard V.L. *The Compact History of the United States Coast Guard.* New York: Hawthorn Books, 1966.

Bonner, Warren D. *The Mighty "E": A Ship and Her Crew.* Orange, CA: Author, 2004.

Buell, Hal. *Uncommon Valor, Common Virtue: Iwo Jima and the Photograph That Captured America:* New York: Berkeley-Penguin, 2007.

Burcusson, David Jay, and Holger H. Herwig. *The Destruction of the Bismarck.* Woodstock, NY: Overlook Press, 2001.

Chambers, John Whiteclay, Frank Anderson, Lynn Eden, Joseph T. Glatthaar, and Ronald H. Spector, G. Kurt Piehler, eds. *The Oxford Companion to American Military History.* New York: Oxford University Press, 1999.

Chandler, David G., and James Lawton Collins. *The D-Day Encyclopedia.* New York: Simon & Schuster, 1994.

Chicoine, Stephen. *Our Hallowed Ground: World War II Veterans of Fort Snelling National Cemetery.* Minneapolis: University of Minnesota Press, 2005.

Cooke, Alistair. *The American Home Front, 1941–1942.* New York: Atlantic Monthly Press, 2006.

Costello, John. *The Pacific War.* New York: Perennial, 2002.

De Quesada, Alejandro, and Stephen Walsh. *The U.S. Home Front, 1941–1945.* Oxford: Osprey, 2008.

Dunnigan, James F., and Albert Nofi. *The Pacific War Encyclopedia.* New York: Checkmark Books, 1998.

Evanson, Christopher. "Looking Back: A Veteran Remembers the First Steps to Racial Equality." *Coast Guard* 4 (2007): 44–47.

Gaffen, Fred. *Cross-Border Warriors: Canadians in American Forces, Americans in Canadian Forces from the Civil War to the Gulf.* Toronto: Canada, Dundurn Press, 1995.

Goodspeed, M. Hill, and Richard R. Burgess. *U.S. Naval Aviation.* Pensacola, FL: U.S. Naval Aviation Museum Foundation, and Hugh Lauter Levin Associates, 2001.

Goodwin, Doris Kearns. *No Ordinary Time: Franklin and Eleanor Roosevelt: The Home Front in World War II:* New York: Simon & Schuster, 1995.

Gurney, Gene. *The United States Coast Guard: A Pictorial History.* New York: Crown, 1973.

Henry, Mark R., and Ramiro Bujeiro. *The U.S. Navy in World War II.* Oxford: Osprey, 2002.

Hickam, Homer H. *Torpedo Junction: U-Boat War Off America's East Coast, 1942.* New York: Dell; Annapolis, MD: Naval Institute Press, 1989.

Hopkins, Daniel J., ed. *Merriam-Webster's Geographical Dictionary.* Springfield, MA: Merriam-Webster, Inc., 2001.

Ingraham, Reg. *First Fleet: The Story of the U.S. Coast Guard at War.* Indianapolis: Bobbs-Merrill, 1944.

"Jack Dempsey." *Coast Guard Celebrities.* U.S. Coast Guard Historian's Office. USCG. http://www.uscg.mil/history/faqs/jackdempsey.asp (accessed March 2001).

Johnson, Robert Erwin. *Bering Sea Escort: Life Aboard a U.S. Coast Guard Cutter in World War II.* Annapolis, MD: Naval Institute Press, 1992.

_____. *Guardians of the Sea: History of the United States Coast Guard, 1915 to the Present.* Annapolis, MD: Naval Institute Press, 1987.

Kaplan, H.R., and James F. Hunt. *This Is the Coast Guard.* Cambridge, MD: Cornell Maritime Press, 1972.

Keegan, John. *Intelligence in War: Knowledge of the Enemy from Napoleon to Al-Qaeda.* New York: Random House, 2003.

Keil, Sally Van Wagenen. *Those Wonderful Women in Their Flying Machines: The Unknown Heroines of World War II.* New York: Rawson, Wade, 1979.

Kennedy, David M., ed., Margaret E. Wagner, Linda Barrett Osborne, Susan Reyburn, and the Staff of the Library of Congress. New York: Simon and Schuster, 2007.

King, Adm. Ernest J. (USN), *U.S. Navy at War, 1941–194: Official Reports to the Secretary of the Navy.* Washington, DC: Office of the Chief of Naval Operations, and the United States Navy Department, 1945.

Klobuchar, Richard. *Pearl Harbor: Awakening a Sleeping Giant.* Bloomington, IN: 1st Books Library, 2003.

_____. *The USS "Ward": An Operational History of the Ship That Fired the First American Shot of World War II.* Jefferson, NC: McFarland & Company, 2006.

Kluger, Steve. *Yank: The Army Weekly: World War II from the Guys Who Brought You Victory.* New York: St. Martin's Press, 1991.

Knauer, Kelly. *V-J Day: America's World War II Triumph in the Pacific.* New York: Time Books, 2005.

Korda, Michael. *Ike: An American Hero.* New York: Harper, 2007.

Lane, Frederic Chapin. *Ships for Victory: A History of Ship Building under the United States Maritime Commission in World War II.* Baltimore: Johns Hopkins Press, 1951.

Larson, C. Kay, and Steven M. Budar. *U.S. Coast Guard Auxiliary: Birth to the New Normalcy, 1939–2007.* St. Louis: National Office of the U.S. Coast Guard Auxiliary; and Nashville, TN: Turner Publishing, 2007.

Larzelere, Alex. *The Coast Guard in World War I: An Untold Story.* Annapolis, MD: Naval Institute Press, 2003.

Layton, Edwin T., and Roger Pineau and John Costello. *And I Was There: Pearl Harbor and Midway, Breaking the Secrets.* New York: W. Morrow, 1985.

Mason, John T. *The Atlantic War Remembered: An Oral History Collection.* Annapolis, MD: Naval Institute Press, 1990.

McGee, William L. *The Amphibians Are Coming: Emergence of the "Gator" Navy And Its Revolutionary Landing Craft.* Santa Barbara, CA: BMC, 2000.

Mercey, Arch A., and Lee Grove. *Sea, Surf and Hell: The U.S. Coast Guard in World War II.* New York: Prentice-Hall, 1946.

Middlebrook, Martin. *Convoy: The Greatest U-Boat Battle of the War.* London: Cassell, 1976.

Morison, Samuel Eliot. *History of United States Naval Operations in World War II.* 15 volumes. Boston: Little, Brown, 1947–1962.

_____. *History of United States Naval Operations in World War II: Aleutians, Gilberts, and Marshalls, June 1942-April 1944.* Vol. 7. Boston: Little, Brown, 1951.

_____. *The Two-Ocean War: A Short History of the United States Navy in the Second World War.* Boston: Little, Brown, 1963.

Morris, James M. *History of the U.S. Navy.* Greenwich, CT: Brompton, 1984.

Murray, Stuart. *Atlas of American Military History.* New York: Checkmark Books, 2005.

Nash, Edgar M. *World War Two USCG Warriors of the USS "Menges" (DE-320).* Modesto, CA: Author, 2003.

Noble, Dennis L. *Lighthouses and Keepers: The U.S. Lighthouse Service and Its Legacy.* Annapolis, MD: Naval Institute Press, 2004.

Novak, Thaddeus D., and P.J. Capelotti. *Life and Death on the Greenland Patrol, 1942.* Gainesville: University Press of Florida, 2005.

Oberg, Tanney E. *Lucky "Sweetbrier."* Bloomington, IN: iUniverse, Inc., 2005.

O'Brien, T. Michael. *Guardians of the Eighth Sea: A History of the U.S. Coast Guard on the Great Lakes.* Cleveland, OH: Ninth Coast Guard District; Honolulu: University of Hawaii Press of the Pacific, 1976.

Ostrom, Thomas P. *The United States Coast Guard, 1790 to the Present: A History.* Oakland, OR: Elderberry/Red Anvil Press, 2004.

_____. *The United States Coast Guard on the Great Lakes: A History.* Elderberry/Red Anvil Press, 2007.

Parrish, Thomas, and S.L.A. Marshall, eds. *The Simon and Schuster Encyclopedia of World War II.* New York: Simon and Schuster, 1978.

Patten, Juliana Fern. *Another Side of World War II: A Coast Guard Lieutenant in the South Pacific.* Shippensburg, PA: Burd Street Press, 2005.

Polmar, Norman. *The Naval Institute Guide to the Ships and Aircraft of the U.S. Fleet.* Annapolis, MD: United States Naval Institute, 2005.

Rachlis, Eugene. *The Story of the U.S. Coast Guard.* New York: Random House, 1961.

Rohwer, Jurgen, and Gerhard Hummelchen. *Chronology of the War at Sea, 1939–1942.* Vol. 1. New York: Arco Publishing, 1972.

_____. *Chronology of the War at Sea, 1943–1945.* Vol. 2. New York: Arco Publishing, 1974.

Ross, Bill D. *Iwo Jima: Legacy of Valor.* New York: Vanguard Press, 1985.

Rottman, Gordon L. *Landing Ship, Tank (LST), 1942–2002.* Illustrated by Tony Bryan. Oxford: Osprey, 2005; New York: New Vanguard, 2005.

Russell, Richard A. *Project Hula: Secret Soviet-American Naval Cooperation in the War Against Japan.* Washington, DC: Naval Historical Center, Department of the Navy, 1997.

Ryan, Cornelius. *The Longest Day: June 6, 1944.* New York: Simon and Schuster, 1959.

Scheina, Robert L. *U.S. Coast Guard Cutters and Craft of World War II.* Annapolis, MD: Naval Institute Press, 1982.

_____. *U.S. Coast Guard Cutters and Craft, 1946–1990.* Annapolis, MD: Naval Institute Press, 1990.

Silverstein, Judy. "Adrift." *Coast Guard* 2 (2006): 28–31.

_____. "USCG Veteran Provided Stars and Stripes for U.S. Marines." *Reservist* (USCG), 51, no. 6. U.S. Coast Guard Historian's Office, USCG. http://www.

uscg.mil/history/weboralhistory/Resni ck_Iwo_Jima.asp (added July 2004). 1–4.

Smith, Rex Allen, and Gerald A. Meehl. *Pacific War Stories: In the Words of Those Who Served.* New York: Abbeville Press, 2004.

Steinberg, Maurice Moe. *Sailor at War.* Philadelphia: Xlibris, 2002.

Symonds, Craig L., and William J. Clipson. *The Naval Institute Historical Atlas of the U.S. Navy.* Annapolis, MD: Naval Institute Press, 1995.

Thomas, Charles W. *Ice Is Where You Find It.* Indianapolis: Bobbs-Merrill, 1951.

Thornberry, Larry. "Fighting Nature: William Halsey's Battle Against a Typhoon." *Washington Times,* National Weekly Edition, June 11, 2007, p. 26.

Tillman, Barrett. *Brassey's D-Day Encyclopedia: The Normandy Invasion A–Z.* Brassey's, 2004.

Tindall, George Brown, and David Shi. *America: A Narrative History.* New York: W.W. Norton, 1996.

Veigele, William J. *PC Patrol Craft of World War II: A History of the Ships and Their Crews.* Santa Barbara, CA: Astral, 1998.

Walling, Michael G. *Bloodstained Sea: The U.S. Coast Guard in the Battle of the Atlantic, 1941–1944.* Camden, ME: International Marine/McGraw-Hill, 2004.

Ward, Geoffrey C., and Ken Burns. *The War: An Intimate History, 1941–1945.* New York: Alfred A. Knopf, 2007.

Waters, John M. *Bloody Winter.* Princeton, NJ: Van Nostrand, 1967.

Westwood, David. *U-Boat War: Doenitz and the Evolution of the German Submarine Service, 1935–1945.* Drexil Hill, PA: Casemate, 2005.

White, David Fairbank. *Bitter Ocean: The Battle of the Atlantic, 1939–1945.* New York: Simon & Schuster, 2006.

Whitlock, Flint. *The Fighting First: The Untold Story of the Big Red One on D-Day.* Boulder, CO: Westview Press, 2004.

Wiley, Ken. *Lucky Thirteen: D-Days in the Pacific with the U.S. Coast Guard in World War II.* Philadelphia: Casemate, 2007.

Willoughby, Malcolm F. *The U.S. Coast Guard in World War II.* Annapolis, MD: United States Naval Institute, 1957/1989.

Zaloga, Steven J. *D-Day 1944.* Illustrated by Howard Gerrard. Oxford: Osprey, 2003.

Articles, Periodicals, Interviews

Barlow, Jeffrey G. "The Navy's Atlantic Learning Curve." *Naval History* (June 2008): 24, 26.

Blankinship, Donna Gordon. "D-Day Veteran Reunited with His Coast Guard Cutter 62 Years after Invasion." Associated Press, June 6, 2006, pp. 1–2.

Browning, Robert M., Jr. *The Coast Guard and the Pacific War.* U.S. Coast Guard Historian's Office, USCG. http://www.uscg.mil/history/h_pacwar.html (accessed February 18, 2008). 5–7, 16, 22.

Cangemy, NyxoLyno. "Coast Guard Lady." *Coast Guard* 2 (2007): 32–35.

Chambers, L.F. "True Blue." *Coast Guard* (March 2005): 36.

The Coast Guard at War: Coast Guard Units in Hawaii, December 7, 1941. U.S. Coast Guard Historian's Office, USCG. http://www.uscg.mil/history/articles/PearlHarbor.asp (updated April 2001). 3–6.

"Coast Guard Personnel: Commandants." U.S. Coast Guard Historian's Office, USCG. http://www.uscg.mil/history/people/ (compiled March 2000). 1–2.

"Coast Guard Personnel: Russell R. Waesche, 1936–1945." U.S. Coast Guard Historian's Office, USCG. http://www.uscg.mil/history/people/RRWaescheSRBio.asp (compiled March 2000). 2.

"Cutters and Craft List." *USCGC Dione (WPC-107).* U.S. Coast Guard Historian's Office, USCG. http://www.uscg.mil/history/webcutters/Dione1934.asp (added February 2003). 1.

"Cutters and Craft List." *USCGC "Taney" (WPG-37/WAGC-37)*. U.S. Coast Guard Historian's Office, USCG. http://www.uscg.mil/history/webcutters/Taney_1936.asp (added July 2003). 6–11.

Fowler, Chuck. "Two World War II Coast Guard Vets Reunite with Their Wartime Patrol Craft." Office of Public Affairs United States Coast Guard, Thirteenth District, 18 May 2007, 1–2.

Frank, Richard B. "Innovation and Determination Ashore." *Naval History* (August 2007): 25–27.

Galluzzo, John J. "Captain Dorothy Stratton Dies at 107." *Life Lines* (Spring 2007), 13.

Grills, Matt. "Just Another Day at the Races." *American Legion* (September 2007), 34–35.

Hamilton, David M. "The Amphibious Revolution." *Naval History* (October 2006), 62–63.

Hobaugh, Jimmie H. "Combined Group Station COTP Duluth Unit History Report," 5 March 1975. United States Coast Guard, Cleveland, OH: United States Coast Guard, Ninth District. Maritime Archives Collection: Coast Guard Files, Jim Dan Hill Library, University of Wisconsin-Superior.

"In Days Gone By." *Duluth News Tribune,* March 11, 1982.

Johnson, Jennifer. "Alex Haley." *Coast Guard* 2 (2007): 1.

Kakesako, Gregg K. "Overdue Honor: New Memorial for the Coast Guard." *Honolulu Star Tribune,* January 20, 2008, p. 1.

Kime, Patricia. "Former Coast Guard Commandant Dies." *Coast Guard* 5 (2007): 38.

Lanier, Rob. "Requiem for a Sailor: World War II Veteran, CGC *Escanaba* Survivor O'Malley Laid to Rest." *Coast Guard* 2 (2007): 41.

Larsen, George C. "Pearl Harbor: A Memory of Service." *The Cutter,* Foundation for Coast Guard History (Spring 2007), 4–7.

McLaughlin, Mike. "Profiles: Intelligence Officer Edwin Layton Had Nimitz's Ear and Guided the Way Across the Pacific." *World War II History* (January 2002), 27–28.

Mehney, Paul D. "Continuing the Tradition." *Guardian of the Great Lakes* (September-October, 1999), Cleveland, OH: U.S. Coast Guard, Ninth Coast Guard District. Maritime Archives Collection: Coast Guard Files, Jim Dan Hill Library, University of Wisconsin-Superior.

Mullen, Mike. "Why Midway Matters." *Naval History* (June 2007): 14–15.

Neas, Derek. "World War II Vets Get to Relive Memories: Highlight of Reunion Will Be Trip Aboard LCT Used at Normandy." *Duluth News Tribune* (Associated Press) and *Minneapolis Star Tribune,* June 6, 2003, B4.

Ostrom, Thomas P. Interview with Dr. Howard A. Andersen, USN Medical Officer, World War II, September 2005.

_____. Interview with Martin L. Jeter, FN1, USCG, 7 February 2007.

_____. Interviews with John Philo, GM2, USN, September 2005, Fall 2007, 23 January 2008.

_____. Interviews with Leonard Jansen, USN/USMC Corpsman, in varied settings and oral presentations between 2005 and 2008.

_____. Personal Correspondence from Seymour L. Wittek, SN2, USCG, 31 May 2006.

"Out of the History Books: A Salute to the Many Heroes of World War II." *Coast Guard* 5, (2007): 1.

"Paper Squadron Sic (VP-6)." Pensacola, FL: National Museum of Naval Aviation. http://naval.aviation.museum.html, 1–8 (accessed January 2, 2007).

Ridder, Robert. "He Saw Four Cruisers Sunk in the South Pacific." *Duluth News Tribune,* May 21, 1944.

"Russell R. Waesche (1936–1945)." *Commandants of the Coast Guard.* U.S. Coast Guard Historian's Office, USCG. http://www.uscg.mil/history/faqs/comm.asp (updated May 2002).

"Russell R. Waesche, Jr., 84, Rear Admiral." *New York Times,* June 15, 1998. http://query.nytimes.com/gst/full-

page.html?res=9804E0DB143DF936A2
5755C0A96E958260&sec=&spon=
(accessed November 2, 2007).

Schnepf, Ed. "SOS: Maligned Cutter *Mohawk* Welcomed to New Home at Key West, Florida." *Sea Classics* (May 2007), 34–35.

Schwaab, C.A., ed. "Project News II: Guardian Spies: The Secret Story of the U.S. Coast Guard and the OSS During World War II." *The Cutter,* Newsletter 22 (Spring 2007), 13–14.

Simon, Ron. "Coast Guard Veteran Followed the Navy During World War II." *Mansfield News Journal,* November 19, 2007.

"The Spirit Lives On." USCGC *Escanaba* home page, Department of Homeland Security. http://www.uscg.mil/antarea/cutter/escanaba/History.htm (accessed October 27, 2007).

"Survival on Land and Sea." Washington, DC: Publications Branch, Office of Naval Intelligence, United States Navy, 1944, 1–187.

Tilley, John A. *A History of Women in the Coast Guard.* U.S. Coast Guard Historian's Office, USCG. http://www.uscg.mil/history/articles/h_womn.asp (accessed January 1999).

"Training Merchant Marines for War: The Role of the United States Coast Guard." *The Coast Guard at War.* U.S. Coast Guard Historian's Office, USCG. www.uscg.mil/history (updated January 2001). 1–6.

"U.S. Coast Guard." *Life* (December 14, 1942), 51–59.

"USCGC *Ingham.*" *Historical Naval Ships Visitors Guide."* Smithfield, VA: Historical Naval Ships Association (2007), 1–3.

"USCGC *Taney:* From World War II to Baltimore Inner Harbor Museum." *Coast Guard News* (2008), 1–2.

Vezina, Meredith R., prod. *The Coast Guard in World War II.* Videotape. Escondido, CA: Traditions Military Videos, 1940s, ca. 1945–1949.

Walling, Michael G. "Dangerous Duty in the North Atlantic." *Naval History* (June 2008), 31.

Index

Numbers in **bold italics** indicate pages with illustrations.